THE HISTORY OF THE

blues

THE HISTORY OF THE blues

BY

FRANCIS DAVIS

 HYPERION

NEW YORK

Library of Congress Cataloging-in-Publication Data
Davis, Francis.
   The history of the blues: the roots, the music, the people: from
Charley Patton to Robert Cray / Francis Davis.
      p. cm.
   "The history of the blues is the companion volume to a three-part
PBS series of the same name" —Intro.
   Includes discography, bibliographical references, and index.
   ISBN 0-7868-6052-9
   1. Blues (Music)—History and criticism. I. History of the blues
(Television program) II. Title.
ML3521.D36 1995
781.643'09—dc 20   94—23370
                                                        CIP
                                                        MN

Designed by Karolina Harris
FIRST EDITION

10 9 8 7 6 5 4 3 2 1

To Fred Below,
the secret architect
of rock 'n' roll,
and to Lonnie Johnson,
subject of one of the great
unwritten biographies

CONTENTS

. . . .

Robert Johnson, *Preaching Blues*

Oh, yeah. Famous man. And he got to be famous since he been gone. He more famous now than when he was alive. . . .

Does this Robert Johnson record sound like Mississippi music to you?

It could be any country or any state, and over the years, I guess it would be. Nowadays, he could be any state or any country. But then [,] that was the kind of music in the South.

From Jas Obrecht, "Spinning the Blues with John Lee Hooker," *Blues Revue Quarterly*, no. 9 (Summer 1993).

INTRODUCTION

. . . .

The History of the Blues is a companion volume to a three-part PBS series of the same name. The series traces the migration of the blues from Mississippi to Chicago; taking advantage of the greater leisure of the printed page, I've included a great deal on the blues in other places. Unlike the TV series, this is an *interpretive* history. In addition to my own research and that of the filmmakers, I've attempted to synthesize much from such experts on the subject as Alan Lomax, Paul Oliver, Samuel B. Charters, Peter Guralnick, Charles Keil, Robert Palmer, Jim O'Neal, Mack McCormick, and David Evans. These are men who have had their disagreements with one another in the past, and it probably goes without saying that they will be taken aback by some of what they read here.

Books on the blues tend to have happy endings, for the same reason that they tend to arrive in the stores in clusters—that is to say, such books typically end by reaffirming the durability of the form and pointing to a widespread revival of interest as evidence, but neglecting to point out that the publication of another book on the blues is itself evidence of that revival, major trade houses not being in the habit of publishing books for which there is no ready market. The most lavish of these books, including the one at hand, tend to be, at least in part, *picture* books. No less than the music they celebrate, these books tend to follow traditional patterns. Along with shots of Charley Patton, Robert Johnson, Bessie Smith, Muddy Waters, and others you'll usually find photographs of anonymous black men and women picking cotton or leading mules down country roads. One reason for this is practical: so few photographs exist of Patton or Johnson or Blind Lemon Jefferson—or of Skip James and Son House as young men—that these stand-ins must suffice. But these photographs also serve an ideological purpose, insofar as the blues is understood to have been originated by black sharecrop-pers much like the ones shown in them. We like to imagine that we can "hear" the blues in these photographs, just as we like to imagine that we can "hear" in the oldest country blues the blisters and stooped backs of the men and women singing them.

This is a view of the blues with which I don't intend to argue, except to point out that despite its origins in field hollers and work songs the blues has from the very beginning been an activity reserved for stolen moments— and to point out that many of its first performers were men exempted from picking cotton by virtue of blindness or some other physical handicap, or wastrels for whom music was a way of avoiding back-breaking labor. For three years beginning in 1921, Charley Patton was even what amounted to musician-in-residence on one Mississippi Delta plantation. Those readers up on their lore will know that Robert Johnson, while still a novice, was supposedly mocked by such older Mississippi guitarists as Patton, Son House, and Willie Brown. Legend goes that he disappeared for a year or so, before astonishing his former tormentors with his newfound prowess. Johnson's own explanation was that he'd struck a bargain with the Devil. More likely, he spent every spare moment practicing, much as Charlie Parker would a decade later, after supposedly being ridiculed off the bandstand in Kansas City. Regardless of whether Johnson's contemporaries bought his story, the point for us ought to be that they took note of his progress.

Charley Patton, 1929
(COURTESY SHELDON HARRIS COLLECTION)

INTRODUCTION

The early bluesmen probably didn't think of themselves as artists, but evidently did think of themselves as musicians. They were impatient with men they considered pretenders, and critical even of some they recognized as peers. Today, when we read descriptions of Charley Patton holding his guitar above his head or behind his back or between his legs—doing everything but picking at its strings with his teeth—we recognize him as Jimi Hendrix's spiritual father. But many of his juke-house contemporaries resented what they described as his clowning. His way of slurring his lyrics also drew censure. Sam Chatmon, of the Mississippi Sheiks, who is believed to have been Patton's half brother, said of him, "Now he plays good, but he just brings that song out like there's somebody choking [him] to death." "A lot of Charley's words, you can be sitting right [next to] him [and] you can't hardly understand him," Son House complained in the 1960s, oddly still speaking of Patton in the present tense some thirty years after his death. Mississippi bluesmen had their own ways of doing things, and what they prized most was a steady, hypnotic beat; to them, the looser rhythms of even so distinctive a Texas bluesman as Blind Lemon Jefferson sounded dead wrong. On the other hand, Howlin' Wolf—who grew up in the Delta as Chester Burnett, and who later carried on Patton and House's traditions in Chicago—once praised Jefferson for his ability to strike "a clear chord," and for not "stumbling in his music like a lot of people do."

If there's a point to be made here, it's that men this ready to criticize one another wouldn't have taken kindly to the implication that any black field hand with a guitar could have sung their songs.

Depending on who we are and what we're listening for, we're likely to hear something else in the blues—and in subsequent forms of black music. "They say, 'I love Bessie Smith.' And don't even under-

Bessie Smith, 1923
(FRANK DRIGGS COLLECTION)

3

stand that Bessie Smith is saying, 'Kiss my ass, kiss my black unruly ass,' "
seethes a black subway rider to a sluttish blonde about to stick a knife in
him in Amiri Baraka's one-act play *Dutchman* (less a murder than a symbolic
castration, given all the sexual hysteria that's preceded it). "If Bessie Smith
had killed some white people, she wouldn't have needed that music."

To which the only sane response is to paraphrase Albert Murray, the
author of *Stomping the Blues* and *The Hero and the Blues*, and ask why, if
Bessie Smith amounted to nothing more than the sum total of the injustice
she suffered as a black woman, was there only one Bessie Smith? Though I
tend to side with Murray, I've deliberately tried to have it both ways in the
main body of this book (entitled "The Blues as Such," after one of his
favorite expressions). Although this "history" section is organized more or
less chronologically and by region—the standard approach to blues evolution—the focus within each chapter is on individual performers, the most
significant of whom I discuss as full-fledged artists, not merely as agents of
tradition or as angry voices of their people.

REGARDLESS of the approach chosen by an author of a book of this
sort, he or she is expected—and the sooner the better—to define the blues
as a musical and lyric form, and to speculate on its possible African origins
and American social matrix. This I do in a long and admittedly episodic
chapter which (fair warning) also includes a good deal of moody, first-
person reportage on a trip I made to Memphis and Mississippi in the spring
of 1993. I'll fudge a bit in turning to the unabridged edition of *The Random
House Dictionary of the English Language* for a definition of the blues as "a
song of American Negro origin, that is marked by the frequent occurrence
of blue notes and that takes the basic form . . . of a 12-bar chorus consisting
of a 3-line stanza, with the second line repeating the first." What needs to
be added is some mention of the basic I–IV–V blues chord structure, and
the information that "blue notes" are defined earlier on the same page as
"flatted note[s], especially the third or seventh degree of the scale, recurring
frequently in blues and jazz as a characteristic feature"—though I might
prefer to define them as musical melanin, pentatonic cargo imported to
America from West Africa, with shiploads of slaves. Finally, what most needs
to be added to this or any other definition of the blues is the proviso, "Not
always."

It's tempting to say that everybody knows a blues song when he hears
one, and maybe I would if not for an incident I witnessed in a pricy New
York supperclub a few years ago. A young black singer named Carmen
Lundy had just finished her rendition of "Street of Dreams"—a pop song

written by Victor Young and Sam Lewis in 1932, and popularized by the crooners Bing Crosby and Morton Downey—when a young white man, obviously drunk, shouted out, "Rock 'n' roll is my *music*, but I could listen to you sing the blues all night!" To countless white Americans, a blues song is any song delivered by a black singer. The same is true, ironically, of countless black Americans, though what we're dealing with in their case isn't a reflexive stereotype, but an ideological belief in the blues as a *sensibility* that pervades all forms of black song—indeed, all aspects of black life.

Whatever their other merits, Amiri Baraka's *Blues People* and Houston A. Baker's *Blues, Ideology, and Afro-American Literature: A Vernacular Theory* are books on the blues by black authors in which you'll find no mention of Charley Patton. Even Murray, in his sage pronouncements on the blues, often seems to be talking about Duke Ellington and Count Basie, not Patton and B. B. King. Though I think that a reader is entitled to greater specificity than such books offer, the problem with definitions is that in practice they inevitably prove to be too loose or too airtight. I know of no definition that answers, once and for all, whether Leadbelly was a folk singer or a bluesman, whether Jimmy Yancey played blues or boogie-woogie, whether Clifton Chenier's music was blues or zydeco, whether Jimi Hendrix's was blues or rock, whether Jimmy Rushing shouting "Sent for You Yesterday" with the Count Basie Orchestra was blues or jazz or both. By now, those aforementioned blue notes have bled into every other form of American music. Good Clinton Democrat that I am, in the pages that follow, I've tried to err in the name of inclusion.

ANOTHER task confronting the author of any work of nonfiction these days is to state his or her "thesis." Not only don't I have a thesis as such; my philosophy has always been to distrust anyone who has just one. I started off with a bunch of ideas I wanted to put to the test, beginning with the notion that the blues is *Southern* music, as well as black music.

"Can't anybody sing the blues if he's a good enough musician and feeling badly enough?" a friend of mine—white, of course—recently asked me.

"Sure, but only after hearing somebody else sing them first," I replied, far too glibly.

The issue of white involvement in the blues is the subject of the final part of this book, titled "Blues Connotation" after a song by the jazz alto saxophonist and composer Ornette Coleman (a great bluesman in his own way). Such discussion usually centers on two questions: whether whites are capable of performing the blues with any credibility; and what it means that the audience for the blues is now overwhelmingly white. Despite my quip, I believe that the answer to the first of these questions is sure, many white performers have, and it's probably no coincidence that most of them have been Southern-born.

I'd offer Elvis Presley as an example, but he was such a complex carbohydrate that maybe it's best to forestall that debate until addressing the issue of rock 'n' roll. Let's consider instead the merits of Charlie Musselwhite, or "Memphis Charlie," as he used to be called, perhaps with the pun intended. I doubt that even the most racially blinkered ideologue would argue with my assessment of Musselwhite as one of the very finest blues harmonica players, a worthy successor to such of his black Chicago idols as Little Walter and Shakey Horton. But I also doubt that even open-minded blues fans appreciate what a relaxed and expressive singer Musselwhite has become since reaching middle age. Not only does it cease to matter whether he's black or white when he starts to sing; it ceases to matter whether the song he's singing is blues or country. He's just a guy singing a song—his song, a Southern song. As for black performers, it's worth considering that Robert Cray is the first major blues performer not to have grown up in the South (if you accept him as major, which you should)—this a full half century after Muddy Waters's departure from Mississippi for Chicago.

The complexion of today's blues audience is worth considering only insofar as music derives its meaning from those who listen to it as well as from those who perform it. This is an issue I explore further in "Blues Connotation"; suffice it to say for now that whites have projected their own meanings on the blues from the very beginning, possibly even giving it its name. "Depressed, miserable, low-spirited," the *OED* gives as figurative meanings for the word "blue," citing references as far back as the 1500s. Maybe the first thing I should have told my friend is that blues songs aren't always *blue*, though white folks have had ample reason for believing them to be.

INSOFAR as I admit to having what others might call a thesis, it finds its fullest expression in the Blues Timeline which concludes this book. No mere endpaper, this Blues Timeline is broken into three columns. The first charts significant dates in blues history; the second lists related developments in jazz, pop, and literature by or about blacks; and the last chronicles leaps in American technology, plus events that represented dramatic gains or setbacks for blacks as a people. At first, my only motive in assembling this timeline was to call attention—in as objective and ocular a fashion as possible—to some of the social forces that have given shape to the blues. I quickly realized, as I began collecting information, that a timeline also served the purpose of putting to rest some of the persistent myths surrounding the blues, such as the one that insists that jazz is its offspring (the evidence

Elvis Presley, early 1950s
(ARCHIVE PHOTOS)

suggests that the two forms evolved independently, though more or less simultaneously, in different parts of the South).

But that's not all my Blues Timeline did, once it took on a life of its own. I found more than I was looking for, not all of it in discographies and encyclopedias, and a good deal of it unrelated to the blues on face value— but only on face value. I hadn't realized, for example, that a mere nine years separated Geronimo's surrender from Edison's invention of the phonograph, nor had I (or anyone I've subsequently sprung the information on) realized that the phonograph came first. One of the most entertaining movies of 1993, though it showed up on only a few year-end best-ofs (it wasn't pretentious enough for most critics), was a Western called *Tombstone*, about the events that led up to the gunfight at the O.K. Corral. *Tombstone* ends with a spoken epilogue in which Robert Mitchum informs us that Wyatt Earp died in 1929, and that the silent movie cowboy stars Tom Mix and William S. Hart were among his honorary pallbearers. What fascinates me about this last detail is its tacit acknowledgment that the years between the O.K. Corral and Earp's death witnessed the invention of mass media that could merge fantasy and reality—dream machinery, of which *Tombstone* is itself a latterday product, that could make a figure like Earp a legend in his own time.

What has this to do with the blues? If we buy the familiar hypothesis that the blues evolved from field hollers and work songs sometime around 1890, the history of the blues almost exactly parallels that of the technology which gave a regionalized America something resembling a national identity by the middle of this century. Part of the appeal of the blues to the alienated white leftist intellectuals who embraced it in the 1930s and 1940s must have been their perception of it (and of "traditional" jazz) as the music of America's last remaining folk culture. Yet the phonograph records on which most of these intellectuals first encountered the blues were themselves evidence to the contrary—emblems of an emerging mass culture in which black Americans were to play no small part, and which would eventually render the very notion of "folk culture" obsolete.

Few readers glancing at what I've included in the Timeline are going to accuse me of attaching too much significance to the fact that Elvis Presley made his recording debut in 1954, the same year that the U.S. Supreme Court ruled segregation in public schools unconstitutional. Seemingly unrelated events can emerge as part of a pattern years after the fact, and *Brown v. the Board of Education* and Presley's covers of Arthur "Big Boy" Crudup's "That's All Right" and Roy Brown's "Good Rockin' Tonight" are now recognized as having signaled a new era in American race relations—an era whose outcome is still up in the air, defined at this point not by the greater contact between black and white that it fostered, but by its failure to do so. Likewise, no reader of this book is likely to raise an eyebrow at my Timeline's suggestion that the urban blues of Muddy Waters and others in his circle was the end result of a mass exodus of rural Southern blacks to industrialized Northern cities in the years between this century's two world wars or that this exodus was itself the result of such factors as war-induced manpower shortages and the introduction of industrial assembly lines and automated farm equipment within a few years of each other.

But I hope to suggest something else with my Timeline, something not as immediately evident or as universally accepted as gospel. In the first two decades of this century, it was possible for a man or woman, black or white, rich or poor, rural or urban, to experience what we now call culture shock without setting foot outside of his or her hometown. Talking pictures, the Model T Ford, and the Kodak box camera were only the half of it. In 1917, Birdseye developed a process for freezing vegetables. Two years later, the initial Piggly Wiggly store—soon to become the nation's first chain of self-service food stores—opened its doors in Memphis. By 1920, no matter where you lived, you could buy what amounted to the same loaf of bread or the same phonograph record. That year, Okeh released Mamie Smith's version of Perry Bradford's "Crazy Blues," the record that identified black America as a *consumer* group and opened the doors for the wholesale recording of black performers. The history of the blues, in one sense, is the history of folk art in the age of mechanical reproduction.

one

PREHISTORY/
THE KIND
OF MUSIC
IN THE SOUTH

························

Such past tenants as Ike Turner, Sonny Boy Williamson, Robert Nighthawk, and John Lee Hooker notwithstanding, the gentleman in question
was probably the most illustrious ever to bed down at the Riverside Hotel,
across from the public elementary school on Sunflower Avenue, in Clarksdale, Mississippi. Which is why Mrs. Z. L. Hill, the hotel's proprietor, had
clipped the article from her local paper and made copies to hand out to her
friends, her guests, and people like me who were just passing through.

**Robert
Nighthawk**
(COURTESY SHELDON
HARRIS COLLECTION)

The author was Howard Stovall, whose byline identified him as spokesperson for the Clarksdale Tourism Commission, and who further identified himself, within his first-person text, as president of the Sunflower River Blues Association. I recognized him as one of the cotton Stovalls—the grandson of William Howard Stovall, the retired colonel on whose sprawling, 5,000-acre plantation just a holler from town Muddy Waters was working as a field hand and tractor driver when Alan Lomax and John Work recorded him for the Library of Congress in 1941. Howard Stovall is a story in himself, a Yale-educated Chicago commodities broker who'd moved back to his ancestral home after being bitten by the blues. But this was a story about John F. Kennedy, Jr., and, indirectly, Mrs. Hill.

"Clarksdale had a distinguished visitor when John F. Kennedy, Jr., son of the late U.S. president, stayed here for one entire weekend," Stovall's article began. "Named 'The Sexiest Man Alive' by *People* magazine, Kennedy is presently working for the district attorney's office in New York City and was traveling here with a friend from law school, Karen Hefler, a lawyer with the NY firm of Cravath, Swaine, and Moore."

Stovall explained that Kennedy and his traveling companion had mentioned to Rex Miller, a New York City photographer who was also a friend of Stovall's, that they were planning a short vacation and would like nothing better than to spend it in the Deep South, hearing the blues on its native soil. Miller, who had visited Clarksdale several months earlier to shoot local musicians for a book of blues photographs, recommended either the annual Sunflower River Blues Festival in Clarksdale or the King Biscuit Blues Festival in Helena, Arkansas, just over the state line. Regardless of which festival they chose, Miller suggested that they stay at the Riverside, which Stovall's article explained was the former site of "the old G. T. Thomas Afro-American Hospital where the Empress of Blues, Bessie Smith, died following a car crash on Highway 61 in 1937," and "the home of many famous blues musicians" since being turned into a hotel and boardinghouse by Mrs. Hill in the 1940s.

Miller had also advised Kennedy and Hefler to look up Stovall, whom they ran into at the Variety Club, in Helena, during King Biscuit.

Inviting them to visit Stovall Farms, I gave them a tour of the area all day Sunday. They were really interested in cotton harvesting. Although the gin wasn't running, we were picking that day, and they got a kick out of seeing the pickers in operation and checking out the bales of cotton on the loading dock.

I explained how the crop developed and how it was marketed.

When they opened their car trunk later on, I saw they had picked two big cotton plants they were planning to take back to the city. They were pretty embarrassed when I saw the plants, but I got a big kick out of it.

Purloined bolls in the trunk of his car? Where on earth was *The National Star*? For that matter, where was Daryl Hannah?

RIDICULE comes with the territory for whomever *People* decrees the world's sexiest man, especially when he's someone those of us old enough to remember November 22, 1963, firsthand persist in thinking of as the little boy in short pants saluting the riderless horse at the funeral three days later. But I shouldn't be mocking JFK, Jr., because I went to Mississippi to sift through the same ruins. Like thousands of visitors to this part of Mississippi, I wanted to see it for myself: the land where, a hundred years ago, if not earlier, the blues took root among those cotton bolls.

American life bulges with ironies, one of which is that the music of a people regarded as worthless except as cheap labor could turn out to be this nation's source music—the yeast that gave rise to rhythm 'n' blues, rock 'n' roll, and a style of popular song unshackled by the restraints of Viennese operetta.

The blues is prototypical American music, circuitous proof of which might be that the Japanese seem to have developed a yen for it. I'm told they travel to Mississippi by the busload to cover the same ground as me and JFK, Jr. It's music with remarkable staying power; if yeast was all it was, it would have sounded its last notes forty years ago, when Elvis Presley recorded his cover version of Arthur Crudup's "That's All Right" and rock 'n' roll surfaced as a distinct entity. Yet if you know where to look, it's still possible to hear blues of every derivation—mostly amplified, yes, but otherwise not far removed from Mississippi at the turn of the century.

We're experiencing a blues revival, certified by the news weeklies as a genuine cultural phenomenon several years ago, when a CD reissue of recordings made by Robert Johnson in the late 1930s was certified gold. If those articles proclaiming the rebirth of the blues sounded familiar, they should have. There's a blues revival every ten or twenty years, it seems, usually coinciding with the end of a decade. In a sense the first of these was in the late thirties and early forties, when blues records distributed almost exclusively to Southern blacks a decade earlier wound up in the hands of white leftist intellectuals who tended to view blues performers as representatives of a rural underclass further disadvantaged by race.

The blues revival of the late fifties and early sixties—the one many of us experienced firsthand—was also political in implication, coinciding as it did not only with a folk music craze but with Southern Freedom Rides and voter registration drives (on the day in 1964 that James Chaney, Andrew Goodman, and Michael Schwerner were murdered in Philadelphia, Mississippi, two teams of young white blues enthusiasts were a few miles away searching for the Delta blues pioneers Skip James and Son House). Politics aside, what now seems significant about this second blues revival is that, although itself only marginally commercial, it pointed to the existence of a college youth market not about to throw its weight behind Steve and Eydie (or to give up buying records and attending concerts altogether) simply because its members felt they had outgrown Top 40 rock 'n' roll. This was the market exploited a few years later by the purveyors of what was termed "progressive" rock, as though to distinguish it from the greasy kid stuff.

The impetus for this blues revival was the publication of Sam Charters's mythopoeic *The Country Blues* in 1959 and his "rediscovery" of the Texas blues singer and guitarist Lightnin' Hopkins that same year. The most avid of that day's blues revivalists, if we may call them that, combed the Southern backwaters looking for the forgotten singers who had first given voice to the blues on records for Paramount and Okeh thirty years earlier. Among the legendary figures they located were Son House, Skip James, Furry Lewis, Lonnie Johnson, and Bukka White, all of whom shook off years of inactivity to give performances as powerful as those they had given as young men. In the process, the blues crusaders also found inimitable but previously unrecorded veteran bluesmen such as Mance Lipscomb and Mississippi Fred McDowell. But most of that period's blues fans never joined the hunt, being satisfied to buy the records of these elder performers and to applaud them and their mostly white progeny in coffeehouses and at folk festivals.

The blues revivalists of the civil rights era tended to be acoustic ideologues, engagé white liberals in the awkward position of rejecting as tainted goods the amplified blues to which masses of black adults in rural as well as in urban areas then still listened. The rigid, qualitative distinction drawn between "country" and "urban" blues must have amused such performers as Lightnin' Hopkins and John Lee Hooker, who were used to changing with the times and giving an audience whatever they perceived it to want. At least this worshipful college-age audience permitted men such as Hopkins and Hooker, whose days as black hit makers were over, to extend their careers. Ironically, by the end of the 1960s, urban blues—exemplified by Muddy Waters and such guitar heroes as Buddy Guy and B.B., Albert, and Freddie King—was all the rage with the Jimi Hendrix and Eric Clapton idolaters who frequented the Fillmores East and West. It was the country performers who were eclipsed.

Much has changed since then. Postadolescents still feel it necessary to differentiate between their rock 'n' roll and someone else's, but the someone else is now their parents rather than their younger siblings—hence "alternative" rock. Today's most ardent blues fans (generally speaking, people in their early thirties or older who were reared on soul and rock but now find themselves alienated by rap and studio-generated pop in which "authenticity" isn't even an issue) tend to be more all-inclusive in their enthusiasm, inclined to regard Son House and Muddy Waters, or even Robert Johnson and Robert Cray, as part of an ongoing continuum. But that isn't the only difference between today's blues revival and previous ones. Nobody's going door to door in Mississippi any more to look for "lost" or undiscovered blues singers; Mississippi's finest are all assumed to be dead or resettled in the North or already recording for small collectors' labels like Rooster Blues and Blind Pig. Yet the sort of fan who years ago would have been content to be a discerning consumer *is* going south, not just to attend festivals but to gaze at the Lula drugstore where Charley Patton is said to have bought his guitar strings, to worship at Muddy Waters's old cabin just outside of Clarksdale,

**Muddy
Waters**
(COURTESY BLUES
ARCHIVE, UNIVERSITY
OF MISSISSIPPI)

to ponder at which crossroads Robert Johnson—half-man, half-myth—sold his soul to the Devil, to visit graves and talk with people like Mrs. Hill. To listen to Waters or Johnson or Patton or Cray on CD isn't enough for some blues fans; they think they hear our identity as a nation bumping around somewhere in those home-brew rhythms.

In terms of the pop marketplace, these pilgrims amount to little more than an over-age demographic blip. You don't see blues videos on MTV, VH-1, or even BET; there's precious little of it on pay channels or PBS. The only network series on which you're guaranteed to hear a smidgen of blues once a week is *Roseanne*, a sitcom about self-proclaimed "white trash" with a gritty harmonica theme under the opening credits; black sitcoms rely on gospel, funk, or toned-down rap to connote blackness. Rap producers sample George Clinton and James Brown, funk's founding fathers. But so far as I am aware, the only one to sample Robert Johnson was the avant-garde composer Neil Rolnick. And though Timberland sells baggy outdoor wear to both yuppies and urban teens, the company uses blues only in its white campaigns. Used to sell products ranging from light beer to a mild laxative called Perdiem, the blues obviously still *signifies*. But what? And to whom?

While we're being realistic, we also need to admit that relatively few of those who bought that Robert Johnson reissue feel obliged to explore Mississippi, and that many of those who do—the world's sexiest man included, for all I know—go because Mississippi has become the cool thing to do after you've tried all the hot new discos and restaurants. You hear conflicting reports on the state of health of the blues. Optimists regard the proliferation of festivals and major label "product" as proof that interest in the blues has never been greater. On the other hand, the dwindling number of black Americans listening to the blues is taken by many to mean that the blues is dead—or (same thing) that it's stopped evolving, in which case the only thing the current revival demonstrates is the gullibility of all those white boys ripping off their neckties and boogying to mojo hand-me-downs. I'll listen to either argument, and agree with either if it's put to me right. But in response to the first, I'm likely to ask what it means that the key figure in this current blues revival is Robert Johnson, who's been dead for over fifty years. In response to the second argument, I'm likely to point out that there still are black people who listen to the blues, especially in the South. I'm also likely to ask why, in a country as racially divided as ours and at a time when black Americans have by and large chosen other forms of musical expression, so many white Americans sense something of their own roots in a music that many of them claim can be performed credibly only by blacks? I don't pretend to know the answer. That the blues spawned rock 'n' roll has something to do with it, certainly. But there's got to be more to it than that, and I guess this is what I went to Mississippi to find out.

Robert
Johnson,
early 1930s
(COURTESY STEPHEN
LaVERE)

MRS. Hill's was my first stop after arriving in Clarksdale from Memphis via Greyhound (a ninety-minute trip lengthened by a delay of approximately an hour in taking off, which my fellow passengers—all of them black, and many of them young women with small children enduring a long, uncomfortable ride from St. Louis or Chicago—seemed to accept as par for the course). Under other circumstances, I might have gone first to see Wade Walton in his barber shop near Fourth and Issaquena Avenue—still Clarksdale's main stem, just as it was sixty years ago, when Muddy Waters was a mannish boy. Walton, now approaching seventy and a barber all of his adult life, used to cut Muddy's hair and Sonny Boy Williamson's, too. He would presumably have stories about them to share. But that wasn't all. Walton is himself a singer, guitarist, and harmonica player who worked Clarksdale's juke joints as a member of Ike Turner's Kings of Rhythm in the late 1940s and recorded for Arhoolie and Bluesville during the blues revival of the 1960s. A musician to the bone, he reportedly sometimes gives favored customers a song to go with their haircut or shave, working up a series of complex rhythms with his razor and barber's strap. On top of all of this, he was vice president of the local chapter of the NAACP during the voter registration drives of the early sixties.

A believer in simultaneity rather than coincidence, I've long wondered how much overlap there was, if any, between those young, white Northerners who descended on Mississippi in the summer of 1964 to register voters and teach in the freedom schools, and those who came to the state around the same time to hunt for bluesmen—conscious sometimes only in retrospect of the jeopardy in which they were putting themselves and the black residents they were seen speaking to. In Mississippi and much of the Deep South then, a Northern license plate was often all the evidence a small-town sheriff needed that a car's occupants were bent on upsetting the status quo. The blues historian Sam Charters, for example, remembers sitting nervously in an Alabama diner whose owner had posted a sign near the cash register giving residents a number to call if they spotted any "nigger lovers."

Clarksdale—a Mississippi town in which there has never been a clavern of the Ku Klux Klan—prides itself on having escaped much of that period's turmoil. But I had a hunch that Walton could tell me different. I wanted to ask him, for example, about the day in 1960 that Chris Strachwitz and Paul Oliver visited him in his barber shop. Also present in the shop that day, along with Walton and the two blues researchers, was the pharmacist Aaron Henry, then president of the local chapter of the NAACP and later head of the state chapter. A few weeks after Strachwitz and Oliver's visit, Henry's pharmacy was bombed—and Oliver persists to this day in believing that this particular attack (one of many directed against Henry during that time) may have been a direct result of his and Strachwitz's conspicuous presence.

If you accept the official version, the blues played absolutely no role in the civil rights struggle of the sixties. It's easy to understand why. Even when topical in nature, blues songs are rarely vehicles of overt protest. (There are exceptions to every rule, and three of the most significant in this case are J. B. Lenoir's "Eisenhower Blues," Floyd Jones's "Ain't Times Hard," and John Brim's "Tough Times," all from the fifties and all indicative of the depth of black discontent during an era officially remembered as having been affluent and complacent.) Of course, there are many ways of hearing the blues, and one of these is as an oppressed race's sublimated *cri de coeur*. Blues singers always seem to be saying more than the words to their songs literally say, and this sometimes encourages us to hear things that simply aren't there. Although not as well known as Langston Hughes, Albert Murray, or Ralph Ellison, the African-American man of letters who has written most perceptively about the blues song form and best caught its pitch in his own work is the poet Sterling A. Brown. One of his most vehement poems is "Frankie and Johnny," which borrows its characters, verse format, and title from a folk song dating back to the early nineteenth century. Though black in origin, "Frankie and Johnny" (or "Frankie and Albert," as it was originally called) has crossed the color line so often that the race of its characters largely depends on who's singing about them. The song has been recorded countless times by performers black and white, but most memorably by the black singer and guitarist Mississippi John Hurt, in 1928. In Brown's version, published in 1932, Frankie is the halfwit daughter of a "red-faced cracker" with "corn silk on her crazy head," and Johnny is a black sharecropper, "a nigger, who never had much fun." Frankie tempts Johnny strictly for diversion, and after yielding to temptation, Johnny winds up dangling from a noose. The poem is brilliant, but there's absolutely nothing like it in the blues. In Hurt's version of "Frankie and Johnny," the couple are lovers who fuck like crazy until Johnny—a "fancy man" heterosexual dandy—makes the mistake of taking up with another woman. Frankie then shoots him dead, and we sympathize with her as she's carted off to jail, because, after all, he was her man and he done her wrong. Race is never mentioned, so we assume that the lovers and the singer all are of the same color.

In his long essay on the blues in *The New Grove*, the aforementioned Paul Oliver, an Englishman who's probably the world's leading authority on the blues, estimates that as many as three quarters of the blues recorded since 1920 are about sexual relationships, often of an aberrant or pathological nature. "The high proportion of these that convey aggression, bitterness, and disappointment suggests that they are symbolic of more profound psycho-sexual problems. Seldom does the blues have more than an oblique element of protest, which is communicated more by canalizing frustration or anger into statements of broken relationships than through overt declarations of resistance or defiance." Well, not exactly, unless you believe that black folks spend as much of their waking hours thinking about white folks as white folks do thinking about them. If a banana is sometimes just a banana, a boll weevil is sometimes just a no-good man and a crawling king snake is sometimes just a stiff prick. In the blues, anything and everything is fair game for double entendre. The blues has never been big on moral or social uplift; the only deliverance most of its singers promise is sexual. At any rate, Oliver concedes that "in this respect [social protest, overt or coded], blues was overtaken by gospel music." Small wonder, then, that the civil rights movement drew its anthems from gospel, given a tradition of songs in which (for example) crucifixion was understood to be a metaphor for lynching, and given the leadership role of black clergymen inclined to look aghast at the dens of iniquity in which the blues was played.

But who knows? In the nineteen sixties, African-Americans rarely turned up on screen except in movies that bannered their social realism in big, bold letters. A typical scenario might have one brother going to Mississippi to join the struggle while the other stays in Harlem and becomes a slave to drugs. But I can imagine a movie from the same period about two *white* brothers from Forest Hills, say, only a year or two apart in age and both in college. Both go to Mississippi on their summer vacations, one to register black voters, the other to track down and record elderly black singers. Aside from their Southern destination, what the two brothers share in common is their record collection—itself a token of their consuming interest in black culture. They go almost the entire summer without seeing each other, until one day they cross paths in Clarksdale, in Wade Walton's barber shop.

And perhaps many paths did cross there. But I'll probably never know for sure. John Mohead and James Butler, local men who were showing me around town, warned me away from Walton. He had gotten religion, they said, and would pick up his razor and chase me or anybody else who came into his shop talking about the Devil's music.

Or, I speculated, maybe he was just god damn sick and tired of strangers showing up to pump him for information about Muddy Waters and Sonny Boy Williamson when he was trying to cut hair.

CLARKSDALE—incorporated 1882, current population just under 20,000—is close to the state's northwestern tip, in an area residents and tourists alike insist on calling "the Delta," though it's nowhere near the mouth of any river. This Delta is approximately two hundred miles of low, flat plain running from Memphis down to Vicksburg, bounded by the Mississippi River to the west and the Yazoo River to the east, and also including parts of Arkansas and rural Tennessee. But this is mere geography. What defines the Delta both as a place and as a state of mind is its topsoil, dark and deep and composed of alluvium deposited by the Mississippi over centuries. It's soil historically associated with cotton, though the Delta hasn't really been a Cotton Kingdom for a long time now. Its landowners today also grow corn, peanuts, soybeans, even rice—but only since being forced to diversify by the invasion from Mexico of the boll weevil in the early days of this century, the introduction of the automatic cotton harvester and the Northern migration of black laborers during World War II, and the gradual spread of cotton production to Asia and the Southwestern United States.

Still in the hands of the Choctaw upon Mississippi's admission to the Union in 1817, and largely swamp and forest until drained and cleared by planters just before the Civil War, the Delta is simultaneously one of the most beautiful spots on earth and an ecological aberration. By dark, the countryside feels isolated, brooding, almost primordial: a place no doubt alive with superstition and myth even before the blues evolved its own, where you can still imagine a Robert Johnson crazy with moonshine and angst—convinced by white people of his worthlessness and by black fire-and-brimstoners of his wickedness, *wickedness*—hotfooting it to a highway crossroads to sell his soul to the Devil in return for prowess on the guitar, believing *to* his soul that he was getting the best of the bargain, by virtue of selling the Devil something the Devil already owned. Yet by day, this same landscape—this Southern Golgotha, where even the crosses men build for themselves are horizontal, not atop churches, but at the intersections of highways and railroad lines—assumes a colossal monotony, with row after row of crops stretching as far as the eye can see to either side of the old Highway 61, whose two narrow lanes might themselves have been drawn with a ruler. The straightness of Highway 61 and the symmetry of the surrounding countryside hardly prepares you for sudden and unmarked swerves like the one just north of Clarksdale, which John Mohead and James Butler believe must be the one that caught Bessie Smith's driver by surprise and caused him to smack into that truck.

There are long stretches of road here with no houses, no hills, no trees: nothing distant and *vertical* to drag the horizon into human perspective. Most of Mississippi's timberland is long gone, 80 million acres of it converted to lumber, and never replenished, in the early part of this century. On the other hand, the river always feels close by, even when you can't see it. Its water is in the damp air, and it seeps into your thoughts. Gazing into the distance reminded me of something, though I couldn't quite figure out what until we climbed out of John's van to take a look at the sharecropper's cabin that Muddy Waters lived in with his family before catching the Illinois Central to Chicago in 1943 (and taking the blues with him, or so the legend goes). I told John and James that what had been working its way to the front of my mind was the time that I'd gone on a whale watch off the coast of Provincetown, Massachusetts. There, in the middle of the ocean, you looked out at the water, and all you saw was water—you couldn't even imagine that somewhere there was land. Here, I said, you had the feeling of being in the middle of something just as infinite, although it was land. My companions pointed out that it was funny I should be thinking about water, because much of the ground we were covering that day belonged to the Mississippi for untold centuries, before the levees were built to curtail its swell.

For someone like me, whose first voluntary exposure to the Bible from Genesis to St. John the Divine was as research for college literary courses (I swear the nuns who taught me catechism were cribbing from *Paradise Lost*), those books are encyclopedias of metaphor, skeleton keys to Western thought. But there are people who grow up actually reading the Bible, especially in the Protestant South—people, both black and white, who accept what I read as lunatic ravings as both prophecy and literal history. Such a view of the Bible entails interpreting *the world* metaphorically, and perhaps explains why so many Mississippians of both races viewed the Great Flood of 1927 (vividly described by Bessie Smith in "Back Water Blues," Charley Patton in "High Water Everywhere," and William Faulkner in *Old Man*) in terms of Noah's Ark—as God's retribution for the sins of man instead of as the river taking back what once belonged to it. The flood left a quarter of a million people homeless. It covered 20,000 square miles and was as much as 50 feet deep. It was followed by earthquakes. The stars of heaven didn't fall unto the earth, and the sky didn't rain hail and fire mingled with blood. But the water did wash up snakes—*serpents*—and for many people that must have been omen enough.

BUILT over a hundred years ago from the wood of a cypress from a nearby forest, and once doubling as a still, Waters's cabin still stands where it always has, just off a side road near the main gate to Stovall's Farm, a few yards away from a cluster of barns and the main silo. Local sentiment favors leaving the cabin here forever, as a kind of roadside shrine, but there's also talk of taking it apart and putting it back together plank by plank inside the Delta Blues Museum, on the first floor of the Carnegie Public Library, in Clarksdale (one of the first things you see on entering the museum is a guitar fashioned from a stray plank of wood from the cabin, custom built for and donated to the museum by Billy Gibbons, of the rock group ZZ Top). All that remains of the cabin is a shell. Originally it faced the road, but tornadoes have twisted it almost completely around, reducing it from four rooms to one. Earth gapes through the wooden floor and the roof is completely gone. Wire netting covers what used to be the front and back doors. The cabin won't be able to withstand the elements much longer, nor is it safe from souvenir hunters and vandals where it is now. (PLEASE . . . DO NOT DEFACE THIS SIGHT! reads a hand-lettered sign posted by Howard Stovall. "We will lay a BIG NASTY MOJO on you if you take anything.") Yet though hardly anything is left of it, the cabin remains imposing somehow, if only because of who once called it home. Whoever built the cabin obviously intended for it to last: peering through the cracks where the wood no longer meets, you can still see the mud that someone used as mortar and for insulation years before Waters was born. I took numerous photographs of the cabin, but the one showing that mud is the one that fascinates me.

Earlier in the day, John had driven us past Tennessee Williams's childhood home, on the "right" side of the tracks in Clarksdale—a popular tourist attraction that particular weekend, what with *The Paris Review* celebrating its fortieth anniversary a hundred or so miles away near William Faulkner's old home in Oxford and the entire Delta swarming with literati (its literature and its music are the two things every Mississippian can be proud of—or are the state's literature and its music the only two things of which its white natives are unashamed?). Try as I may, I can't remember much about the Williams house beyond that it was gabled and possibly three stories high, with fenced-in hedges and white columns in imitation of the architecture

Exterior of Muddy Waters's
cabin
(FRANCIS DAVIS)

Interior of Muddy Waters's
cabin
(FRANCIS DAVIS)

of a period that was long over by the time ground was broken on this or
any of the surrounding houses. I couldn't imagine living there, either.

THOUGH all of them caution that no one knows for certain, just about
every historian willing to venture an opinion on the matter believes that this
exotic land put to ordinary use is where the blues evolved from field hollers,
work songs, spirituals, ragtime songs, country reels, and Anglo-Scottish

23

ballads sometime around 1890. The evidence begins with the fact that so many of the performers who have shaped the blues over the decades were born or spent their formative years in the Delta, including Charley Patton, Robert Johnson, Son House, John Lee Hooker, Muddy Waters, B. B. King, and Howlin' Wolf. No other region of the South can claim as many famous names.

There's further evidence, anecdotal and suppositional as well as circumstantial. Who doesn't know the famous story of W. C. Handy "discovering" the blues while waiting for a train in the sleepy Delta town of Tutwiler, Mississippi, in 1903? The errant son of a black Alabama minister (a genteel ex-slave whose view of race relations was based on the principle that "in a community of cultured white folks, there will be found a similar group of colored people"), Handy was by then leading the Mahara Minstrels, a "conventional, respectable" orchestra whose book of operatic overtures and popular tunes was probably no different from that of most of that day's

W. C. Handy
(COURTESY OF RAY
AVERY'S JAZZ
ARCHIVES)

white ensembles of similar size and instrumentation. The Minstrels were based in Clarksdale, which is presumably where Handy was headed. His train was several hours late, Handy tells us in *Father of the Blues*, his 1941 autobiography, and he was trying to catch some shuteye when he noticed that "a lean, loose-jointed Negro had commenced plunking a guitar beside me while I slept."

> His clothes were rags; his feet peeped out of his shoes. His face had on it some of the sadness of the ages. As he played, he pressed a knife on the strings of a guitar in a manner popularized by Hawaiian guitarists who use steel bars. The effect was unforgettable. His song, too, struck me instantly.

Goin' where the Southern cross' the Dog.

> The singer repeated the line three times, accompanying himself on the guitar with the weirdest music I had ever heard. The tune stayed in my mind. When the singer paused, I leaned over and asked him what the words meant. He rolled his eyes, showing a trace of mild amusement. Perhaps I should have known, but he didn't mind explaining. At Morehead, the eastbound and westbound met and crossed the north and southbound trains four times a day. This fellow was going where [the Southern railroad crossed the Yazoo Delta Railroad, nicknamed "Yellow Dog" by black Mississippi sharecroppers], and he didn't care who knew it. He was simply singing . . . as he waited. This was not unusual. Southern Negroes sang about everything. Trains, steamboats, steam whistles, sledge hammers, fast women, mean bosses, stubborn mules—all became subjects for their songs. They accompany themselves on anything from which they can extract a musical sound or rhythmical effect, anything from a harmonica to a washboard.

Or, Handy might have added, a penknife, the neck of a bottle that had been reshaped over flame into a "slide," or any other makeshift device intended to extract from the strings of a guitar a wailing sound like the voice of the man playing it—an instrumental technique associated with the blues in general, but especially with the Mississippi variety.

"In this way, and from these materials, they [African-Americans in Mississippi, in the early twentieth century] set the mood for what we now call the blues," concludes Handy, before relating a similar anecdote, probably from around the same time.

> I was leading the orchestra in a dance program [in Cleveland, Mississippi] when someone sent up an odd request. Would we play some of our "native" music," the note asked. This baffled me. The men in this group could not "fake" and "sell" it. They were all musicians who bowed strictly to the authority of printed notes. So we played for our anonymous fan an old-time Southern medley, a medley more sophisticated than native.

Stephen Foster and the like? Handy doesn't say, and neglects to give the year. But let him go on.

> A few moments later, a second request came up. Would we object if a local colored band played a few dances?
>
> Object! That was funny. What hornblower would object to a time-out and a smoke—on pay? We eased out gracefully as the newcomers entered. They were led by a long-legged chocolate boy and their band consisted of just three pieces, a battered guitar, a mandolin and a worn-out bass.
>
> The music they made was pretty well in keeping with their looks. They struck up one of those over-and-over strains that seem to have no very clear beginning and certainly no ending at all. The strumming attained a disturbing monotony, but on and on it went, a kind of stuff that has long been associated with cane rows and levee camps.

Sure sounds like the blues, right down to its substitution of variations in pitch for conventional harmonic development—what a schooled musician like Handy would perceive as "disturbing monotony." The songs that the archeologist Charles Peabody reported hearing his black workers improvise from scratch on a dig near Stovall's Farm in 1902 sound like the blues from his descriptions of them, as do the verses collected by the folklorist Howard Odum in Lafayette County, Mississippi, between 1905 and 1908. But there's more from Handy, who goes on to tell us that he "commenced to wonder if anybody besides small town rounders and their running mates would go for such music."

> The answer was not long in coming. A rain of silver dollars began to fall around the outlandish, stomping feet. The dancers went wild. Dollars, quarters, halves—the shower grew heavier and continued so long I strained my neck to get a better look. There before the boys lay more money than my nine musicians were being paid for the entire engagement. Then I saw the beauty of primitive music. They had the stuff the people wanted. It touched the spot.

All the best stories are apocryphal, especially any told by Handy, who wasn't just one of the new century's most important bandleaders, composers, and musical publishers, but also, in common with men like Henry Ford, a bootstrap entrepreneur savvy enough to know that the creation of personal myth came with the territory. Even so, these two stories are endlessly rich. Frequently quoted to substantiate the existence in Mississippi of something very much like the blues well before the publication of Handy's "Memphis Blues" in 1912, they wind up telling us much else about black life around the turn of the century. Just as the unconfirmed story that Harlemites gave Handy the cold shoulder when he brought his band to New York in 1918 supplies one of the first examples we have of an emerging difference in musical taste between African-Americans in the South and those in the

North, so the tale set at Tutwiler Station supplies one of the earliest documented instances we have of a schism between African-Americans of different social classes—and of the ambivalence with which members of either class regarded the other. Handy's preoccupation with the anonymous Negro's bare feet and tatters is obvious enough, but there's also his sentimental description of the man's face containing "some of the sadness of the ages." Just as telling is the man's rolling of his eyes and his "trace of mild amusement" at finding a brother so obviously without a clue. I almost wrote "a brother with no more clue of what was what than the average white man," but Handy's second story suggests that white men in Mississippi in the early 1900s knew more than we've been inclined to give them credit for knowing, if only about the blues.

That seductive shower of "dollars, quarters, halves" in Handy's second story recalls the first chapter of Ralph Ellison's *Invisible Man*, in which Ellison's unnamed "I"—a black high school senior who admits that "when I was praised for conduct I felt a guilt that in some way I was doing something that was really against the wishes of the white folks"—is invited to repeat his valedictory speech to a gathering of Greenwood's white civic and business leaders. The gathering turns out to be a smoker, and before being allowed to deliver his speech, Ellison's hero is forced to compete against nine of his darker, more physically developed schoolmates in an old-fashioned battle royal with a few extra twists. He and the others are led into the ring, where first they're taunted by a lewdly gyrating blonde from whom they have to avert their eyes, then ritualistically blindfolded before being given the signal to clobber one another. They go at one another "like drunken dancers, weaving to [their] rapid drum-like blows," until our stunned and bloodied hero regains enough of his composure to play one attacking group against the other, "slipping in and throwing a punch then moving out of range while pushing the others into the melee to take the blows blindly aimed at me." Then, sensing one rival after another leaving the ring, he realizes that he's been set up: this is to be a fight to the finish between him and Tatlock, "the biggest of the gang" and probably the meanest. Tatlock beats our hero to a pulp, but the tournament doesn't end there. A small rug is rolled out and all nine of the boys are pitted against one another again, this time in diving for the "coins of all dimensions and a few crumpled dollars" scattered on the rug.

There's more, of course, but it's those gold coins that fascinate me, much as they do Ellison's narrator, and much as they did Handy. Am I making too much of their appearance in both stories, one fictional and one ostensibly fact? Undoubtedly. But at the very least, Handy's story should dissuade us of the romantic notion that the blues was something African-Americans cooked up in secret. Whites have enjoyed black music from the beginning, and there have never been very many secrets between the races in the South. Likewise, the opening chapter of Ellison's subversive picaresque amplifies

27

something discreetly hinted at in Handy and in newspaper ads of the early nineteenth century which emphasized the musical abilities of slaves for sale: that so far as Southern whites were concerned, Negroes gave the best return on the entertainment dollar.

"Mighty seldom I played for colored," Sam Chatmon, Charley Patton's half brother and a member of the Mississippi Sheiks, once explained to a BBC interviewer. "They didn't have nothing to hire you with."

WHAT is evidence but things arranged in such a way as to mean what we want them to mean? The blues turn up in too many other places around the same time to support the theory that this music was once exclusive to Mississippi. Ma Rainey told the folklorist John Work that she first heard the blues—or a bone-scraping moan song she later identified as such—in a small town in Missouri in 1902, when she was traveling with a tent show. "She tells of a girl from the town who came to the tent one morning and began to sing about the 'man' who left her," Work reported in his *American Negro Songs*, published in 1940.

> The song was so strange and poignant that it attracted much attention. "Ma" Rainey became so interested that she learned the song from the visitor. . . .
>
> The song elicited such response from the audiences that it won a special place in her "act" as an encore. Many times she was asked what kind of song it was, and one day she replied, in a moment of inspiration, "It's the Blues."

There's evidence to support the existence of the blues in New Orleans around the same time, though the city ultimately became more identified with jazz. In the magazine *Jazz Review* in the late 1950s, a Louisiana surgeon named Edward Souchon published an essay on the jazz trumpeter King Oliver which also included a good deal of Souchon's personal reminiscence of growing up in New Orleans around the turn of the century. Souchon, who was white, remembered his family's black maid singing "an admixture of Creole folk songs, church hymns, and up-to-date hits of the late 90's or early 1900's" as she prepared meals, though the sample verse he gives—an early version of "Alabama Bound," later popularized by Leadbelly—suggests that she was singing the blues. If we're to believe what Jelly Roll Morton and other New Orleans musicians have told us about her, so was Mamie Desdoumes, a piano-playing Creole prostitute missing two fingers from her right hand who was legendary for singing the same song from morning till night. Morton told Alan Lomax that she was the one who "first really sold me on the blues."

Even Handy, after describing his fateful encounter in Tutwiler Station, goes on to allow that his "fondness for this sort of thing" began a decade or so earlier in his hometown of Florence, Alabama, and that the verses he heard in Mississippi were "set to a kind of earth-born music that was familiar throughout the Southland." And Howard Odum collected early examples of the blues in Georgia as well as in Lafayette County, Mississippi.

What about the staggering number of great Mississippi bluesmen? Aren't the twenties and thirties recordings of Charley Patton, Son House, and Skip James in themselves evidence of the Delta blues' superiority, if not its primacy? Before answering yes, we have to take into account to what extent our perception of the past has been colored by contemporary taste. "When people from Australia or Japan or Italy say, 'Oh, I love the blues,' they're not talking about Southwest blues styles, the Georgia twelve-string players, ragtime Piedmont styles, or whatever," notes Dick Waterman, one of the men who rediscovered Son House. "It's the Delta blues. If you say, 'Who do you like?' they'll name Robert Johnson, Muddy Waters, John Lee Hooker, Howlin' Wolf, Son House."

CD reissues have played an inestimable role in the blues revival of the 1990s. So far, however, the focus has been on Delta blues and its electrified Chicago offshoot, to the virtual exclusion of Georgia, Texas, and California. In most instances, commercial recordings are the only empirical evidence we have of what the blues from any given region sounded like at any given point. Yet as often as not, records mislead us. Record companies are tricksters—modern technological equivalents of Légba and Èsù, the African gods of the crossroads, who delight in playing pranks on the unwary. The tricks started with Mamie Smith's recording of Perry Bradford's "Crazy Blues" for Okeh, which sold a then-incredible 75,000 copies within the first month of its release in 1920, mostly to black record buyers who represented a hitherto untapped market. Usually cited as the first blues record, "Crazy Blues" is more accurately a synthesis of the blues and black vaudeville; it's significant that the same performer had made her record debut earlier that year singing "That Thing Called Love" and "You Can't Keep a Good Man Down," two songs Okeh intended for Sophie Tucker until yielding to Bradford's entreaties to record a black singer. The trickery was in presenting record buyers with the synthesis first: country blues performers weren't recorded in great number for another six or seven years, and Charley Patton—believed to be the prototypical early bluesman—had to wait until 1929 (and then had, in common with Ma Rainey, the misfortune to record for Paramount, a company whose inferior acoustic recording technique distances him from us today, making him sound like a wraith or a figment of some blues scholar's imagination, whereas Robert Johnson and Bessie Smith, who made electrical recordings for what ultimately became Columbia, still sound like they're in the same room with us).

All of the elements we've come to identify with the blues—including twelve-bar verses, with the second line echoing the first, and I–IV–V chord progressions moving back and forth from the tonic to the subdominant—seem to have fallen into place by the time that the country bluesmen started to record. But was this the logical culmination of a folk process, or did records instantly codify the blues by virtue of their mass distribution? Vast portions of the rural South were without indoor electricity until almost midcentury; the lights went on only after the Tennessee Valley Authority harnessed the region's waters into dams and reservoirs. But you didn't need electricity to play a Victrola. By 1930, up to a third of the families in the poorest, most remote areas of the South owned one.

Although bridgeless and twelve-bars-long instead of thirty-two, the blues otherwise resembles American popular song. It's possible, however, that this apparent similarity is a byproduct of the three-minute duration imposed on the blues by the 78 rpm phonograph record: published versions of some early blues include a dozen or more choruses. Perhaps the most widely read of the early essays on the blues was Abbé Niles's introduction to a seminal collection published by W. C. Handy in 1926. Niles began by reminding his readers that what most of them probably still thought of as a new Tin Pan Alley concoction had actually originated years earlier among "illiterate and more or less despised classes of Southern Negroes: barroom pianists, careless nomadic laborers, watchers of incoming trains and steamboats, street-corner guitar players, strumpets and outcasts." Perhaps too romantically put, but a sentiment with which most of us would today be inclined to agree. "A spiritual is a matter for choral treatment; a blues was a one-man affair, originating typically as the expression of the singer's feelings, and complete in a single verse," Niles went on, and although probably even his most informed readers accepted his dichotomy as valid, he was on far shakier ground. That same year, Vocation recorded Blind Joe Taggart, the first of a proliferation of "guitar evangelists," whose solo hymns to Jesus were a far cry from those of the Pace Jubilee Singers, the Dinwiddie Colored Quartet, or any of the early gospel choirs with whose recordings Niles was presumably familiar. (Taggart, about whom little is known, occasionally recorded with his wife, Emma, or his brother, James. But neither he nor any of the "guitar evangelists" who followed—the best remembered of them are Washington Phillips and Blind Willie Johnson—ever recorded with a choir.) Black sacred music wasn't always choral in the 1920s, and blues and other forms of black secular music weren't always "one-man" affairs. In 1927, the Memphis Jug Band made its recording debut, followed a year later by Gus Cannon's Jug Stompers, and in 1930 by the Mississippi Sheiks, the most important of the black string bands.

For whatever reason, the record companies of the 1920s favored unaccompanied singer-guitarists. As a consequence, our image of the early bluesman is that of a solitary drifter trusting only his guitar—the first of an alienated species. Yet we have the testimony of Son House that he, Charley Patton, and Willie Brown often performed together. Record companies of the 1920s were also partial to singers from the Mississippi Delta and Memphis, perhaps owing to the proximity of the former to the latter, and the latter's short distance via rail to Chicago, which then still rivaled New York as the fledgling record industry's hub. It was usually more expedient for a company to send its representative to the Delta than it would have been to send him to, say, Dallas or Fort Worth—likewise more expedient to bring a singer from the Delta to Chicago than to pay his fare all the way from Texas. This remained true even after the success of the Texas singer and guitarist Blind Lemon Jefferson's "That Black Snake Moan," in 1926 (a fast seller not just in the rural South, but also in those Northern cities in which there was already a sizable black population). Regardless of how they may have thought of themselves, male country blues singers were folk performers, not professional entertainers, in the eyes of record company field representatives. Much like the field hands who bought their records, blues singers were assumed to be in plentiful supply, virtually interchangeable, and willing to work cheap. They were the record industry's equivalent of unskilled labor.

"Their repertoire would consist of eight or ten things that they did well, and that was all they knew," Frank Walker, who supervised many of Columbia's early rural recordings, once explained to the writer Mike Seeger. "So, when you picked out the three or four [songs] that were best in a man's so-called repertoire you were through with that man as an artist. [That] was all. . . . You said goodbye. They went back home."

Walker was an astute judge of talent, the man who signed Bessie Smith for Columbia in 1923 and the country singer Hank Williams for MGM twenty-five years later. In a way, though, it hardly mattered *which* singers he or another company's field representative recorded, so long as they recorded the blues. And it was usually more feasible for them to record singers from Mississippi.

THIS is where the suppositional evidence comes into play, and it requires a leap of faith. In Northwest Mississippi to this day, you'll occasionally spot a homemade instrument called the diddly-bow, an extra-thick broom straw or piece of baling wire stretched taut and extended vertically along the side of a barn, with a small rock serving as a bridge. You play the diddly-bow by striking unusual pitches up and down its length. Though this can be done by snapping it in different places with your fingers, the method favored in Mississippi involves rubbing it with a bottleneck that's been reshaped over flame into what's called a "slide." Generations of Delta guitarists, famed for their slide and bottleneck techniques, have started off playing the diddly-bow, and a young Mississippian named Lonnie Pitchford has developed into something of a diddly-bow virtuoso. But it's essentially a children's toy, and much has been made of its resemblance to the one-stringed instruments favored in West Africa, and of the fact that it's found only in Mississippi.

The diddly-bow is undoubtedly part of what William Ferris, the author of *Blues from the Delta* and the director of the Center for the Study of Southern Culture at the University of Mississippi, has in mind when he says that the Delta retained "one of the richest veins of African presence in this nation." Ferris doesn't say so, but others have concluded from such evidence that the blues was, in effect, something that black Mississippians *remembered* from Africa, well over a century after their ancestors were brought to the New World in chains. It's supposed to follow from this that the bluesman is a sort of latterday African *griot*, and that the blues *must* have first been played in the Delta because no other style of blues sounds *blacker* or more African—no other early regional sound betrays fewer echoes of Europe or retains so little of ragtime's punctilious syncopations. The proof of the Delta blues' direct link to Africa is supposed to be in the hearing: in the moans and irregular vocal accents of the Delta blues singers, in the polyrhythmic density of their one-chord drones, in their music's very *pitch*—the way Charley Patton or Son House or Bukka White or Tommy or Robert Johnson will sing a note not in the Western diatonic scale, then work his slide over the strings of his guitar to achieve the same effect instrumentally.

"The way the guitar equals the voice, people like that," B. B. King, whose blues are urban and electric but still redolent of his Delta birthplace of Indianola, Mississippi, told Charles Keil almost thirty years ago, during a backstage interview ultimately published in Keil's *Urban Blues*. "The two make one, and it fits together."

The two make one, and it fits together: one man playing the roles of preacher and congregation, internalizing the African tradition of call-and-response. But not only is this not unique to Mississippi, it's not even unique to the blues. The foremost exponent of slide guitar in the twenties and thirties was Blind Willie Johnson, a Texas street evangelist who presumably never laid hands on a diddly-bow. Johnson was also the most "African" of early black singers. In his 1981 book *Deep Blues*, Robert Palmer reminds us that many of the African masks now valued as art objects were once components of ritual, "the visual aspect of a masking procedure that also involved modifying the voice." Some masks, according to Palmer, had special mouthpieces through which their wearers would sing or hum in order to produce a buzzing sound that was taken as evidence of possession by a god or spirit. More frequently, especially in those regions of West Africa which imported the greatest number of slaves to the American South, the "masker" would simply resort to "deep chest growls, false bass tones produced in the back of the throat, strangulated shrieks, and other deliberately bizarre effects" in order to disguise his voice. "Since such extreme vocal modification had primarily religious or ritual associations in West Africa," Palmer observes, "it's interesting to note that it figured more prominently in black American sacred singing than in secular music." As examples, Palmer—whose thesis, in a nutshell, is that Delta blues is the "deepest" and most African blues of all—gives the occasional sacred recordings made by such early Mississippi bluesmen as Charley Patton, Son House, and Rubin Lacy. But this is only after conceding that "we encounter [this tendency] most frequently in the early recordings of guitar-playing evangelists such as the Texan Blind Willie Johnson."

REGARDLESS of what it's supposed to prove or disprove about the Delta's role in seeding the blues, to hear the blues as a West African import creates its own share of confusion. In the absence of recorded evidence, we can't even trace the blues back to slavery, much less Africa—especially not if we insist on a Delta birthplace for the blues, given that the Delta was largely unsettled land before the Civil War. What *can* be traced to African sources is the field holler, described by the folklorist Frederick Law Olmstead as "a long, loud musical shout, rising and falling and breaking into falsetto." (The earliest description we have of the music of African-Americans is the earliest we possibly could have—that of a writer named George Pinckard, who witnessed the arrival in Savannah, Georgia, of a shipload of slaves from Guinea and uncharitably characterized their chanting as "a wild yell devoid of all softness and harmony.") Whether in Senegal or in the Delta, a holler would be answered by a shout from a worker elsewhere in the field; it therefore stands to reason that these shouts and hollers evolved into the collective work song—with its chanted, rhymed couplets—and that the work songs evolved into the blues.

Or does it? According to most ethnomusicologists, the work song came first. Another problem is that although the blues is the final link in this evolutionary chain, it was the first to be commercially recorded and disseminated. This makes it difficult to gauge the extent to which the work songs and hollers recorded by John and Alan Lomax for the Library of Congress after 1933 were influenced by commercial recordings of the song form to which they supposedly gave birth. There's even a recording of hollers made in Clarksdale in 1941 on which one of the unnamed singers is believed by some to be none other than Son House.

To make matters more confusing, African music is beginning to betray the influence of the blues. Take the case of Ali Farka Touré, a native of Mali in his middle fifties who's recognized as a master of the one-string *gurkel*. "American blues, to me, just means a mix of various African sounds," he has said, expressing a romantic point of view probably held by more Ameri-

John Lee
Hooker
(FRANK DRIGGS
COLLECTION)

cans than Africans. "It's not American music, it's African music directly imported from Africa." Touré is a fan of John Lee Hooker. "[The first time I heard him] I didn't actually think he was American," Touré told the British music critic Philip Watson in an interview published in *The Wire*. "As I was listening to him I picked up my traditional guitar and played exactly the same thing, and it was after that that I thought I should do more with my music because he was producing something second hand. I decided that I should show people where this music came from."

You see the problem. Though the echo of Hooker's music in Touré's is often pointed to as evidence of Africa's influence on the blues, it's really the other way around. But this is all becoming solemn and theoretical, and that's no good—that can be deadly. Raymond Chandler once advised that the best way to satisfy a reader's craving for action was to have a man enter the room holding a gun. A .38 snub nose being a little beyond my reach, I'll brandish a . . . pigfoot, in the belief that a little absurdity never hurt anyone.

Civilization's most ignominious delicacy, the pigfoot was the morsel Bessie Smith yelled for (along with a bottle of beer) in one of her most famous songs. John Mohead called my attention to a whole jar of them when we stopped for beer and gasoline at a roadside grocery and filling station somewhere between Clarksdale and Memphis. He assumed he was showing me something I'd never seen the likes of before, something with the potential to amuse or nauseate me. I explained to him and James that I used to frequent a black jazz club up north that kept jars of them on the bar for customers to gnaw on with their drinks. Not only that, when I was a kid in Philadelphia, my grandmother used to send me to the corner grocery for them and a slimy cold cut packaged as "souse" meat, made from parts of a pig I didn't even want to know about.

The pigfoot is commonly thought of as "soul" food, the assumption being that it and hog jowls and the like were something Southern blacks developed a taste for out of necessity, on account of whites saving all the good parts of the pig for themselves. But such victuals have long been dietary staples of poor Southerners regardless of race. There was nothing remotely "down-home" about my grandmother. Her parents were from Liverpool, and she was as Irish as Paddy's proverbial pork chop. She had no black friends (or enemies), and if she was ever south of Baltimore in her entire life, she never told me about it. Even so, despite being Roman Catholic, she shared Celtic roots (and a preference for calories over nutrition) with the Delta's white settlers, who were mostly Irish, English, and Scottish. Am I merely trumpeting my own ethnic group by guessing that the pigfoot was something African-Americans chewed on after seeing the Irish do so? Nobody's ever mentioned spotting one in Africa, and they do eat them in Ireland, where they're called "crubeens." At any rate, a visit to a typical British pub ought to be enough to convince you that the Irish are the race most adamantly opposed to letting any limb or internal organ of a slaughtered animal go to waste, no matter how revolting.

But enough about the pigfoot. Let's talk about the banjo, the origins of which involve absolutely no guesswork. Most Americans probably think of it as a primitive forerunner to the guitar. Those who know something of jazz history might be especially prone to thinking so, given the banjo's use in jazz rhythm sections of the 1920s. Johnny St. Cyr played one on Louis Armstrong's first Hot Five recordings in 1925. Just five years later, the banjo had all but disappeared from jazz ensembles, having been replaced in many instances by rhythm guitar. The only present-day jazz groups in which you're likely to find one are semiprofessional Dixieland ensembles of the straw-hat-and-sleeve-garters variety. The banjo has never played much of a role in the blues, despite being the instrument strummed by a number of early black rural recording stars, including Papa Charlie Jackson and Gus Cannon. About the only style of music in which the banjo is still prominent is bluegrass, and as a result of this, when we think of the banjo, we're likely to think of white country folks.

At this point, the banjo practically shouts "cracker!" (or Northern old-tyme folkie). Yet it's actually an African import, related to the guitar only

35

insofar as the latter is itself of Arabic origin. Closer to a gourd than to a lute in both pitch and construction, the five-string American banjo is a direct descendent of an instrument played by the Wolof tribe of West Africa called the *halam* or the *konting*. It's played essentially the same way, by use of a technique musicologists call "frailing" and bluegrass players call "clawhammer," in which the player sustains a drone on an open-tuned string with his thumb while strumming a rhythm pattern or melody with the other four fingers.

The banjo was introduced to America by black slaves. It crossed over to white culture via blackface minstrel shows, musical revues in which white performers wearing burnt cork on their faces would spoof blacks, sometimes affectionately, sometimes viciously. By no means exclusive to the South, minstrel shows started about two or three decades before the Civil War; the first minstrel tune identified as such to make a dent in the national consciousness was Tim Rice's "Jump Jim Crow," published in 1830 and based on a song Rice had heard sung by a black stable hand in Louisville, Kentucky.

Blackface minstrel shows invite automatic comparison with the portrayal of women by men in Elizabethan theater, but there are other, less obvious parallels. In David Cronenberg's chimerical 1993 film adaptation of David Henry Hwang's *M. Butterfly*, Hang's make-believe Chinese geisha—a man masquerading as a woman to compromise a French diplomat under official sanction of the People's Republic, but clearly someone of indistinct gender who might be dressing as a woman and having sex with men anyway— asks the female Red Guard who's giving the orders if she knows why women are traditionally played by men in the Peking Opera. The good little soldier mumbles something about this being a carryover from "reactionary" times. "No," Butterfly tells her, walking away, "it's because only a man knows how a woman is supposed to act."

And only a white man knew how a "coon" was supposed to act. Minstrels are still with us, though they now forgo the burnt cork. Mick Jagger, the most famous of contemporary minstrels, sings and struts as though trying to get in touch with his Inner Negro. Minstrelsy was an embarrassing chapter in American history that retains its power to disturb us because white wish fulfillments have a way of becoming black reality. What is the TV show *Martin* if not a contemporary coon show aimed largely at blacks? (Granted, what looks like Tomming to me might strike black viewers as riotous comedy making knowing use of black show-business traditions. We've reached a point in our history where whites are more easily embarrassed than blacks by this sort of thing.) What distresses many people about rap, in addition to the music itself (or what some might describe as an absence of music in the conventional sense), is the zeal with which its performers and its impressionable young audiences embrace bad-nigger stereotypes, on stage and off. In retrospect, even the black militancy of the 1960s can be viewed as a form of minstrelsy. In a recent issue of the *Village Voice*, a black man calling himself Inb Kenyatta, an inmate serving a sentence of 21 years to life for the attempted murder of a New York City cop, described boarding a subway in the late sixties wearing a colossal Afro and a beige dashiki over a shirt showing a clenched black fist—"trying to be Black for black folks," in his own words. Is it possible that he was trying to be Black for white folks, too? Presumably paraphrasing him, the reporter Kathy Dobie writes, "Then five white girls got on the train and they went oohh! too and skittered down to where Kenyatta was standing and grabbed the straps next to him."

According to Rudi Blesh and Harriet Janis's *They All Played Ragtime*, one popular minstrel stereotype was "the good-natured simpleton." Another was "the Negro dandy, who wore the habiliments and the customs of his white 'superiors' so absurdly." From this description, the joke might have been on those laughing the loudest. Did it occur to whites of that day that the so-called Negro dandy might have been spoofing them? Nineteenth-century minstrelsy can be seen as both a perpetuation of a cruel status quo and the first sign of change, a form of theater and a form of drag, an entry into a world in which black could be white, white could be black, anything could be itself and simultaneously its opposite. As a defining episode in American race relations, the minstrel show is a rich and ambiguous topic. On a musical level, minstrelsy was the sincerest form of flattery. Minstrel shows provided scores of white Americans with their first taste of black music, no matter that it was secondhand and often presented as travesty. No doubt there were white minstrels who were earnest in their appreciation of black song forms and reasonably accurate in their interpretations of them. The appearance on stage of make-believe blacks ultimately paved the way for authentic black performers, albeit in burnt cork and white lip paint at first. ("The canny Negro," Blesh and Janis speculate, "turned *his* vision of the burnt-cork divertissement into a subtle but devastating caricature of the white *Übermensch*, employing the blackface like an African ceremonial mask, and through the whole thing insinuated his way onto the white stage.") In any event, the first white man to go on stage strumming a banjo was blacking up in ways he could hardly have been aware of. Minstrel tunes, beginning with Rice's "Jump Jim Crow," which has survived as "Turkey in the Straw," were usually accompanied by a dance step; the best and most popular of the white "nigger minstrels" prided themselves on the "authenticity" of both their music and their terpsichore. The first black minstrel to achieve renown was one William Henry Lane, a supple dancer who performed under the name "Juba" in the 1840s and is extolled in Charles Dickens's *American Notes*.

Minstrel shows were often literally drag shows, with white male performers dressing up as Negro "wenches." The practice of blacking up black performers seems to have started sometime around 1881, when P.T. Barnum hired a black dancer to replace John Diamond, the white star of his minstrel revue.

Fearing that white audiences would take as an affront the presence on stage of an actual Negro, Barnum smeared the man's face with burnt cork, painted his lips white, and outfitted him with a comically wooly wig—all of this to pass him off as a white man *imitating* a black, and therefore a genuine *artist*, not just someone doing what came naturally. This goes to show that Barnum was being conservative when he estimated that there was a sucker born every minute. It also goes to show that as "blackness" has become a form of masquerade for whites, "authenticity" can be a form of self-caricature or drag for blacks—thus Public Enemy, Martin Lawrence, and our subway radical.

YOU see where all this talk of pig's feet and banjos has led us. Neither can tell us where the blues started, or when. But each helps us to frame, if not answer, the equally important question of *how* the blues came to be.

Like the pigfoot and like the banjo, *songs* were items of Southern racial exchange. Many of the first black performers to be marketed as "blues" singers were, to their own way of thinking, no such thing. By their own reckoning, they were "songsters." In addition to blues, they sang folk ballads, work songs, hymns, ragtime numbers, minstrel and "coon" songs, cakewalks and other dance tunes they and their audiences called "reels" or "break-downs," and their own versions of the popular tunes of the day. Except for the blues—and frequently *including* the blues—this repertoire was more or less identical to that of the period's rural white performers.

The question of who was a bluesman and who was a songster is a tricky one, given that the market created for rural blues by the success of Blind Lemon Jefferson in 1926 probably resulted in many a country songster leaving a good deal of his material back home when he went to Memphis, Atlanta, or Chicago to record. Even Charley Patton favored variety in his repertoire, though he tended to rework everything he sang—including spiri-tuals—into one sort of blues or another. But we can say with absolute certainty that "Ragtime Texas" Henry Thomas—born around 1874 and one of the eldest-born black singers to be recorded—was a songster who only occasionally sang the blues. So was Blind Blake, variously associated with Georgia, the Carolinas, and Chicago, but essentially (in the words to one of his songs) "a travelin' man, staying alone and doing the best I can"—a nominal bluesman whose influential guitar style clearly owed something to ragtime pianists. Other songsters included Papa Charlie Jackson, who is believed to have been from near New Orleans, and who became the first rural black singer to be recorded, in 1926 (he gave us the first recorded versions of "Spoonful," "Alabama Bound," and "Shake That Thing"); Frank Stokes, a professional blacksmith from Memphis who formed a guitar duo with Dan Sane and more or less introduced the blues to Beale Street; and

Frank Stokes
(COURTESY SHELDON
HARRIS COLLECTION)

Jim Jackson, of Hernando, Mississippi, who began his career with a traveling medicine show and briefly became famous enough to land a cameo in King Vidor's 1929 movie *Hallelujah!* With the possible exception of Leadbelly, the ex-convict who achieved fame among white intellectuals with his booming voice and twelve-string guitar in the late 1930s, long after black musicians like himself had stopped calling themselves songsters, the best-known songster of them all was probably "Mississippi" John Hurt, from the tiny Delta town of Avalon, near Greenwood.

Hurt was an intriguing figure, a lifelong farmer who recorded a mere twenty songs at three different sessions for Okeh Records in 1928, when he was already in his late thirties, and then was unheard from again until being "rediscovered" in Avalon, in 1963. At that point, he was still tilling the fields and—much to the delight of acoustic blues purists—still singing and playing the same songs he'd recorded thirty-five years earlier in much the same way, oblivious to the forces that had led most professional bluesmen to change their repertoires and style of presentation. Following his rediscovery, Hurt became a favorite in coffeehouses and at folk festivals. Before his death in 1966, he even appeared on *The Tonight Show* with Johnny Carson. But he might never have recorded at all if not for the intervention of two of his white neighbors from Avalon, a guitar-and-violin duo who called themselves Narmour and Smith, and who recommended Hurt to their producer at Okeh.

Among those twenty songs that Hurt recorded in 1928 was a version of "Stagolee," a tale then already seventy years in the public domain and definitely of African-American origin—of a cold-blooded killer unintimidated by the law or the prospect of his own death (he winds up ruling Hell with an iron fist). "Stackolee" isn't a blues, exactly, though Hurt utilizes blues tonality and his version is, in fact, called "Stack O'Lee Blues" (probably his producer's phonetic approximation). The same song was a number-one hit for Lloyd Price in 1958; Price based his version on that of Leon T. Gross, a New Orleans singer and pianist who recorded it under the name "Archibald" but copyrighted it under his real name. In all its many versions, this is the song that Greil Marcus goes on about at length in his chapter on Sly Stone in *Mystery Train*, calling it "a story that black America has never tired of hearing and living out," and identifying Stagolee as the mythological prototype of the militant ex-cons who made their voices heard "when the civil rights movement got tough," and of the stylish pimps, drug dealers, and all-around bad motherfuckers who ran rampant in the black exploitation movies of the early 1970s. (*Mystery Train* was written too early for Marcus to take note of "gangsta" rappers.) Hurt's interpretation is cautionary, surprisingly gentle in light of the violent events depicted in the lyrics, which culminate with Stagolee's calm execution of a man who had the audacity to beat him at craps and try on his Stetson hat. "Police officer, how can it be? You can 'rest everybody, but cruel Stagolee?" Hurt sings, clearly on the side of law and order.

Depicted with a mixture of fear and admiration in the many versions that have followed Hurt's, Stagolee offers a clue to black America's potential for self-delusion, for self-loathing disguised as pride. Yet one of the song's earliest recorded versions was by Frank Hutchinson, a white singer of Irish extraction from North Carolina who recorded it in 1927, after learning it from Furry Lewis, a black Memphis songster who also recorded it the same year.[1]

---

1. According to Paul Oliver, in his *Songsters and Saints*, there was an actual "Stack Lee" whose racial background was as confused as the origins of the song that bears his name. A cabin boy on the Anchor Steamboat Line, he was one of many black children fathered illegitimately by Stacker Lee, a white Confederate officer and heir to a fleet of riverboats. Though Oliver doesn't say so, Stack Lee may have believed that sharing his name with a powerful white father granted him license to kill with impunity, so long as his victims were black. In any case, this is one of those instances in which it's difficult to say where fact ends and legend

This underscores the point made earlier, that the repertoire of the typical black country songster of the 1920s was more or less identical to that of white rural performers of the same period. Of course, there was nothing "typical" about Mississippi John Hurt, very possibly the best of the breed. The typical black songster was probably someone like Leslie Riddle, a singer and guitarist from North Carolina who didn't record until the blues revival of the 1960s, and who might be completely forgotten now if not for his early relationship with A. P. Carter, the patriarch of the Carter Family, the legendary white country harmony group whose most famous members were Mother Maybelle Carter and her daughter, June, the wife of Johnny Cash. The Carters never made a secret of the fact that they learned many of their songs from Riddle, a black man whose name was as unfamiliar to most blues fans as it was to devotees of country music.

It's important to remember, though, that Riddle himself performed many songs believed to be of Irish and Scottish origin. This raises the possibility that some of the songs he taught the Carters were on the second leg of a round trip. Paul Oliver theorizes that post-Reconstruction segregation laws forced Southern blacks to fall back on their own cultural resources, allowing the blues and other forms of black music to flower in relative isolation. There's clearly some truth to this. But what outsiders such as Oliver and myself are prone to overlook is the fact that, in the first half of this century, whites and blacks were in closer contact in the South than in the North, Jim Crow laws notwithstanding. In a cotton economy such as the Delta's, the two races were economically dependent on each other to an extent then unimaginable in the North: floods and boll weevil infestations spelled disaster for everyone, landowner and sharecropper or tenant farmer alike. In 1889, following the random killing of an estimated twenty-five black citizens in Leflore County, Mississippi, by a white mob reacting to rumors of an armed black insurrection, the county's cotton planters offered refuge to any black seeking it. These planters weren't motivated by social conscience. They were pragmatists "opposed [to] annihilating people who within a few weeks could pick their cotton," as the historian William F. Holmes puts it.

To be sure, the Delta's peculiar economy practically guaranteed white enmity toward blacks: it was all right for the proverbial redneck to joke that picking cotton or clearing lumber was work unfit for a white man, but probably no joking matter that he would never be hired for such a job anyway, so long as there was a black man forced by circumstances to pick cotton for practically nothing. There's a streak of white Southern sentimentality that insists whites and blacks got along just fine before the agitations of the 1960s. Maybe they did, but generally only if blacks kept their place. Northern blues fans visiting Memphis, usually on their way to or from

begins. You keep running into them in the blues—and only someone with no relish for mystery would have it any other way.

Mississippi, flock to A. Schwab's dry goods store on Beale Street, where such items of voodoo invocation as mojo powder and John the Conqueror roots are displayed directly across the aisle from votive candles and clerics' collars—as you stand there browsing next to black middle-aged shoppers who take this sort of thing seriously, you feel like you're penetrating the darkest mysteries of the blues. But on the mezzanine that Mr. Schwab maintains as a combination curio department and museum are a variety of large metal signs of the sort that used to hang on the walls of country stores, showing grinning Sambos devouring this manufacturer's pancake syrup or that manufacturer's watermelon freeze—reminders of how virulent Southern racism could be even at its most casual and unintended.

One sign, for Genuine Bull Durham Smoking Tobacco, presents a tableau so busy, so bizarre, that you can't even guess what it was meant to signify. It shows a black mammy on a rocker in front of a general store, pigs and chickens in a nearby yard, and a black youngster with a slingshot in his back pocket saying, "My, it sure am sweet tasting," as a bull with enormous testicles follows him down the road. To the first-time visitor from elsewhere in the United States, the Deep South is a foreign country, inscrutable to anyone who doesn't know its customs. In practically any of Beale Street's many record and souvenir shops, you can buy figurines or even waist-high ceramic statues of portly, bandannaed mammies that would bring pickets out in the North. They're usually right there in the display window, next to busts of Elvis and souvenir-size sacks of King Biscuit Flour. I was told by everybody I asked that blacks buy as many of them as whites.

Whatever the nature of their relationships, whites and blacks living in close proximity in cramped little Southern towns known only to census takers and the post office were able to keep few secrets from each other. They smelled each other's food and heard each other's music. Rock 'n' roll is supposed to have come screaming and kicking to life as the lovechild of blues and country-and-western in the early 1950s. But blues and country may themselves have been among the fruit of an earlier back-of-town rendezvous, between the field holler and the rhymed, Scots-Irish narrative ballad.

BLUES fans go to Memphis for the same reason they go to Mississippi, to stare at things that aren't there any more. The sign outside 315 Beale used to read "P. WEE'S," and every musician in Memphis knew where to find the door, even if he couldn't remember the number. The joint was ostensibly a pool room, but the billiards tables and pool cues were a front for a never-ending back room craps game. Anybody needing to get in touch with a musician for whatever reason knew to call Pee Wee's first. The Italians who owned the place would even take messages. Where Pee Wee's used to be is now the headquarters of the Memphis chapter of the National Academy of

Recording Arts and Sciences, the Grammy people. The former site of the Monarch Club, the hangout of W. C. Handy and his cronies, across the street at 340, is now the Memphis Convention and Tourist Information Center—fitting, because Beale Street, black Memphis's former hub, where a black man with a little bit of money in his pocket could shop for clothes or have his hair cut by day and engage in any manner of illicit activity by night without white folks paying much mind, has been transformed into a blues theme park, a tourist lure, several blocks of clubs, takeout windows, and souvenir shops for suburban and out-of-town white boys on the prowl. By day, Beale Street feels dead, still hung over from the night before. About the only reminder that Beale once served humdrum, daytime needs is Mr. Schwab's wood-floored dry goods store, open for business since 1876 and still selling blues records and mojo paraphernalia along with ketchup, over-alls, and grain.

Memphis was one of the Southern cities rural blacks flocked to in the decades before manpower shortages brought about by World War I and consequent restrictions on foreign immigration (down from 1.3 million in 1914 to just over 100,000 three years later) made the North a realistic option for most of them. Once the exodus from the South began, Memphis remained a way station for many Northern-bound blacks, and Beale Street was the one place in Memphis where they could be themselves. In an informative and entertaining half-hour movie that they'll run for you at the Center for Southern Folklore (an oasis of reflection at 152 Beale), B. B. King, who arrived in Memphis after World War II, says, "When I got to Beale Street, it was like a fantasy come true. I didn't think of Memphis as Memphis. I thought of Beale Street as Memphis." (Though he himself is long gone from Memphis, King now owns a club on Beale, as does Jerry Lee Lewis.)

But Beale Street no longer feels very magical, even by night. The strip's jewel used to be the Palace Theater, on the northeast corner of Beale and Hernando, directly across from the statue of W. C. Handy in the small park that bears his name. Like most of the businesses on Beale in its heyday, the Palace was white-owned. But when it opened its doors in 1907, it was one of the first theaters in the South in which blacks weren't restricted to faraway balcony seats. The theater was segregated, but it was for *them*. Though everyone from Bessie Smith to James Brown played the Palace over the years, the big events were the "Midnight Rambles" every Friday, when the theater's shapely chorus girls would perform a late show for curious whites, and the Amateur Night competition hosted by Rufus Thomas every Tuesday, with performers such as B. B. King and Big Mama Thornton at the very beginning of their careers. Elvis Presley nearly caused a riot at the Palace in 1956, though he was there merely to lend his support to a local black radio station's annual Goodwill drive, not to perform: "A thousand black, brown, and beige teenage girls in that audience blended their alto and soprano voices in one wild crescendo of sound that rent the rafters, and took off like scalded cats in the direction of Elvis," Nat D. Williams, a popular black Memphis newspaper columnist who moonlighted as a disc jockey for WDIA, later reported, bewildered and perhaps somewhat chagrined by the sight of black girls swooning over a white performer.

The Palace is long gone, demolished in the late 1960s, by which time the beginnings of integration had spread black nightlife thin and whites no longer felt safe strolling Beale in the wake of the riots that followed Dr. Martin Luther King, Jr.'s, assassination. But the Orpheum Theater is still there, at the foot of Beale, down by the river. The weekend I was in Memphis, it was hosting a road company production of *The Phantom of the Opera.* Close by was a blues karaoke bar where, after tanking up with beer, you could pretend that you were Howlin' Wolf or somebody equally as *baad.* If present-day Beale Street could talk, the message it might belch would be that the night belongs to Michelob.

Still, karaoke bars and *tchachka* shops are better than the rubble Beale Street was reduced to in the name of urban renewal in the late sixties. The late Albert Goldman, a boorish author of poison-pen biographies of Elvis Presley, Lennie Bruce, and John Lennon (he was always arm-wrestling with cadavers and winning), once complained that Memphis's only contribution to the blues was in commercializing it. To which the only sensible rebuttal might be to point out that because the blues is a form of popular music, commercialization wasn't such a bad thing. "The blues had a baby, and they called it rock 'n' roll," Muddy Waters used to sing; if so, Memphis was the maternity ward, and the record producer Sam Phillips was the obstetrician. Sun Studios, on Union a few blocks north of Beale, where Phillips turned Memphis into one big echo chamber, doesn't have a revolving door, but maybe it should: you imagine a succession of pomaded bluesmen walking in and a succession of pompadoured rockabillies walking out in an evolutionary blur on a sunny afternoon around 1954. B. B. King, Howlin' Wolf, and Bobby "Blue" Bland were all in Memphis around that time, and so were Elvis Presley, Jerry Lee Lewis, and Carl Perkins. But Memphis was a musical crucible long before that, and remained one long after—it was where Gus Cannon and Will Shade brewed up an intoxicating blend of the blues and minstrel melodies with their jug bands in the teens and twenties, and where Booker T. Jones and a handful of Stax/Volt session men devised a pop music slicker than the blues and funkier than Motown some forty years later.

You can't walk a block in downtown Memphis without coming across a hole-in-the-wall record store advertising itself as a blues museum. Without its musical heritage, the city would have no identity at all. I stayed a few blocks from Beale in a Ramada Inn across the street from the Peabody, one of the South's oldest and most fabled luxury hotels, and still a thriving convention site. Yet except for Beale, the streets surrounding the Peabody were empty and eerily silent, clean by Northern standards but *vacated*—as grim and apocalyptic as an abandoned warehouse. One whole mile of Poplar Street, which I saw from a speeding bus, seemed composed of nothing but pawnshops, bail bondsmen, and Western Unions. Elvis was everywhere I looked, wherever merchandise was for sale: Elvis shot glasses, Elvis jigsaw puzzles, shrink-wrapped facsimiles of newspapers headlining his death. I half expected there to be a painting of him in my room at the Ramada, like there was in the fleabag that Joe Strummer, Rick Aviles, and Steve Buscemi holed up in after robbing a liquor store and shooting its owner in Jim Jarmusch's *Mystery Train*. I myself began to feel a little bit like Elvis in a movie directed by Michelangelo Antonioni: anomic and self-absorbed but careful to end every sentence I uttered with "Sir" or "Ma'am," the way Elvis did and everybody in Memphis also seems to, no matter whom he or she's talking to and no matter what he or she's saying. Southern politeness is no myth, yet the panhandlers on Union Street were the most aggressive I've encountered anywhere—or maybe just the most desperate. One, asking me if I liked the blues (white guy, right?) as I crossed the street from the Greyhound Station to my hotel, whipped out a harmonica and offered to play Bill Doggett's "Honky Tonk" for me if I gave him a dollar. All he was able to give me was a dollar's worth of wheeze—the two of us standing there in the middle of traffic in a city with the blues that's forgotten how to sing.

ON the other hand, it rained the entire time I was in Memphis, and the steady drizzle may have chilled my thoughts, along with the early spring air (it's not the heat, it's the humidity; it's not the barometric pressure, it's the pathetic fallacy). Unable to sleep on my final night in town, alternately gazing at the TV and out the window at the puddles on the roofs in back of the hotel, I found myself thinking about the Delta. It's one thing to scoff at the notion that the blues is a Delta import when all you're doing is listening to records and poring over books, but another matter when you're actually there, walking the ground Patton and Johnson once walked, and breathing the same air.

The Delta's blues singers were the genre's transcendentalists, their lyrics pondering the nature of faith, the purpose of life, the inevitability of death. Something about the Delta inspired introspection on the part of men whose lives allowed little time for it. Folks there tell you it's on account of something in the water, and that whatever it is, it also gave birth to the blues. But the Mississippi rips through several states, and belongs to none of them. Without being mystical about it, I believe that the proof of the Delta's formative role in the blues is in that fabulous soil, to which most blacks of Patton's generation were indentured no less than their parents had been to their masters.

The two most important phrases in a black sharecropper's life in the first half of this century were "the furnish" and "the settle." The furnish was the tangible goods a landowner supplied a cropper family in the spring, before planting: this usually included fertilizer, seed, a mule or two, and farm machinery, in addition to clothing, shelter, and a line of credit at the plantation commissary or a local store. The settle, paid off after the crop went to market in late fall, was the cropper's half of the profit from his allotted piece of land, minus the furnish and whatever interest the landowner decided to charge on it. This arrangement almost never worked to the sharecropper's advantage. Actual figures are provided in Charles Sawyer's *The Arrival of B. B. King.* In 1939, when King was fourteen, his grandmother, Elmora Farr (by then the head of King's household), received $32.05 in furnish (including $2.05 for fertilizer) from Edwayne Henderson, a Kilmichael, Mississippi, dairy farmer who also grew cotton on his land and kept meticulous financial records. At 8 percent interest, Farr and her grandson started the season $34.61 in debt. Their small share of the market value of that year's crop was $25.27; they earned another $10.00 doing odd work in the Henderson home, bringing their net income for the year to a grand total of 66 cents. During the off season, Farr drew another $16.75 from Henderson to see her and King through the winter; this included $8.00 for doctors' bills for the ailing Farr, who died of what sounds like tuberculosis in January, owing Henderson $3.63 once the cost of her funeral was added to her ledger and a percentage of the farm subsidy Henderson received from the federal government was applied to her portion of the crop. Henderson wrote off Farr's debt as a loss. King, left on his own after his grandmother's death, ended the following year $7.54 in debt, though Henderson—no monster— marked his account paid in full.

Debts were carried over year to year, so that a family of sharecroppers (or even a tenant family able to supply its own animals and equipment) often faced the prospect of working for nothing. At least they had a roof over their heads and stood a chance of clearing a few dollars if that year's crop was good. The alternative to this cotton feudalism was homelessness, or working under a similar arrangement for even less money on depleted farms in the Mississippi hills. We're used to tracing blues evolution from Mississippi to Chicago, the Northern city to which scores of Delta singers and guitarists and harmonica players and pianists migrated as part of a larger black exodus starting in the last decade of the nineteenth century and reaching a peak between the two world wars. This is why the blues fascinates sociologists who otherwise have no ear for music: it provides a kind of soundtrack to the gradual urbanization of a once largely rural people. What even musicologists sometimes overlook, however, is that the blues may have resulted from an earlier migration *within* Mississippi—from the fallow hill country to the fertile Delta. In the late 1800s and early 1900s, blacks streamed into the Delta—not just from the hills, but from other parts of the South—for jobs on its plantations, sawmills, and lumber and turpentine camps, bringing as their only baggage the varied musical traditions of their different starting points, and making the Delta something of a black cultural melting pot.

This influx to a region where little value was placed on black life (at least under slavery, Negroes had counted as salable *property*) helped to create what David Evans, a professor of music at Memphis State University and the author of *Big Road Blues*, describes as "the conditions of an urban ghetto spread out over a rural landscape." If anything, this is an understatement. Urban blues isn't the only aspect of black city life that can be traced back to the Delta—just the most providential. Despite the wealth of a small group of landowners, the Delta was a poverty-stricken region even during its roughly fifty-year reign as America's Cotton Kingdom. Poor whites experienced their own hardships, but black life was a nightmare of rootlessness and self-destruction from which black America still hasn't fully awakened. Most marriages were common-law and understood to be temporary. Hopelessly in debt to a landowner, an entire family might steal away by dead of night to another plantation where, as likely as not, they would eventually find themselves in the same situation. Just as frequently, the man of the family would flee on his own, leaving his latest woman and their children to fend for themselves while he rode the rails or started another family on a plantation a few miles away. Birth control was then in its primitive stages, but practically unheard of among the Delta's black population. Someone who considered himself a family man would deliberately sire as many children as possible, believing that a large brood meant more hands picking cotton and therefore a bigger annual settle—but not calculating that every son or daughter meant another mouth to feed on a small furnish. Children attended school only during the off season, and only until they were old enough to join their parents and older siblings in the fields. Many children never saw the inside of a schoolhouse at all. The infant mortality rate, among both blacks and whites, was the highest in the nation. Tuberculosis and venereal disease were epidemic, and many men and women spent every penny they made on moonshine. Murder was a fact of life, and though no statistics on black-on-black violence are available, there is reason to believe they were staggering. The unwritten law in the backwoods gambling dens in which the blues was performed was that you could kill anybody you pleased and the authorities would look the other way so long as your victim was a fellow Negro and not a good worker.

These shacks in which the blues began its transformation from a form of self-expression to a form of entertainment were called juke houses. *Juke* is an African retention, a word meaning "evil, disorderly, wicked" in Bambara, a language spoken in parts of the Congo. Absorbed into English via Gullah, the language of blacks in the Georgia Islands, it has since acquired multiple meanings, all redolent of sinful pleasure: to juke is to dance (or to rumble, if 1950s movies about street gangs can be trusted); a juke box is a gaudy neon-and-chrome pop-music dream machine; a juke house—frequently doubling as a brothel—was a place to drink, gamble, wreak havoc, and dance to the blues. No wonder the Delta's black churchgoers and strivers considered the blues itself to be sinful. Yet the blues, like most subsequent forms of black music (arguably including rap), was a way of smiling through (or sneering at) adversity, a people's attempt to alchemize poison into medicine, all the deliverance hoped for or needed by the men and women who played it or merely danced and indulged their desires to its hypnotic accompaniment.

A second black migration within Mississippi was already in motion by the time the early Delta blues we hear as a touchstone of black plantation life was recorded in the late 1920s. This slow but steady migration from the plantations to nearby small towns occurred simultaneously with the migration that everyone knows about—the one that brought the arrival in the North of an estimated 6.5 million blacks from all over the South in the years between 1910 and 1970, ultimately changing the complexion of America's Northern urban areas and making race a national, rather than just a Southern, issue. As late as 1940, over three quarters of America's black population was Southern—though, in the case of Mississippi, no longer 100 percent rural. There was less need for blacks as manual laborers on the Delta's plantations after the introduction of the row tractor by International Harvester in 1922; still less need for them after the mechanical cotton picker went into widespread use just after World War II. By then, many of the smaller plantations that had once competed with larger operations such as Stovall's had folded anyway, victims either of the Great Depression of the 1930s or of competition from the Southwestern United States. The final blow was the use by an increasing number of planters, beginning in the late 1950s, of chemical defoliants, which eliminated even the need for hand-chopping of weeds between rows.

The Great Migration is frequently assumed to have been a byproduct of Northern industrialization, and of black perception of the North as the symbolic equivalent of the promised land spoken of in the book of Exodus. But no matter how vehemently Mississippi plantation owners may have opposed black migration at first, theirs was one state that supplied its own push. When Muddy Waters boarded that train in 1943, the Delta that Charley Patton had known no longer existed. And when Waters plugged his guitar into an amplifier in Chicago a few years later, the transformation of the blues from a rural folk idiom to an urban popular music had already been under way for several decades—a slow and tentative process, much like the migration itself.

•

MISSISSIPPI blues didn't just pack up one day and head for points north, leaving no trace of itself in the Delta or the hills. In Bentonia, a town on the Delta's southern perimeter, half in the hills, where Skip James spent most of his life, his contemporary Jack Owens—now closing in on ninety, but still performing fairly regularly, usually with the harmonica player Bud Spires—carries on James's tradition, playing an intricate, percussive guitar style and singing in a falsetto voice somehow both measured and possessed. (With his bright eyes and seamed, skull-like face, Owens is worth any number of books on the history of the blues.) Among the middle-aged musicians still living in the Delta and playing regularly in its juke joints are Junior Kimbrough, Frank Frost, and Big Jack Johnson, all of whom have modest national followings. But play their records for someone without telling him what he's hearing, and he's likely to guess it's something from Chicago—something derivative of Muddy Waters or Howlin' Wolf or Sonny Boy Williamson's recordings for Chess. The blues has completed a kind of reverse migration, via radio and the phonograph.

But music never travels alone, and other signs of a reverse migration that has quietly been taking place over the last few decades include a roadside shack near Clarksdale that was once a juke joint but was recently torn down by the police as a crack house, and the occasional graffiti you see around town for the Disciples and the Vice Lords, Southern branches of Chicago street gangs—many of whose local members, in fact, were born in Chicago. In *The Promised Land*, Nicholas Lemann follows the progress of several of Muddy Waters's Mississippi contemporaries who, like him, migrated to Chicago in the 1940s, initially thinking they had arrived in Canaan. A surprising number of them are back in Clarksdale now, along with their children, grandchildren, and even great-grandchildren, having been as luckless in the Midwest as in the South.

In one of those ironic reversals common to American life, many first- or second-generation Southern migrants now view the North as the place where black life went horribly wrong. A 1993 article in the *Chicago Tribune* told the story of Frederick Alston, a fourteen-year-old member of a street gang on Chicago's South Side sent by his mother (herself a Southern migrant) to live with relatives in Kosciusko, Mississippi, in an attempt to straighten him out. The story was part of a series on a murder epidemic among black Chicago teenagers, to which Alston himself fell victim soon after his return to the South Side. But Alston had stayed out of trouble in Kosciusko, and might have remained there if he hadn't been prevented from enrolling at the local high school by the very state laws designed to prevent white students from establishing temporary residency in a county in order to avoid attending integrated schools. (Ironically, Kosciusko High—the only public school in a town of 8,000 whose courthouse displays a monument to the Confederate dead—would have been the first integrated school the Chicago-born Alston had ever attended.)

This story isn't unique: the principal of Kosciusko High told the *Tribune* that he and other Mississippi school principals constantly field calls from Northerners hoping to rescue their children from inner cities by sending them to school in the South. But a more typical scenario might be that of a child born to an unwed mother in the North and raised in the South by a grandparent, the entire family drifting rootlessly back and forth—not just dispossessed, but spiritually displaced. In a sense, "reverse" migration is a misnomer for this little noted social phenomenon. Chaos in the black family structure—a bitter inheritance of the sharecropper system, if not slavery—has prevented the Northern migration of the first half of this century from ever having been completed once and for all.

Blemished with listing shacks and atrophied mobile homes, vast portions of the Delta countryside today more than ever fit Evans's description of an urban ghetto spread over a rural landscape. The nation's most chronic poverty can be found here, atop the nation's most fertile soil. The most depressing example might be Jonestown, an almost completely black town of 1,500 people not twenty miles northeast of Clarksdale. Three quarters of Jonestown's adult residents are women, and a full half of its citizens are children under the age of fourteen. In a town in which full employment is estimated to be only 5 percent, fathers have gradually disappeared. Median family income in the Delta is half the national standard, and the median for black families is just half that of whites. The infant mortality rate is the highest in the nation, far exceeding that of many Third World countries. There are few jobs. Between the end of World War II and 1980, the number of farms in the Delta decreased from 105,037 to 6,561. The remaining cotton plantations still provide a few jobs, paying choppers an average of $4.25 an hour for work that paid only $3.00 a day as recently as twenty-five years ago. But the work is seasonal, and cotton season lasts only a few months. What used to be a cotton economy, then a farm economy, is now what Lemann discreetly calls a government economy—that is, a black welfare economy.

Blues scholars of the 1960s tended to be gripped by an optimism that expressed itself as pessimism. Viewing the blues as a byproduct of black America's poverty and deprivation, they concluded that the entry of the black masses into mainstream American life would spell the end of the blues as a distinct form of music. Looking at the Delta's hardest-hit counties or Chicago's South Side today, we can say with a bitter laugh that these blues enthusiasts needn't have worried, at least not for the precise reason that they did. But no one could have foretold that—in yet *another* ironic reversal—

the blues would thirty years later become a source of pride for white as well as black Mississippians, and an actual source of *revenue* for the state.

By Delta standards, Clarksdale is fairly prosperous. There has always been wealth there, a small portion of it black. The town might be doing all right even without the influx of tourists, but this steady stream of outsiders is responsible for Clarksdale being one of the few towns in Mississippi in which revenues from sales taxes have actually risen over the last few years. Practically anybody with free time on his hands can pick up a few extra bucks showing tourists where the relevant tombstones are. I was lucky to hook up with two white guys close to my own age whose passion for the blues and knowledge of its lore made them ideal guides. Driving people like me around the Delta has become a second livelihood for James Butler, an antiques dealer by trade, and John Mohead, a pecan grower and avocational blues guitarist. The only problem was that they didn't know what to charge me for their time, never having shown an *individual* around before—only groups, mostly Japanese. We finally settled on a fair price for their Saturday afternoon, though I sensed that they felt awkward taking anything from me at all, once we became friends. In any case, John bought the beer.

THEY figured I'd enjoy meeting Mrs. Hill, and I did. In one of the photos that ran with the newspaper article she showed me, she and JFK, Jr. clasped hands on the Riverside's front steps, beneath a sign proclaiming her establishment the "Home of the Delta Blues." If you like, Mrs. Hill can sell you a T-shirt or a baseball cap bearing the same legend.

The Riverside's interiors are spotless, though the sun streaming in the front window doesn't brighten the place up, but just makes it seem more faded around the edges—like a photograph from another era, so old that looking at it requires imagination, not memory, to relate it to the contemporary world. Mrs. Hill is a dark, tiny woman who wears her gray hair in a bun and looks at least a decade younger than her eighty-some-odd years. She's gracious and softspoken and endlessly patient—used to busloads of strangers dropping in unannounced to see the packed suitcase Robert Night-hawk left behind when he checked into a Helena hospital to die in 1967, and the first-floor room believed to be the one in which Bessie Smith lay hemorrhaging, her ribcage smashed and her right arm torn loose at the elbow, in the early morning hours of September 26, 1937 (it's the only one of the Riverside's twenty-five rooms unavailable for occupancy). You can tell, though, that Mrs. Hill lays down the law to her transient clientele. COOKING IN ROOMS STRICTLY PROHIBITED BY THE LANDLADY & THE FIRE MARSHALL, reads a hand-lettered sign in the basement corridor, giving the impression that it's Clarksdale's local ordinances that are in compliance with Mrs. Hill's housekeeping, instead of the other way around. And who's to say? She's

Mrs. Hill, or better yet, *Ma'am*, and a white Northerner such as I would no sooner dream of calling her by her first name (or even asking it) than he would of talking to her or any of the folks in Clarksdale about the *Mississippi* blues. The adjective is superfluous, because south of Memphis, there's assumed to be no other kind.

Sitting across from me on a wicker chair in a front room that doubles as her parlor and office, Mrs. Hill talked about Bessie Smith: about her dangling jewelry and fringed gowns, the spell she could put on an audience, the *naughtiness* of some of her songs (did I detect a blush?), the excitement around Clarksdale when Mrs. Hill was a young lady and Bessie would return to her hometown with one of the tent shows.

"Someone from Europe sent me this letter today," Mrs. Hill said, abruptly changing the subject and handing me a tissue-thin air-mail envelope with a German postmark. "He's writing some kind of book, and he wants to know about a Champion Jack Dupree. Do *you* know anything about him?"

"Champion Jack" Dupree—famous as a barrelhouse piano player, but also a graduate of the same waifs' home as Louis Armstrong, a Mardi Gras Indian, a hobo, a prizefighter, a cook, a bootlegger, a comedian, a World War II POW, and a painter at one point or other in the years between his birth in 1909 (according to his passport) or 1910 (according to Sheldon Harris's generally reliable *Blues Who's Who*) and his death in 1992. Although Shakespeare was Champion Jack's favorite author—the one he frequently misquoted between numbers, anyway—he had a thing or two in common with Charles Dickens, who supposedly used to sit at his writing desk weeping or doubled over laughing at his own prose. Champion Jack also had a thick slick of ham in him, though in his case it was probably a butt portion (one of his most popular songs was called "Stick Out Your Can, Here Comes the Garbage Man"). Just as Dickens was his own most sympathetic reader, Dupree was often his own most receptive audience, especially after following the example of countless black jazz musicians and becoming the first American bluesman to emigrate to Europe in the late 1950s (the story goes that he decided to stay when a uniformed British customs inspector addressed him as "sir"). "Not seldom did he wipe a tear from his cheek when he sang about his orphan childhood, about prison loneliness, never growing up in a family, not having a home for so many years," a German writer named Norbert Hess recalled in his liner notes to *New Orleans Barrelhouse Boogie*, a CD reissue of Dupree's 1940–41 Okeh recordings that I'd been listening to before heading south. Champion Jack's life was the stuff of legend—or half-cocked fable. His father was originally from the Belgian Congo, his mother part-Creole and part-Cherokee, and he and his four siblings lost both parents when the Ku Klux Klan torched the Dupree family store. Or so he usually told interviewers, except for the one time he speculated that the fire was an accident: his folks sold oil for kerosene lamps and the fire started from a spontaneous explosion in one of the oil drums.

For a man who tended to play piano like the boxer he once was (a Golden Gloves champion with over a hundred professional bouts to his credit, including—we are asked to believe—a spot on the card in New York in 1936 before the first Joe Louis–Max Schmeling title fight), Champion Jack could deliver a vocal with surprising understatement. This, more than any other aspect of his Tin Pan New Orleans piano style, may have reflected the influence of Leroy Carr, the Indianapolis-based singer and pianist whose 1928 "How Long—How Long Blues" (with the guitarist Scrapper Blackwell) heralded the transformation of the blues from rural folk to sophisticated urban pop (it was the first blues record Muddy Waters remembered listening to over and over again as a child). I recalled reading that Champion Jack, by his own recollection, had arrived in Indiana in 1935, just in time to rub elbows with Carr, who died from the effects of alcoholism that April. I also recalled looking at the publicity photo of Dupree from around 1940 on the back cover of the booklet that came with *New Orleans Barrelhouse Boogie*.

Champion
Jack Dupree
(COURTESY ALTA
SIMMONS
COLLECTION, BLUES
ARCHIVE, UNIVERSITY
OF MISSISSIPPI)

In it, he was young and pomaded and trying his best to look like a penthouse serenader in white dinner jacket and black tie. Seeing this photo a few years after his triumphant homecoming at the 1991 New Orleans Jazz and Heritage Festival, where he captivated the crowd with his very *age*, it was somehow disorienting to see him ungristled—without his cigar, his mouthful of gold teeth, and his Indian headband and moccasins.

Was Champion Jack one of the dozen or so most important bluesmen? Hardly. He might not even rank in the top hundred, despite having been the first New Orleans blues pianist to be recorded (albeit in Chicago, after his exposure to Carr had wiped away some of the traces of such proto-Crescent City ticklers as Tuts Washington and Willie "Drive 'em Down" Hall) and despite having been one of the progenitors of rhythm 'n' blues and rock 'n' roll (there's an unmistakable echo of his "Shake, Baby, Shake" in Jerry Lee Lewis's "Whole Lot of Shaking Going On," and both Fats Domino's "The Fat Man" and Lloyd Price's "Lawdy Miss Clawdy" are descended from his "Junker Blues"). He was essentially a journeyman who too often got by on his considerable charm as a ribshack raconteur.

With which I suppose there was nothing wrong, insofar as he gave his audiences a good time and seemed to be having one himself in the bargain. Despite its origins as folk expression and its present status as a subject for academic inquiry, the blues has always been understood by its performers and audiences to be above all else a form of *entertainment*. Sometimes we need a Champion Jack to remind us of that, and of something else besides. Given the sociological bias of most writing on the blues, we tend to discuss the work of its performers in terms of their country birthplaces, or in terms of the cities in which they first make their marks. But look at Champion Jack. Never really a country boy, he was born in the Bayou, died in the Rhineland, and was all over the map in between—in Chicago, New York, London, Denmark, and who knows where else? He wasn't the only one, either. For every bluesman you can name who spent practically his whole life within a few miles of his hometown, I could name a dozen others who just couldn't stay put. Maybe that's why some of them became musicians in the first place, to leave places like Clarksdale far behind.

So yeah, as a matter of fact, I did know a thing or two about Champion Jack Dupree, whose travels never seem to have landed him in Mississippi—which, ironically, might have been why Mrs. Hill needed to inquire about him.

"He was from Louisiana," I told her, knowing that was all she needed to hear.

"I didn't think he was from here," said Mrs. Hill, no blues oracle, just an old woman who knows what she knows.

She took the letter back from me and put it under a lace doily, with the rest of that morning's mail.

two

THE BLUES AS SUCH/NO SUCH THING AS THE BLUES

CHAPTER 1

• •

COON SHOUTERS AND TITULAR BLUES

One of the topics most frequently addressed in blues songs is the blues itself. Personification being a technique frequently employed by blues singers, regardless of whether they recognize it as a literary concept, the blues is also a familiar *character* in their songs—walking like a man, thumbing a ride, bidding the singer good morning, and implying that it's going to be around for a good long spell no matter what the singer does to chase it away. Those who write about the blues also tend to grant it human characteristics. It's born in Mississippi before the turn of the century, wanders around the South a little bit, spends a considerable amount of time in Texas, then turns up in Chicago just in time to father rock 'n' roll. It dies a natural death around 1960, but—stubborn old cuss that it is—rises up like Lazarus every ten years or so.

Of course, nothing is that simple—which is why this portion of our narrative begins in a New York recording studio before returning south. Let's just say the blues has a large extended family and bears a strong resemblance to many of its relatives. Especially in its younger years, it was frequently sighted in places it may or may not have been, and mistaken for blood relatives long since forgotten.

ACCORDING to most experts, the first blues record was "Crazy Blues," a song composed by Perry Bradford and recorded for Okeh Records by Mamie Smith and Her Jazz Hounds (a five-man combo possibly featuring the unrelated stride pianist Willie "The Lion" Smith) on August 10, 1920. Then again, some of the experts will tell you that "Crazy Blues" isn't *really* a blues, by which I think they mean that it's not *the* blues. It's what might be called a "titular" blues—a song (in this case, a torch song) utilizing blues tonality and twelve-bar structure, and alluding to the blues as a mood or inclination, but essentially a pop number rather than a blues in the self-defining way that a song by Robert Johnson or Muddy Waters is.

"Crazy Blues" was hardly the first of these blues-in-name-only. Bradford, a black music-store proprietor and all-around hustler from Chicago who was known to bend the truth to his own advantage, copyrighted it in 1915, five years before Smith's recording, but claimed to have written it as "The Nervous Blues" in 1912. This earlier date is significant, because we know for a fact that a trio of titular blues were published that year. The most famous of these is W. C. Handy's "Memphis Blues," which Handy had written on commission three years earlier (as "Mr. Crump Don't 'Low It") in an effort to get out the black vote for E. H. Crump, a successful mayoral candidate who pledged to clean up Beale Street. (Crump won the election and went on to become one of the South's most powerful political bosses, though he apparently neglected to listen very closely to Handy's original lyrics, which were clearly on the side of sin: "We don't care what Mr. Crump don't 'low/We're gonna barrelhouse anyhow.")

Mamie Smith
(FRANK DRIGGS
COLLECTION)

But two other composers, one of them white, beat Handy to the copyright office. The composer of the very first copyrighted "blues" was Hart Wand, a white Oklahoma violinist and bandleader whose "Dallas Blues" was so named because its melody gave a black porter who worked for Wand's family "the blues to go back to Dallas." This was followed a few months later by "Baby Seal Blues," a negligible item by the black vaudeville performer Arthur "Baby" Seals and the ragtime pianist Arthur Matthews. (Another song written in 1912, though not published until the following year—and not recorded until 1915—was the blackface minstrel Leroy "Lasses" White's crude "Nigger Blues." But in a sense, the very first blues was the twelve-bar opening verse to the pop song "Oh, You Beautiful Doll," which was published in 1911.)

In 1913, Handy—having been finagled out of his royalties from "Memphis Blues" and desperate for another hit—composed "Jogo Blues," a number he soon decided was "over the head of the average pianist and too difficult for the average orchestra." "Jogo," he tells us in his autobiography, was slang for Negro, and he seems to be implying that the tune was too idiomatic— too *black*—to catch on with white orchestras and sheet-music buyers. "Jogo Blues" would be of little interest to us today if not for the fact that its composer, resolving to combine "ragtime syncopation with a real melody in the spiritual tradition," and to use "all that is characteristic of the Negro from Africa to Alabama," refashioned it into the most celebrated titular blues of all.

"St. Louis Blues," published in 1914, is one of the most enduring American songs: more popular than "Star Dust," "Body and Soul," "Summertime," "Tea for Two," and even "White Christmas," if we are to judge from its number of recorded versions between the two world wars. It's also something of a compositional pastiche, though intentionally so. "When 'St. Louis Blues' was written the tango was in vogue," Handy explained in *Father of the Blues*. "I tricked the dancers by arranging a tango introduction, breaking abruptly then into a low-down blues." Only the first and third strains of "St. Louis Blues" employ traditional twelve-bar blues structure. The second strain (the bridge, as it were, which begins "St. Louis woman, with your diamond ring") is an unambiguous tango, and despite Handy's symphonic leanings, the song's overall construction is that of classic ragtime, right down to its internal syncopations.

Nothing about "St. Louis Blues" was original except for Handy's élan in tossing together these seemingly disparate elements. The song is a virtual melting pot, and therein its power as well as its charm. "My eyes swept the floor anxiously, then suddenly I saw the lightning strike," Handy later wrote, recalling his band's first performance of the tune, at the Alaskan Roof in Memphis. "The dancers seemed electrified. Something within them came suddenly to life. An instinct that wanted so much to live, to fling its arms and to spread joy, took them by the heels."

You sense that this is the one passage in Handy's autobiography in which he wasn't exaggerating. Years later T-Bone Walker, speaking for the majority of blues musicians, said of "St. Louis Blues," "That's a pretty tune, and it has kind of a bluesy tone, but it's not the blues. You can't dress up the blues." Still, to those white dancers in Memphis that night in 1914, Handy's tune must have sounded absolutely primal—the first genuinely American song, even its tango elements coming across as essentially African-American in nature and increasing the song's lure of social upheaval and the shattering of sexual taboos. (It's worth noting, in passing, that the tango itself, within its native Argentina, was like the blues in terms of its underclass origins and its eventual domination of that country's musical sensibility.)[1]

I N what sense, then, did "Crazy Blues" represent a breakthrough, coming as it did six years later? A clue lies in those bands and singers who recorded "St. Louis Blues" within a few years of its publication. The first hit version of Handy's masterpiece was in 1916, an instrumental by the Prince Orchestra, a society band led by a pianist who claimed to be a distant relative of the second and sixth presidents of the United States. In addition to its version of "Joe Turner's Blues," another Handy composition drawn from traditional sources, the Prince Orchestra's other hits that year included "Hello, Hawaii, How Are You?" and "The Star Spangled Banner." The first vocalist to have a hit with "St. Louis Blues," three years later, was Al Bernard, a vaudeville comedian billed as "The Boy From Dixie," who recorded it again in 1921, this time accompanied by the Original Dixieland Jazz Band, the same group whose 1917 "Livery Stable Blues" is generally recognized as the first jazz record.

The best of the early recorded versions of "St. Louis Blues"—it rivals Bessie Smith's 1925 interpretation for sheer abandon—reached number one on the charts just two weeks after Mamie Smith made "Crazy Blues." This was by Marion Harris, one of whose earlier hits was a nifty little number called "Everybody's Crazy 'Bout the Doggone Blues (But I'm Happy)." Largely forgotten now, Harris was among the most popular singers of her day, and one of the most creative; Will Friedwald, in *Jazz Singing*, credits her with initiating the practice of setting lyrics to improvised jazz solos (in the manner of the bebop

1. An out-of-print record well worth the hunt (though it won't come cheap) is *Blues Revisited: A Unique Series of Authentic Performances by the Legendary W. C. Handy* (Heritage), a ten-inch LP from 1953 on which Handy, then approaching eighty and completely blind, offers utterly charming interpretations of "Memphis Blues," "St. Louis Blues," and others of his most famous songs, accompanying himself on guitar and trumpet on a few of them (now available in cassette only, on DRG Records, New York, N.Y. New title: *W.C. Handy—Father of the Blues, a Musical Autobiography*).

singers Eddie Jefferson, King Pleasure, and Jon Hendricks) with her 1934 interpretation of Bix Beiderbecke and Frankie Traumbauer's "Singing the Blues."

Though she sang with genuine blues feeling, Harris was white—as were Prince, Bernard, the members of the Original Dixieland Jazz Band, and (of equal, if not greater, significance) the public to whom their records were addressed. Yet in the music business as in any other, green has always been the only color that mattered. Victrolas—or "talking machines," as many still called them at the time—were sold to whomever could afford them, and by the late 'teens, this included an ever-growing number of black consumers, especially in larger cities.

In 1916, the *Chicago Defender*, the nation's largest black weekly, with a circulation of roughly a quarter of a million, including subscribers in the rural South, noted that black Americans, like the rest of their countrymen, were paying hard-earned money for records by Caruso and Tetrazini but were unable to ask dealers for records by "Mme Anita Patti Brown, Mr Roland Hayes, Miss Hazel Harrison, Miss Maude J. Roberts, [and] Mr. Joseph Douglas." These were black concert performers whose names mean nothing to us now (save for Hayes's), except to reveal the paper's sense of itself as the voice of an emerging black bourgeoisie and its miscalculation of the musical tastes of the overwhelming majority of its readers. (Ironically, Mme Anita Patti Smith, whoever she was, made her recording debut in September 1920, several months after Mamie Smith, who, for whatever reason, was billed as "Mamie Smith, Contralto" on *her* first release.) Also in 1916, the *Defender* asked for a count of its readers who owned Victrolas, presumably to demonstrate to skeptical record companies the potential market for releases by black performers.

According to Robert Dixon and John Goodrich, the authors of *Recording the Blues*, the *Defender* never published the results of its survey—in fact, never again raised the issue. But its editors weren't the only ones to sense that black Victrola owners represented a vast, overlooked market. This is where Perry Bradford entered the picture. After knocking on many doors, he finally persuaded Fred Hager, the recording manager for Okeh Records, an upstart company then still in its first year, to take a gamble on himself and Mamie Smith.

How *much* of a gamble it actually was is open to conjecture. According to legend, Hager braved a threatened boycott by white music-store owners. But he and Bradford were nothing if not savvy. Bradford, in particular, had been around. He must have reckoned, as did Hager, that a black woman singing in what could be advertised as an authentic Negro style would find a ready market not only among blacks, but among whites who purchased records such as Harris's "I'm Gonna Make My Hay While the Sun Shines Down in Virginia" and Ted Lewis's "The Blues My Naughty Sweetie Gives to Me," and who regularly went "slumming" in Harlem or attended the

61

white-only "Midnight Rambles" at black theaters. In a roundabout way, the success of Harris, Lewis, and even Al Jolson opened the door for black singers to record, just as the blackface minstrels of the nineteenth century had opened the door for black stage performers.

Whatever Hager's motivation in recording Smith, the facts are these: on St. Valentine's Day in 1920, Smith, accompanied by white sidemen and then already in her late thirties, recorded "That Thing Called Love" and "You Can't Keep a Good Man Down," Bradford songs originally earmarked for Sophie Tucker. When issued a few months later, these failed to generate quite the sensation that Bradford had hoped for, but sold sufficiently to warrant bringing Smith back into the studio to record "Crazy Blues" in midsummer.

As already noted, "Crazy Blues" sold 75,000 copies within a month of its release in November, an astonishing figure for the time. Its sales pointed to the existence of a "colored" market which was soon euphemized as the "race" market (the word may have carried a double meaning, signifying "ours" to blacks and "raciness" to whites), eventually putting record companies on the trail of rawer, more idiomatic blues singers like Ma Rainey, Bessie Smith, Blind Lemon Jefferson, and Charley Patton. Still competing with sheet-music publishers for marketplace supremacy, the fledgling record industry topped 100 million units in sales for the first time in 1921, thanks in no small part to the participation of black Americans to whom sheet music had meant nothing, requiring as it did both conventional literacy and the ability to read music—not to mention access to a piano. (Records instantly transformed what folklorists would persist for decades in approaching as an oral tradition into an *aural* tradition.) By 1927, some five hundred race records were being released annually, including gospel performances and sermons—but not including jazz, which generally wasn't marketed by record companies in their race series, perhaps because it was acknowledged to have wide crossover appeal to whites.

At first, "Crazy Blues" and other early race records—most of them by women singers who, like Smith, were veterans of theatrical vaudeville and traveling tent shows, and who recorded with jazz instrumentalists—were distributed only to dealers in black urban areas. But as a result of ads in the *Defender* and other Northern black newspapers with large rural Southern readerships, record companies found themselves doing a booming mail-order business. The discovery of this market inevitably led to the recording of rural blues performers such as Patton, Jefferson, Son House, and Blind Blake. (A 1926 Paramount Records ad describes Jefferson's music as "real, old-fashioned blues, by a real, old-fashioned singer," as though to imply that the music recorded as blues up to that point was actually a synthesis of folk blues, vaudeville, and jazz, which it pretty much was. On another level, though, what we now think of as "the blues" was initially a trope, a

marketing concept, a handle on the enormous changes then taking place in black music.) Record company field representatives, dispatched to the Deep South, didn't record only blues; many race ads describe blues and gospel releases side by side. Nor did they record only black performers on their visits to small Southern villages and towns. Many of the earliest recorded examples of what we now call bluegrass were another side effect of "Crazy Blues."

We might like to think that performers as crucial to the evolution of American music as Ma Rainey, Bessie Smith, and Blind Lemon Jefferson would have eventually been recorded anyway—that if Smith hadn't emerged as a pioneer in 1920, one of them would have sooner or later. But who can say for sure when this would have occurred, if not when it did? A decade later, in the squeeze of the Great Depression, phonograph records became luxury items for Americans of all races, but especially for blacks. By 1932, record sales had plummeted to just 6 million for the entire year, and Southern field trips had virtually ground to a halt.

MAMIE Smith, who was practically born in a trunk, having begun her career in vaudeville as a foil to a white act called the Four Dancing Mitchells as a child in her native Cincinnati, is inevitably described as a beauty by her black show-business contemporaries. Talking about her to the British writer Derrick Stewart-Baxter long after the fact, the late Victoria Spivey remembered her as having "pearly teeth" and "big sparkling eyes," and as dressing for the stage in sequins and rhinestones "plus a velvet cape with fur on it." Smith's photographs remind us that standards of female beauty were very different then. In them, she just looks fat. One gathers that success was not kind to her. According to Stewart-Baxter, in his *Ma Rainey and the Classic Blues Singers*, Smith was rumored to have earned over $100,000 in royalties during her career. "She spared herself practically nothing: fancy cars, expensive furnishings and a procession of lovers filled her life," Stewart-Baxter writes. "Her escapades and temperamental outbursts were food for the gossip columnists." She was living large, as they say now, but her success as a recording artist was short-lived. Though she remained a popular live attraction until the Depression, her last hit record was in 1923: "You've Got to See Mama Every Night (Or You Won't See Mama at All)," with Coleman Hawkins, by then a regular member of the Jazz Hounds, on tenor saxophone. An edition of the *Defender* from 1929 reported that she was set to star in a movie called *The Blues Singer*, though this never happened. She did appear in a few black films in the late thirties and early forties, including one called *Paradise in Harlem*, in which she sang an updated version of "Crazy Blues" retitled "Harlem Blues" (not to be confused with the Handy composition of that name). She died virtually penniless in 1946, at the age of sixty-three.

ALL forms of music are evolutionary, and this makes it difficult to pinpoint "firsts." By Greil Marcus's reckoning, if practically no one else's, the first rock-'n'-roll record was "It's Too Soon to Know," a sobbing ballad that was a big hit in 1948 for a black group from Baltimore called the Orioles. Writing about it in a 1993 issue of *Rolling Stone*, Marcus likened what he imagined was its initial impact to that of Elvis Presley's "That's All Right" in 1954, Aretha Franklin's "I Never Loved a Man (The Way I Love You)" in 1967, and Nirvana's "Smells Like Teen Spirit" in 1992—"a shock, a dead-in-your-tracks *what* was *that?*, a sound that was stylistically confusing and emotionally undeniable."

The author of such far-ranging books on music as *Mystery Train, Lipstick*

Traces, and *Dead Elvis*, Marcus is a rock critic who delights in playing the role of intellectual provocateur—an essayist who allows his imagination free rein in exploring the ways in which pop music reflects and periodically transforms American myths and values. This might be his greatest asset as a critic, this ear he has for ruptures and conjunctions. But along with an extremely patchy knowledge of pre-1950s pop, it's often his greatest weakness, too—he wildly overreaches, frequently hearing things that simply aren't there. "The song drew a line," he says of a record which—although chillingly beautiful—is far too mannerly, far too derivative of the Ink Spots and the Mills Brothers, to suffice as an early example of doo wop, much less rock 'n' roll. As he usually is, however, Marcus is onto something in hearing in certain records, including those with which he compares "It's Too Soon to Know," "a quality of contingency" in which more than just the future of pop seems to be hanging in the balance. "Nothing would ever be the same again," Marcus says of the Orioles hit, and he's not far afield in ascribing such powers of divination to a pop record. He just has the wrong song.

But who can say which is the right one? If ever a record seemed to merit Marcus's apocalyptic hyperbole, it would be "Crazy Blues," which—largely on its reputation as the first commercially recorded blues by a black singer—was inducted into the National Academy of Recording Arts and Sciences Hall of Fame in 1994, along with Bob Dylan's "Blowin' in the Wind," the Beach Boys' "Good Vibrations," Tony Bennett's "I Left My Heart in San Francisco," and the Miles Davis 1957 album *Miles Ahead*. Smith's recording clearly dwarfs these others in historical significance. Yet heard today, it sounds like a period novelty, a vaudeville moan essentially no different from those recorded in the same era by such white female singers as Marion Harris and Sophie Tucker. If anything, Smith lacks Harris's rhythmic finesse and Tucker's steamroller pizzazz. Despite its place in legend, it isn't one of those songs that transcends its moment in the process of defining it ever after.

Yet who knows? It could be that Smith's recordings do her as little justice as her photographs. Spivey said of her that "her full voice filled the auditorium without the use of mikes like we have today. That was singing the blues!" We'll have to take Spivey's word for this, because the only crackle we hear in "Crazy Blues" more than seventy years later is the sound of surface noise from the needle digging into the original master disk, the only thunder the imagined plunk of black people's coins dropping on record dealers' counters to begin a new chapter in American commerce.

"**CRAZY** Blues" didn't "draw a line," in the sense that Marcus talks about, but to give Bradford and Smith their due, it did sharpen one already drawn by Handy and others in the first two decades of this century, when the technology that's made everything since then part of our virtual memory was still in its primitive stages. Most of them were stage performers for whom the passage of time has proved to be the ultimate fourth wall. The surface noise on the recordings they made almost as souvenirs for their live audiences is a cobweb that can't be blown away.

Smith's wasn't the first black voice to be captured on record. In 1902, Victor issued six titles by the Dinwiddle Colored Quartet, described by Dixon and Goodrich as "a group that sang in a quite authentic Negro style, without the European influence that marked the work of other early gospel groups." The authors of the otherwise unimpeachable *Recording the Blues* go on to add, somewhat dubiously, that "it was to be another eighteen years before another recording of authentic black music ["Crazy Blues," in other words] appeared on the market."

But what's "authentic," and who decides?[2] One of the first performers to record—on tinfoil disks in 1877, the year that Thomas Edison patented the phonograph—was George Washington Johnson, a freed slave whose "The Laughing Song" and "The Whistling Coon" were among the largest-selling cylinder recordings of the 1890s. As his titles suggest, Johnson was a cackling stereotype—the Negro as eunuch, an object of white mirth. He's better forgotten, but not so Bert Williams, a major recording artist from his debut in 1901 to his death in 1922, and a headliner with the Ziegfeld Follies for much of that time.

Taking advantage of the only way into show business available to black performers of his generation, Williams did himself up for the stage in burnt cork and white lip paint; it could therefore be argued that his popularity helped to perpetuate the demeaning black stereotypes it should have dispelled. Yet Williams's artistry was far more complex than that of any other black performer to that point (he was a gifted mime as well as a singer, which should give some idea of his range), and so was his presentation of himself as a black man. Despite retaining the outer trappings of minstrelsy, Williams never stooped to pandering. He often recited his lyrics in lieu of singing them, alternating between a homey Negro dialect and the oracular diction of the frustrated Shakespearean he no doubt was. His recordings—two dozen of which are spread over the four multidisc volumes of Pearl's *Music from the New York Stage 1890–1920*[3]—are full of what one suspects both blacks and astute whites of his time interpreted as knowing winks.

2. For future reference, we should note that when employed by whites to describe black music, "authentic" used to mean "rural," but as now employed by both whites and blacks, in the face of rap, has increasingly come to mean "ghetto."
3. *Music from the New York Stage 1890–1920*. Vol. I: *1890–1908*, Pearl GEMM-CDS-9050-2; Vol. II: *1908–1913*, Pearl-GEMM-CDS-9053-2; Vol. III: *1913–1917*, Pearl-GEMM-9056-8; Vol. IV: *1917–1920*, Pearl GEMM-CDS-9059-61. Each of these is a three-disk set. (Available from Koch International, 177 Cantiague Rock Road, Westbury, NY 11590.)

Eleonora Duse declared Williams his country's finest actor, W. C. Fields called him "the funniest man I ever saw," and Booker T. Washington decided that "Williams has done more for the race than I have." His "Unlucky Blues" and "I've Got the Sorry I Ain't Got It, You Could Have It If I Had It Blues" were vaudeville numbers, merely titular blues. But his "You Can't Get Away from It," from 1914 (not included on the Pearl collection, unfortunately), was, as Ann Charters points out in her 1970 biography, *Nobody*, "one of the earliest recordings that anyone did with a real feeling of 'swing' to it." This is one of many numbers on which Williams might easily be mistaken for Fats Waller, whose rascally vocal style he obviously influenced. He may have influenced Louis Armstrong's vocal approach, too: on the final chorus of his 1905 recording of "Nobody," his tale-of-woe signature tune, he suddenly turns the tables on the trombonist who's been mocking him with a baleful obbligato, stretching out and flatting his vowels as though playing a slide instrument himself. In doing this, he displays a sense of timing— comic as well as musical—that makes him seem a spiritual father not only to Armstrong but to Redd Foxx and James Brown. It's the seminal performance we want "Crazy Blues" to be: stylistically confusing, emotionally undeniable, a bridge between the world as we know it and as it once was.

THOUGH Williams had little company as a black recording artist in the two decades before "Crazy Blues," he wasn't exactly breaking ground when he joined Ziegfeld in 1910. Twelve years earlier, there was a show called *A Trip to Coontown* entirely written, performed, and produced by blacks. The music was by Bob Cole, who subsequently teamed with J. Rosamond Johnson (the composer of "Lift Ev'ry Voice," the "black national anthem") and James Weldon Johnson (more famous as the author of *The Autobiography of an Ex-Colored Man* and as a collector of Negro folk songs and spirituals) to write two more black musicals—*The Shoo-Fly Regiment*, in 1907, and *The Red Moon*, in 1909—and several others for all-white casts. This period witnessed numerous other black shows, among them *In Dahomey* (1903) and *Bandanna Land* (1908), both of which starred Williams and his stage partner, George Walker.

But all of this happened during what's sometimes referred to as the Ragtime Era, a period that now seems as remote as colonial times—whereas all aspects of popular culture from the 1920s remain vivid and alive to us on account of the sound movies and electrical recording techniques introduced in that decade. Because many of us now in our forties or younger were first exposed to ragtime via Gunther Schuller and Joshua Rifkin's interpretations of Scott Joplin on labels such as Angel and Nonesuch, we tend to think of ragtime as a genteel musical exercise, a charming attempt at "classical" music by its day's black bourgeoisie. But ragtime was a pop craze of the late 1890s, introduced to New York not by Joplin but by such journeymen black pianists and songwriters as Irving Jones and Ben Harney. Ragtime borrowed its harmonic schemes and its marchlike tempos from Europe, but the syncopations that marked it as new were African-American in origin, possibly derived from the music of rural fiddle and banjo players.

The dance sensation of those years was the cakewalk, a step whose black ancestry was broadly acknowledged in such song titles as "A Coon Band Contest," "Whistling Rufus," and "Blackville Society." By 1913, the fox trot was all the rage, thanks in no small part to the success of "Ballin' the Jack," written by Chris Smith, a black songwriter who had started his career with a traveling medicine show. This was also the era in which Vernon and Irene Castle popularized ballroom dancing, further liberating American music from the constraints of the waltz; though the Castles were white, their musical director was James Reese Europe, a black composer who teamed with Ford C. Dabney, the black music director of the Ziegfeld Follies, to write "The Castle Walk" for them.

As much a mythical locale as an actual jumble of offices along New York's West Twenty-Eighth Street, Tin Pan Alley of the late 1890s and early 1900s was America's street of dreams, the place where the sons of Irish and Jewish immigrants channeled their assimilationist fantasies into song, contributing to the naturalization of American popular song as their end of the bargain. But scant attention is paid to the role played by the Alley's black craftsmen, probably because the folklorists who have told us most of what we know about early black music—reluctant, most of them, to discuss music shaped by market forces rather than a folk process, as this would require admitting that blues is a form of pop—have focused almost exclusively on rural forms. A more obvious reason is that no one is eager to revive such items as Ernest Hogan's "All Coons Look Alike to Me" (1896) and the many Negro dialect songs by Ben Harney, a black man who passed for white. Yet Harney's "You Been a Good Old Wagon, But You Done Broke Down" (1895) marked a turning point in the evolution of American popular song, according to no less an authority on the subject than Alec Wilder. The "coon" songs of the Ragtime Era, which achieved their greatest popularity more or less simultaneously with such malarky as "Too-ra-loo-ra-loo-ral" and "My Wild Irish Rose," helped to blacken the beat of American popular music long before rock 'n' roll—long before "Crazy Blues," for that matter. These were the songs that George M. Cohan, Irving Berlin, and George Gershwin used as models for their own "blues," rhythm, and ragtime songs. As unsavory as such songs seem to us now, they're as essential a part of the American musical-and-racial puzzle as field hollers and work songs, forms of which we have copious recorded examples. But few among us can claim to have heard a genuine coon song—nor are we likely to in the future, to judge from the furor that greeted Ben Vereen's tribute to Williams at Ronald Reagan's first inaugural, in 1981.[4]

Such was the influence of black songwriters in the early years of this century that Irving Berlin once felt compelled to point out that not all of Tin Pan Alley's composers and lyricists were Negroes. "Many of them are of Russian birth or ancestry," he added. "All of them are of pure white blood."[5]

Not all of them, Irving. By Mississippi's "one drop" law, American popular song would have been legally black almost from the beginning. Including Perry Bradford's, no fewer than four black-owned publishing firms set up shop on Tin Pan Alley between 1903 and 1920, a period during which the real money to be made in the music business was still in sheet music, not in records, and when all but the most famous singers were essentially glorified song-pluggers. Sheldon Brooks's "Some of These Days," Spencer Williams's "I Ain't Got Nobody," Tony Jackson's "Pretty Baby," James P. Johnson's "If I Could Be with You One Hour Tonight," and John Turner Layton and Harry Creamer's "After You've Gone" were among the songs published by black composers during this period. These were followed, all within a few years, by Layton and Creamer's "Way Down Yonder in New Orleans," Eubie Blake and Noble Sissle's "I'm Just Wild About Harry," Maceo Pinkard's "Sweet Georgia Brown," Will Marion Cook's "I'm Coming, Virginia," Eddie Green's "A Good Man Is Hard to Find," and James P. Johnson's numbers for *Running Wild*, the show that popularized the Charleston.

These are songs we're likely to think of as belonging collectively to our grandparents, rather than to individual composers and lyricists. Such songs seem raceless to us now (except, perhaps, for "Sweet Georgia Brown," by dint of its association with the Harlem Globetrotters and Ray Charles); indeed, their composers and lyricists no doubt strove to leave race out of them, in order to guarantee the widest possible sheet-music sales. Yet these numbers represented the next step after coon songs. Something about their rhythms—combined with the fact that so many of them were introduced

---

4. About that troublesome word: In *Juba to Jive: A Dictionary of American Slang*, Clarence Major guesses that "cooning," as initially used by rural Southern whites, meant "stealing as opposed to robbing." "Although 'cooning' may to some degree refer to the fact that raccoons were known to steal food, it probably also stems from the widespread southern mythical belief that all blacks were thieves." Major further speculates that "black use of 'coon' was picked up from derogatory white use probably as early as the 1650s. Blacks used 'coon' with the same sort of self-irony and affection with which they use words such as 'nigger' and 'sambo.'" This raises the interesting possibility that black lyricists of the Ragtime Era used "coon" much the way that rappers now use "nigger." It also raises the equally fascinating possibility that blacks heard these songs differently from whites, interpreting them not as songs in which they were objects of ridicule but as songs expressing a *black* point of view.
5. Quoted in Lawrence Bergreen's *As Thousands Cheer*.

on record by either Marion Harris or Sophie Tucker, white women who emulated black vocal styles and were frequently billed as "coon shouters" in their day[6]—ought to tell us that these songs, too, were initially understood to be "coon" numbers.

In making such a fuss over "It's Too Soon to Know," Greil Marcus trades on what he assumes to be the richest of ironies, that this song performed by a black vocal group was written by a young Jewish woman named Deborah Chessler. For Marcus, this collaboration signaled the beginning of "marginalized, ghettoized voices from blues and country now confronting the entire nation, demanding that it respond in kind." But Chessler and the Orioles were actually reversing a process begun by the likes of Sheldon Brooks and Sophie Tucker in an era that's now a blank to everyone but specialists in early twentieth-century arcana. It remained for Mamie Smith to expose three decades of American pop as having been largely a ventriloquist act. And hers was hardly the only new voice to make itself heard once her titular blues went on sale.

6. The original "coon shouter"—at least the first woman to be so billed—was May Irwin, a Broadway star originally from Canada who introduced "The Bully," a song in which she took the point of view of a tough "Tennessee nigger," in the 1895 show The Widow Jones. (It, too, is included on Vol. I of Music from the New York Stage.) Irwin, the leading lady in the first of the "white" musicals written by Cole and the Johnsons, also popularized "Ta-Ra-Ra-Boom-Deray," a seemingly innocuous little ditty whose origins have been traced to a black Kansas City brothel.

CHAPTER 2

. . . .

BLUES VAUDEVILLIANS, JUG BANDS, AND MEDICINE SHOW SONGSTERS

I talked to a fellow, an' the fellow say,
"She jes' catch hold of us, somekindaway.
She sang Backwater Blues one day:

    'It rained fo' days an' de skies was dark as night.
    Trouble taken place in de lowlands at night.

    'Thundered an' lightened an' the storm begin to roll
    Thousan's of people ain't got no place to go.

    'Den I went an' stood upon some high ol' lonesome hill,
    An' looked down on the place where I used to live.'

An' den de folks, dey naturally bowed dey heads an' cried,
Bowed dey heavy heads, shet dey moufs up tight an' cried,
An' Ma lef' the stage, an' followed some de folks outside."

Dere wasn't much more de fella say:
She jes' gits hold of us dataway.
               —Sterling A. Brown, "Ma Rainey" (1930)

She was born in Georgia, traveled all over this world," Memphis Minnie tells us in her 1940 song of the same title, implying homespun beginnings and subsequent fame and fortune, but leaving it to the reference books to supply the mundane particulars. The "she" of Brown's poem and Minnie's song was born Gertrude Pridgett in Columbus, Georgia, in 1886, the daughter of black minstrel show performers. She first achieved word-of-mouth celebrity among her own people as a member of F. S. Wolcott's Rabbit Foot

Minstrels soon after the turn of the century, and later barnstormed the rural South as the featured attraction in her own vaudeville revue (along with her husband, William "Pa" Rainey, himself a song-and-dance man), eventually making a name for herself in the cities as a headliner of many of the shows packaged by the Theater Owners Booking Association (TOBA for short, and many of the black performers swore that the initials stood for "Tough on Black Asses"). Although she didn't begin to record until 1923, she was probably the first blues singer identified as such by the black public, having added blues songs to her repertoire as early as 1902, if we can believe the story she told the folklorist John Work. The Great Depression halted her career, as it did the careers of most of the women singers who recorded in the aftermath of "Crazy Blues" ("Nobody Knows You When You're Down and Out," recorded so memorably by Bessie Smith in 1929, could have been the theme song for all of these woman.) But Ma Rainey, a homely woman who reportedly detested her nickname, had invested her earnings more wisely than most of her rivals. Retiring from show business and returning to her hometown, she immersed herself in church work and managed the two movie theaters she had bought in the nearby town of Rome, until her death of a heart attack in December 1939.

Memphis Minnie, on the tribute she recorded six months later, ignores these details in her hurry to tell her listeners all she thinks they really need to know, that the subject of her song is "the best blues singer people has ever heard." She delivers this encomium in the present tense, as if to say: Sure, Ma Rainey's dead and gone, and she was off the scene for five years before that, but nobody now singing the blues is as good as she was, and nobody ever will be.

Then, as an example of the powerful effect of Ma Rainey's blues on anyone who heard them, Minnie describes her own reaction to "Bo-Weavil Blues," Rainey's 1923 wail over those twin scourges, crop-destroying insects and cheating men. "Every time I hear that record," Minnie says, accompanying herself with a guitar line that might be the sound of her shaking her head in wonder, "I just couldn't keep from cryin'."

Ma Rainey just got to Memphis Minnie, somekindaway.

A vaudevillian to the core, Ma Rainey apparently put on quite a show, traveling the country with her own stage backdrops, including one showing a giant eagle like the eagle on the twenty gold coins she wore as a necklace, and another emblazoned with the Paramount Records logo. Rainey had already been on the road—traveling "all over this world," or as much of it as was available for conquest to a black performer of her era—for a quarter of a century when she finally entered a recording studio, and as though to underline her newfound status as a recording artist, she would often materialize on stage from a huge cardboard Victrola. However much this may have thrilled her audiences—this equation of Ma Rainey in the flesh with the mystery of recorded sound—it's likely to strike us as incongruous today. No singer of Rainey's period owed less of her following to records. She was

Ma Rainey, 1923
(FRANK DRIGGS COLLECTION)

a favorite of black audiences long before she recorded, and we listen to her today with the understanding that even her most powerful recorded performances—those on which she outshouts the crackle seemingly endemic to 1920s Paramounts—were made when she was well past her prime.

No, as we are given to understand it, Ma Rainey's genius was in convincing the country people whom Brown describes as flocking to hear her—"ridin' mules" or "packed in trains," "flivverin' in" from the lumber camps, the "blackbottom cornrows" and "de little river settlements"—that she was simultaneously one of them and one of a kind. (Insofar as this is what pop stardom is all about, she may have been the first black pop star.) A large part of her appeal to her people was in her material, an assortment of songs drawn from folk sources and originals in the same tradition, unblushing in their treatment of human sexuality and unself-consciously rural in their allusions to fortune tellers, bo weevils, and chain gangs—songs that were a far cry from the sophistication of "Crazy Blues." Though she tended to record with jazz instrumentalists, she often performed live with country jug bands. But there must have been more to it than that. Perhaps her fans recognized in her roar something of their own inexpressible hopes and frustrations. And perhaps they identified with something else about her, something hinted at in the physical descriptions we have of her.

"I couldn't say that she was a good-looking woman," Thomas A. Dorsey, her longtime pianist, once said of her, trying to be chivalrous and not quite succeeding. Everyone else who knew Ma Rainey described her as plug ugly, a short and stubby woman with a big rear end and broad features that didn't quite match. What usually goes without saying is that she was also quite dark: a *black* black woman, in other words, for whom there would have been little point in attempting to emulate white standards of feminine beauty. Who can say? Perhaps the sight of her prancing on stage in sequins and plumes, the trappings of glamour, as though *she just didn't care* sent a message to her fans that they needn't care what the white world thought of them, either. Then, too, that eagle and those gold pieces must have been potent symbols to audiences without much money of their own: Ma Rainey was nigger-rich, in that day's parlance, and proud of it.

That prop Victrola wasn't the only thing incongruous about her. It seems odd, to say the least, that a woman so enamored of opulence and finery, a woman notoriously promiscuous and widely rumored to be bisexual, would have devoted the last few years of her life to the Lord's work. But Ma Rainey was no simple creature.

"People sure look lonesome since Ma Rainey been gone," Memphis Minnie observes in the last verse of her song, not needing to explain *which* people. "But she left little Minnie to carry the good works on." Memphis Minnie will be discussed in a later chapter; what's significant here isn't her boldness in offering herself as a replacement for Ma Rainey, but that women singers of Minnie's generation were aware of their lineage. They recognized Rainey not just as a performer nicknamed "Ma," but as a matriarch.

•

Bessie Smith
(FRANK DRIGGS
COLLECTION)

RAINEY'S only peer among women singers of her era was Bessie Smith, who, though eight years younger, also began her recording career in 1923. An irresistible bit of legend—not the last we shall encounter on the subject of Bessie Smith—was that Rainey "discovered" Smith in the latter's hometown of Chattanooga, and took her on as a protégée. Smith did, in fact, break into show business as a singer and tap dancer with the Moses Stokes minstrel show in 1912, a troupe which at that time starred Ma and Pa Rainey. But the person who interceded on Smith's behalf was probably her elder brother, Clarence, the show's MC.

In any case, the truth of the matter seems to be that Smith saw Rainey as an adversary. For those of us who grew up with rock 'n' roll in the fifties—a decade in which rhythm-'n'-blues hits were routinely "covered"

75

by white performers and usually bowdlerized in the process—the very notion of the cover version stinks of racism. We overlook that era's twangless cover versions of hillbilly records, including some of Hank Williams's biggest hits. And we forget that black singers then still frequently turned in their own versions of white pop hits. The "cover"—now increasingly a postmodernist transgression, a bold reinterpretation, even a travesty—was, in the fifties, when the phrase seems to have originated, merely a reflex: a remnant of an earlier day in which a hit song was a more important commercial property than a hit record and the goal of music publishers was to secure as many recorded versions as possible, in order to cater to different markets. Smith became, in her own way, the fledgling recording industry's first great cover artist, perhaps at the urging of her producer, Frank Walker, and the pianist and songwriter Clarence Williams, who claimed to have discovered her.

Smith wasn't trying to tap into other markets with her covers; she was aiming to beat the original singers at their own game. Smith's very first hit— it sold an estimated 750,000 copies—was her version of "Down Hearted Blues," a song written by Alberta Hunter and recorded by her with modest success just a few months earlier. Smith continued this process of picking and choosing among the songs of her competitors throughout the twenties, and it was said that black record buyers of that day, on hearing a song that they liked by another woman singer, would wait a few months for Bessie's version before plunking their money down. For whatever reason—personal animosity between her and Rainey, or just a sense that Ma was her most formidable rival—Smith tore into Rainey's "Backwater Blues" and "Moon-shine Blues" with particular relish when she covered them in 1924. Smith was a more flexible singer than Rainey, more sophisticated in her repertoire, though no less earthy in her delivery (try to imagine Rainey doing "A Good Man Is Hard to Find," "Alexander's Ragtime Band," or, for that matter, "St. Louis Blues") and so sure of herself rhythmically it hardly mattered that she insisted on recording without drums. Thanks to the rhythmic thrust of her phrasing, she was more at ease than Rainey in the company of jazz instrumentalists, who for their part counted themselves among her most ardent admirers.[1]

1. The sidemen on her various records included Louis Armstrong, Fletcher Henderson, Coleman Hawkins, Bubber Miley, and Sidney Bechet. As it did Rainey's, the Depression more or less ended her recording career. But the record producer and high-born liberal gadfly John Hammond, who also adored her, brought her back into the recording studio after a two-year absence, for what proved to be her last session. "Nobody wants to hear blues no more," Bessie insisted. "Times is hard. They want to hear novelty songs." Hammond called on the husband-and-wife team of Coot Grant and "Socks" Wilson to write four novelties for Smith which "would not be too far from the blues," including "Gimme a Pigfoot." The band he enlisted to accompany her included Benny Goodman, Chu Berry, and Jack Teagarden. "Jack Teagarden was flying," Hammond recalled in *John Hammond on Record*, his 1977 memoir. "He had dreamed of recording with her and thought he never would."

Smith had a larger following than Rainey in the North, and a much larger white audience. Chiefly through the efforts of Carl Van Vechten, a white novelist, photographer, and *Vanity Fair* opinion maker, she became a darling of café society (an ornery and extremely reluctant darling, to be sure) and a goddess of the Harlem Renaissance. She even appeared on Broadway, singing "If the Blues Don't Get You" in *Pansy*, a revue that lasted just three performances, in 1929. Brooks Atkinson, of the *New York Times*, called it "the worst show ever written," but raved about Bessie—as did Wilella Waldorf of the *Post*, whose review described how Bessie was called upon by the audience to sing her one song "over and over to wild applause, likewise executing sundry dance steps at intervals by way of variety" until "[announcing] breathlessly that she was tired and that she was too fat for that sort of thing, anyhow, whereupon she was allowed to retire." That same year, at the height of her fame, she also made her only movie, starring in *St. Louis Blues*, a short in which she wailed Handy's famous song and portrayed a woman done wrong and unable to do anything about it *but* sing.

In real life, she probably would have floored the bastard who plays her for a sucker, as she is said to have once floored Clarence Williams in an argument over money (she also once took a swing at Fania Marinoff Van Vechten, whose sisterly hug she misinterpreted as a lesbian pass). What Bessie does in *St. Louis Blues* isn't exactly acting, but you're never going to see a woman with more screen presence, or more unrefined sexual energy. Shoulders sagging but feet firmly planted when her man slams that door, she manages to seem at once vulnerable and massive, a confusion of herself and every woman—at least every black woman—angry at having been born into a world where men hold all the cards.

Like Rainey, Smith carried plenty of excess flesh. But she was tall, and her heft was seen as evidence of an appetite for life that was essentially carnal. The white clarinetist and proto-hipster Mezz Mezzrow, clearly infatuated with her, as most musicians were, remembered her as "just this side of voluptuous, buxom and massive, but stately too, shapely as an hourglass, with a high-voltage magnet for a personality." Her appeal was more frankly erotic than Rainey's or that of any other woman singer of the twenties—including Lucille Bogan, who sometimes recorded as Bessie Jackson, and whose material was far more sexually explicit. The story goes that Smith would occasionally pick out a man in her audience and "walk" him—that is, fix him with her eyes and give him the impression that she was singing only to him, until he left his seat and started up the aisle to the stage in a trance, heeding her siren call. One of my favorite stories about her is almost certainly apocryphal. It's the one told by her biographer, Chris Albertson, about the time that she stood with her hand on her hip and faced down a group of white-robed Klansmen who made the mistake of attempting to collapse the tent under which she was doing her show. This story ends with

Lucille Bogan
(COURTESY SHELDON HARRIS
COLLECTION)

her yelling threateningly, "You just pick up those sheets and run," then bawling out her frightened stagehands for being "a bunch of sissies." Not for nothing was Bessie nicknamed "the Empress."

LIKE Elvis or JFK, Bessie Smith was one of those larger-than-life figures now most famous for having died. Even the way in which she's supposed to have met her end turns out to be apocryphal. She bled to death after being refused admission to a white hospital, following a traffic accident on a dark stretch of road in rural Mississippi, in 1937—they might not be able to tell you the year or the town, but even people who have never heard a record by Bessie Smith can tell you that she died needlessly, a victim of institutional racism. The story—first reported by John Hammond in *Down Beat* soon after the incident—just won't go away; it turned up most recently in Alan Lomax's *The Land Where the Blues Began*, most of which can be taken as gospel. But the part about the white hospital is something that Lomax should have recognized as folklore.

Here's what actually happened, according to Chris Albertson's well-researched biography. Smith was injured—her arm torn loose at the elbow—when the car in which she was traveling as a passenger (a Packard driven by Richard Morgan, the last of her many lovers, and the uncle of the vibraphonist Lionel Hampton) sideswiped a slowly moving truck on Highway 61, near Clarksdale, Mississippi, about seventy miles south of Memphis, in the early morning hours of September 26, 1937. As she lay bleeding, Bessie was tended to by Dr. Hugh Smith, a white Memphis physician who was on his way to a fishing trip when his car was flagged down by the uninjured Morgan. After covering her wounds, Dr. Smith moved Bessie to a shoulder of the road, out of further danger from oncoming traffic. He then sent his companion to search for a home with a phone, in order to summon an ambulance. After waiting for an ambulance for about twenty minutes, Dr. Smith and his friend decided to transport Bessie to a Clarksdale hospital themselves. They had removed their fishing tackle from Dr. Smith's car, which was still in the middle of the road, where he had screeched to a halt, and placed Bessie on the back seat, when they heard another vehicle speeding toward them. It was a car carrying a young white couple who had been drinking and weren't about to slow down. They smashed into Dr. Smith's car, driving it straight into Bessie's Packard and throwing their own vehicle into a ditch.

Two ambulances eventually arrived almost simultaneously, one answering the call of Dr. Smith's friend, the other sent by the driver of the truck involved in the first collision, who had reported the accident on arriving in Clarksdale. These ambulances carried Smith and the injured white couple to segregated Clarksdale hospitals less than a quarter of a mile apart. At that time, in that place, no one would have considered taking Bessie Smith to a white hospital. Not that it would have made any difference: neither of Clarksdale's hospitals was equipped to save a patient who had lost as much blood as she had.

She might have lived if the truck driver had stopped and taken her straight to a hospital, if Dr. Smith hadn't wasted time waiting for an ambulance, if the white couple had slowed down. But all of this amounts to poor judgment, not racism. So how did the legend start that her real cause of death was segregation, and why do people still believe it? Because it was believable. Hammond didn't originate the story; he was merely the first to tell it in print, after hearing it from several musicians. It's become a story perversely cherished by older black Americans, who take its moral to be confirmation of a bitter truth: that even one of their own as celebrated as Bessie Smith was just another nigger to whites.

Smith was buried in an unmarked grave in a suburb of Philadelphia. Over the years, numerous collections were taken up, numerous benefits staged, for the purpose of buying her a headstone. But just like the rumored $80,000 settlement from the biscuit company whose goods were being transported in that truck Morgan sideswiped, the money from these benefits disappeared into the pockets of Smith's husband, Jack Gee, an ex-policeman with the scruples of a pimp who continued to use her as a cash cow even after her death (while she was still alive and riding high, he funneled a large part of her earnings into launching the career of Gertrude Saunders, his showgirl mistress). Bessie finally got her headstone in 1970, the singer Janis Joplin splitting the cost with a registered nurse from Philadelphia who had cleaned house for Bessie as a little girl. By that time, the woman frequently hailed as the greatest blues singer of them all had herself become a blues of the saddest, most agonized sort.

WOMEN dominated the first few years of blues recording, the five or six years just after the success of "Crazy Blues." Ma Rainey and Bessie Smith were not only the most popular of what are now generally referred to as the "classic blues singers"; they are the only two whose reputations have survived from their time to ours. Their contemporaries haven't been as lucky, in part because the very qualities that endeared them to black audiences of the 1920s—their glamorous wardrobes and practiced stagecraft, their mastery of jazz and vaudeville as well as blues, their sense of themselves as part of show business—places them out of bounds to folklorists. Ma Rainey and Bessie Smith are the only ones we now read much about, because nobody would be foolish enough to question their authenticity. But in their own day, Rainey and Smith vied for the loyalty of black audiences with dozens of women singers, the most unjustly overlooked of whom might be Ida Cox, whose billing as "the uncrowned queen of the blues" echoed the sentiment of many of the musicians who accompanied her.

"That's what they called her," the pianist Sammy Price once noted, "and that's what she was." Cox, who was born in Knoxville in 1889 and died there in 1967, a few years after resuming her recording career with a session on which she was accompanied by Roy Eldridge and Coleman Hawkins, combined vaudevillian flair and sophistication with a keening delivery that sounded straight from the farm. Her voice was harsh and somewhat nasal in quality, but surprisingly supple; as hair-raising and hypnotic as the drone of a Delta slide guitar. She wrote many of her own songs, and her lyrics were often morbid in nature and sometimes macabre, full of coffins and bone orchards and walks to the electric chair. Her best-known song was probably "Wild Women Don't Have the Blues," still an ironic anthem of sorts for female blues performers. Like Smith and Rainey, she drew heavily on country folk traditions. Also in common with them, she was a total original.

WHEN Negroes were finally allowed to appear in minstrel shows and drama-tizations of *Uncle Tom's Cabin* in the years after the Civil War, they inherited roles originated by whites in blackface. Audiences thus had fixed notions of what a black man on stage was supposed to represent. So, perhaps, did America's first black stage performers, who emulated those whites who sought to emulate *them*—right down to the burnt cork and watermelon grin.[2] Early blues recording followed a similar pattern, with many of the black women singers who followed Mamie Smith delivering numbers that might have been written for Sophie Tucker or Marion Harris in a manner not far removed from theirs. Sara Martin, a singer from Kentucky who, like Ma Rainey and Mamie Smith, was already in her late thirties when she began to record, and whose theatrical diction revealed her lengthy tenure in vaudeville even when she sang a number as salty as Porter Granger's "'Tain't Nobody's Bus'ness If I Do" or her own "Mean Tight Mama," was frequently billed as "the black Sophie Tucker," and not without reason.

All manner of black women singers recorded the blues, or someone's notion of the blues, in the 1920s, many of them versatile stylists later identified with other forms of music. Ethel Waters, for example, is remem-bered today as the star of Broadway and the movies, a singer who played as large a role as Louis Armstrong and Bing Crosby in shaping American pop between the two world wars. But she started off as "Sweet Mama Stringbean," a handmaiden of sorts to Bessie Smith, and one of the first performers to record for Black Swan, a black-owned label which boasted of being "the race's own record" (W. C. Handy was one of its founders). Waters's Black Swans were blues and marketed as such, as were the early recordings of Alberta Hunter, who later appeared on stage in at least one production of Kern and Hammerstein's *Show Boat*, and later enjoyed a vogue as a cabaret singer in the 1970s.

Martin, Waters, and Hunter were typical of those singers of the 1920s who moved blithely from blues to pop and jazz then back again, effectively making a mockery of such distinctions. But also popular around the same time were women whose styles were rougher and more rural, with fewer

2. Interestingly enough, one of the first actors to portray Uncle Tom—at a time when blacks were still assumed to be too thick to memorize text or deliver it intelligibly—was T. D. Rice, the white man whose "Jump Jim Crow" had started the minstrel craze. As Eric Lott points out in his *Love & Theft: Blackface Minstrelsy and the White Working Class*, "Rice's path from celebrated Jim Crow in the early 1830s to sympathetic Uncle Tom twenty years later highlights the improbable political geometry of blackface minstrelsy." And lest you think I'm exaggerating or speaking metaphorically when I say that black minstrels emulated whites emulating them, consider the following (from an 1845 playbill quoted by Lott): "The entertainment [will] conclude with the Imitation Dance, by Mast. Juba [the aforementioned William Henry Lane, the first widely known black minstrel], in which he will give correct Imitation Dances of all the principal Ethiopian Dancers [i.e., white "nigger minstrels"] in the United States. After which he will give *an imitation of himself* [emphasis added]."

traces of vaudeville and Tin Pan Alley. The best of these women each tended to become identified with a particular kind of lyric. Sippie Wallace—the sister of George and Hersel Thomas, Texas pianists who were among the first to play boogie-woogie, and herself one of the first regional performers to build a national reputation—offered what amounted to sisterly advice in the form of country homilies. (In the 1970s, her "Woman Be Wise" became one of Bonnie Raitt's first hits.) Lucille Bogan, a singer of narrow expressive range whose records gained immeasurably from Walter Roland's spinning, ragtime-inflected piano accompaniments, specialized in songs about prostitution. She was the raunchiest of the women singers of her era, maybe the raunchiest ever; on a version of "Shave 'Em Dry" recorded in 1934, but (too racy even for the race market) not released until more than fifty years later, she bragged that she could "make a dead man come," going on to explain that "I fucked all night and all the night before, baby, and I feel just like I want to fuck some more." (Compared to which, Liz Phair's "I'll fuck you 'til your dick is blue" comes off like tense flirting.)

Victoria Spivey, though she, too, performed her share of bawdy ditties ("Black Snake Blues," "Deep Sea Diver," and the like), emerged as something of a moralist, with such topical numbers as "T.B. Blues" (about the discrimination faced by victims of tuberculosis during the epidemic of the late 1920s) and "Dope Head Blues" (possibly the first song to warn of the addictive powers of cocaine). Spivey's lyrics were almost as incisive as Ida Cox's.

Other black women singers in an era dominated by them included the mysterious Bessie Tucker, who recorded a harrowing shout called "Penitentiary" in 1928, but about whom little else is known; the relatively delicate-voiced Clara Smith, who enjoyed the distinction of being the only singer to record duets with Bessie Smith (to whom she was not related); Edith Wilson, a cabaret and Broadway trouper who eventually played the role of Kingfish's mother-in-law on radio and Aunt Jemima on TV; and Lucille Hegamin, the light-skinned "Georgia Peach" who became the *second* black female artist to record, in November 1920, just three months after "Crazy Blues." Hegamin's subsequent "He May Be Your Man (But He Comes to See Me)" was one of the era's most spirited romps, and the godmother of a long line of such songs about black women competing with one another for men, the most recent example of which is Me'Shell NdegéOcello's "If That's Your Boyfriend."

O N May 15, 1929—the day after opening on Broadway in the ill-fated *Pansy*—Bessie Smith recorded the definitive version of "Nobody Knows You When You're Down and Out," a riches-to-rags lament first sung by its composer, the vaudeville comedian Jimmie Cox, six years earlier. The stock market crash was still five months away; even so, it's tempting to hear what proved to be Smith's last big seller as the wail of an entire nation, and as a swan song for herself and her kind of singer. The decline of the women blues vaudevillians was as swift as their ascent, hastened even before Black Friday by the introduction of talking pictures in 1927, which resulted in the construction of Deco movie palaces equipped for sound but not necessarily outfitted with runways and orchestra pits; movies were now a show unto themselves, and Al Jolson might as well have been pronouncing last rites over vaudeville with his cry of "You ain't heard nothing yet."

Not all of these blues vaudevillians followed Ma Rainey's example and put their feathers and rhinestones into storage. Most of them continued to travel the country performing. In those days, entertainment was something you left the house for, and Americans—both black and white—continued to do so during the Depression, at least to the extent that they were financially able. But live entertainment was increasingly a luxury in a country in which approximately 20 percent of the population was on public assistance by the end of 1935, including more than half of the black population of some Northern cities. (This at a time when the economy was supposedly on the road to recovery. The plight of Southern blacks was even worse, owing in part to an unforeseen consequence of an attempt by the Agricultural Adjustment Administration to boost market prices by limiting supply. Federal subsidies to farmers and cotton growers to let their land stand idle resulted in the letting go of millions of field hands and sharecroppers, creating widespread homelessness. Many sharecroppers and tenant farmers found themselves in the ironic position of hoping that they would end the season in debt, so that their landowners would keep them on the following year.)

In the face of such abject poverty, phonograph records became luxury items. A number of record companies went bankrupt or into receivership. Those that continued to target blues releases to a black buyership increasingly focused their efforts on self-accompanied rural singer/guitarists who wrote their own material or drew it from traditional sources. It wasn't as though black audiences of the 1930s suddenly outgrew their infatuation with female blues vaudevillians. It was just that singer/guitarists from Mississippi or Texas or the Carolinas were cheaper to record. Unlike the women, they didn't require songwriters or backup musicians. They sometimes didn't even require a recording studio.

HISTORY is an ideological tug of war, subject to contemporary shifts of emphasis. The stock of the women singers who introduced the blues on records in the 1920s has been subject to wild fluctuation in the decades since. The first books to deal with the blues in a substantive manner were histories of jazz published in the 1930s and 1940s; these typically treated the blues as an early ancestor of jazz, often including an early chapter in which Bessie Smith and Ma Rainey—largely, one suspects, on account of their taste in sidemen and the family resemblance of their music to jazz—were extolled to the virtual exclusion of Blind Lemon Jefferson and Charley Patton. With the blues revival of the 1960s, the pendulum began to swing the other way. Although still regarded as an embryonic form of jazz, the blues is increasingly viewed as a music with its own traditions, which once happened to dovetail those of jazz.

This is the point of view that makes more sense, one to which I myself subscribe. But carry it too far and it encourages downplaying the contributions of the female vaudevillians as somehow tangential to the evolution of the blues. There are obligatory chapters on these women in present-day histories of the blues, much as there once were in histories of jazz; given an intellectual climate in which no male writer except for the most gleefully splenetic wants to be accused of sexism, it would be unthinkable to omit discussion of the blues women of the 1920s altogether. Yet it says something about the extent to which their stock has fallen that even in· the thick of what we're told is a commercial blues revival, there's not a single domestic CD exclusively devoted to the recordings of Ida Cox, Victoria Spivey, or Lucille Hegamin. Or Mamie Smith, for that matter.

Sexism doesn't seem to me to be the culprit here, though I do think that one reason for this oversight is that the women named (and most of the others, including Rainey and Bessie Smith) were singers who weren't also instrumentalists—the typical blues fan is male, and boys do tend to place a high value on being good with your hands. But I think it finally has more to do with a subcultural consumer anathema not peculiar to blues purists. Despite its recent surge in popularity, the blues remains a minority taste, a passion understood only by fellow initiates. Those who choose the blues over all other forms of music, in common with those who choose jazz or anything else not on the charts, are sometimes suspicious of, sometimes hostile toward, music bearing more than one label. A devotion to the blues needn't entail antipathy toward jazz or pop, but it frequently does. The image of the early blues that many of us have grown to cherish is the contradictory one of it as both a solitary activity and a dispossessed people's alternative to suffering in silence. It is assumed to have been only incidentally a form of entertainment. So, when we think of a blues singer of the 1920s, the image we see is that of a man in overalls holding a guitar within shouting distance of a cotton plantation, not the confusing image of a woman in sequins fronting an entourage of jazz musicians under a tent or a proscenium arch.

Yet this was an image fondly embraced by black audiences of the teens and twenties. A modern definition of a star is a figure upon whom audiences project *meaning*, revealing in the process their own fears and anxieties, as well as their own desires. We still don't know for sure if Ma Rainey and Bessie Smith were bisexual, or if this was a rumor started by men who spitefully assumed that women as domineering as these two, singing song after song about cheating men, had to be trying their luck someplace else. Thanks to the protractive capabilities of film and sound recordings, a star's real audience has become posterity. The character of Shug Avery in Alice Walker's *The Color Purple*—the blues diva as life force and lesbian dream lover, sexual enabler as well as racial uplifter—shows that what we might call a star's dreamlife doesn't cease with his or her death; the dreams just become wetter and more absurd. On the other hand, it's not surprising that Walker should identify so closely with Ma Rainey and Bessie Smith. Like Walker, they were black women frequently accused of lining up according to gender rather than race, of signifying on black men in their songs, portraying them in such a way as to reinforce negative stereotypes of them as sexually profligate and just smart enough to be devious—a source of embarrassment to their women, when not an actual danger to them.

As in country music, the battle of the sexes is one of the most popular themes in the blues, the difference being that in the blues (and in black music in general, up to and including rap) the age-old rift is widened by the social and economic restrictions imposed on black men, who frequently see themselves as victims of symbolic castration. The blues itself is a battleground, with women the targets of misdirected resentment not only in blues lyrics but in interpretations of blues history. It's often said that the reason black women preceded black men into the recording studio was that whites found black women less threatening, the point being that it's traditionally been easier for black women to find work, whether as domestics, receptionists, or musical icons. It's likewise often said that—as B. B. King put it to Charles Keil, in attempting to explain the dearth of women blues singers after Ma Rainey and Bessie Smith—"any girl in a choir who's got any kind of voice can make more money as a pop singer or in the good clubs, or even calling herself a jazz singer, than she can by going into the blues," such opportunities presumably having been denied male performers.

Maybe. But a simpler and more convincing explanation for the relative scarcity of women blues singers since 1929 is that the death of vaudeville pulled the props out from under them, almost literally. Without the theaters and tent shows, both the presentation of the blues and the lives of its performers became extremely catch-as-catch-can. The mental image we have of the average blues performer of the 1930s isn't so far from the truth: a nomad riding the freights from town to town, performing in railroad stations or disorderly juke houses or wherever there was a crowd, keeping one eye out for the law and the other for coins tossed in his direction. Ma Rainey and Bessie Smith had roamed the country, too; but never alone with just a harmonica or guitar, always chaperoned—as it were—by pianists, comics, jugglers, dancers, ticket takers, and stagehands. Those days were over.

•

85

BEFORE they ended, however, the women blues vaudevillians helped to change the course of American popular music, loosening up both its rhythms and its inhibitions. They introduced countless listeners in other parts of the country to the music of the rural South, simultaneously treating their fans back home to the spectacle of wealth and glamour at a time when there were no black movie stars or professional athletes. They gave many record buyers their first real taste of hot jazz. Not least of all, their success made it possible for the rural male performers to record.

In tracing the evolution of the blues, it's important to keep reminding ourselves that records fail to tell the whole story. To some extent, "the blues" as we now define it—not just a kind of *song*, a musical form—was a byproduct of the Great Depression and the death of vaudeville, events which halted in progress and postponed until Louis Jordan's success in the 1940s the merger of rural folk and show-business traditions audible in the music of the women blues vaudevillians. Even so, evidence suggests that the blues was being sung long before any examples of it were recorded, and records themselves bedevil any attempt on our part to impose a semblance of chronology on the music's internal development. We draw a distinction between blues singers and songsters, recognizing the latter as transitional figures who performed many types of rural songs in addition to the blues. But we don't know exactly when this transition began, because the recording of both songsters and bluesmen started at roughly the same time. To black record buyers of the twenties and thirties, all of these men were blues singers—or more likely, just singers. Distinctions between different kinds of black singers were applied retroactively, and not by the performers themselves or the people who bought their records.

If we agree not to count George Washington Johnson, the first rural black musician to make a record under his own name was Sylvester Weaver, a guitarist from Georgia who was brought to New York to accompany Sara Martin on one of her dates for Okeh, in November 1923. Martin's producer must have liked what he heard from him, because Weaver wound up recording two solo numbers, "Guitar Rag" and "Guitar Blues," at the tail end of the session. Though Weaver would later sing on record, these tunes were instrumentals. The first of the country men to emerge as something of a record star was Papa Charlie Jackson, a dapper singer who accompanied himself on an oversized, six-string banjo and made his debut with "Papa's Lawdy Lawdy Blues," in 1924. Jackson subsequently recorded dozens of charming, if slightly bowdlerized, versions of traditional black country folk songs. He's believed to have born in New Orleans around 1890, though little is known about him for certain, other than that he was a veteran of the medicine shows that once crisscrossed the South selling tonics and elixirs high in alcoholic content to people prevented by local ordinances or religious conviction from simply buying a bottle of hooch.

"Papa"
Charlie
Jackson
(COURTESY SHELDON
HARRIS COLLECTION)

In terms of the variety of entertainment it offered—singers, shake dancers, magic acts, comic routines, dramatic recitations, playlets based on Shakespeare, *Faust*, and the Bible—the turn-of-the-century medicine show was vaudeville in miniature, vaudeville on a buckboard. It also resembled a latterday minstrel show, with black performers sometimes forced to appear before white audiences in lampblack and burnt cork. Despite this indignity, the folk singers who traveled with such shows gained much from them. These shows exposed them to songs and black song styles of regions other than their own, making them walking repositories of American vernacular music. Unlike the women vaudevillians, Papa Charlie Jackson, Jim Jackson, Pink Anderson, and the other medicine show songsters were essentially folk singers, only semiprofessionals. But the medicine shows molded them into well-rounded entertainers. Mississippi John Hurt, whose versions of "Stagolee" and "Frankie and Johnnie" and importance to the blues revival of the 1960s were discussed in Part I of this book, was an exception to the rule: a farmer who became a professional musician only toward the end of his life, so diffident in manner that it's impossible to imagine him holding a townful of strangers spellbound from a soapbox or the back of a wagon. Most of the others were seasoned crowd-pleasers by the time their voices were heard on record.

Descended from England, the medicine show was a small-town, turn-of-the-century American institution. These shows played to both black and white audiences, and occasionally featured performers of both races. There were white songsters, though we might not think of them as such. The most obvious example is Jimmie Rodgers, the man frequently hailed as the father of "hillbilly" or country-and-western music. Rodgers started his career with the medicine shows, sometimes performing in blackface and often paired with Frank Stokes, the black Memphis songster (and professional blacksmith) from whom he is suspected to have learned much of his repertoire. Rodgers's series of "Blue Yodels" and his many songs with "blues" in their titles made no secret of his debt to black music. One of his most popular records was "In the Jailhouse Now," said to have been a favorite of black medicine show performers long before he and any of them recorded it. (Based on a verse included only on a 1924 version by the black jug bandleader Buford Threlkeld, Paul Oliver speculates that it may have begun life as a minstrel show "coon" song.) Rodgers didn't just take: black performers were as enchanted as anyone by the falsetto yodel he indulged in on refrains, and the Mississippi Sheiks' 1930 "Yodeling, Fiddling Blues" is practically a homage to him.

Roy Acuff, Dock Boggs, Fiddling John Carson, Frank Hutchinson, and Uncle Dave Macon were other white country performers who worked the wagons as white songsters. Hank Williams was once a songster, too, though a few decades after these others. According to Paul Oliver, Buster Keaton broke into show business as a blackface minstrel with a traveling medicine show.

In most cases, though, blackface was superfluous. The medicine shows created a climate in which blackness rubbed off. Though prevented from meaningful contact by both custom and law, whites and blacks in rural areas increasingly shared a taste in music—another way of saying that what was eventually called "country" and what was eventually called "the blues" shared a similar genesis in these medicine shows. This similarity became even more pronounced after the annexation of the Hawaiian Islands in 1896, an event that not only aroused a wave of patriotic fervor and triggered visions of paradise on the part of most Americans, but also resulted in a lingering musical craze—one that saw both white country pickers and black slide guitarists adapting as best they could the string-bending techniques and plangent sound of Hawaiian guitarists.

By the time black performers started to be recorded in appreciable numbers, many of them already had substantial followings among whites. DeFord Bailey was a Nashville hunchback who was a songster in spirit, though not actually a singer. He was a harmonica virtuoso admired for his ability to conjure up a cackling hen, a contented lover, or a speeding locomotive with nothing more than his breath and fingers. In 1925, he became a featured performer on the WSM Barn Dance, a Nashville country music radio program that eventually went national as the Grand Ole Opry, an institution we're likely to think of as having always been lily-white. Bailey stayed with the Opry for sixteen years, during which time he was treated in a patronizing manner (introduced on air as "our little mascot"), but emerged as a favorite of listeners. He fell into oblivion after being dismissed from the WSM in 1941, supposedly for his lack of initiative ("laziness" was the way it was actually put) in learning new numbers. He was clearly a victim of racism, but at least one of his records was released by RCA Victor in both its "race" and "country" series, the latter representing the company's attempt to exploit his popularity with the Opry's rural white listenership.

Lest Bailey be dismissed as an anomaly, let's show that he wasn't by citing an example even more extreme—though probably apocryphal. Legend has it that Jaybird Coleman, another black harmonica-playing songster and occasional jug bandleader, was, for a few years in the 1930s, managed by the Ku Klux Klan.

CONTRARY to what some reference books say, "Ragtime Texas" Henry Thomas, who was born to former slaves in the bottomlands of the Sabine River in 1874, wasn't the eldest-born black performer to be recorded singing in what everyone would agree was a "genuine" Negro style. That honor goes to Johnny "Daddy Stovepipe" Watson, a singer, guitarist, and harmonica player, who was born in Alabama in 1867 and who—after many decades on the road with minstrel and medicine shows—made his first recordings for Gennett in May 1924, just six months after Sylvester Weaver's debut. These and many of Watson's subsequent recordings included second vocals by his wife, "Mississippi" Mary; they are of interest to us now only as relics.

The twenty-five numbers that Henry Thomas recorded for Vocalion over a two-year period beginning in October 1927 are a different story altogether: historical documents whose vitality remains undiminished by time. These are among the most evocative recordings of their period, not least for what they suggest about the years preceding them—they amount to a virtual palimpsest of black vernacular music of the late nineteenth and early twentieth centuries.

Thomas's life, insofar as we know about it, reads like the artful invention of an author intent on combining in one individual the appeal of antiquarian music and the romance of the open road. He was a hobo, a man on the move in a day when it was still possible to assume that anyone who was homeless was that way by choice. Refusing to be tied down to the land and opting for a high-speed mobility that must have struck people of his generation as nothing short of miraculous, Thomas traveled wherever the railroads could take him—and seldom in a boxcar.

"Ragtime Texas was a big fellow that used to come aboard at Gladewater or Mineola or somewhere in there," a former railroad conductor once told the liner note writer Mack McCormick. "I'd always carry him, except when he was too dirty. He was a regular hobo, but I'd carry him most of the time. That guitar was his ticket."

Travel was a constant theme in Thomas's songs, and no wonder. Though he apparently never worked the medicine wagons, he was an archetypal songster in terms of the range and transitional nature of his repertoire, which included country stomps, ragtime numbers, prison songs, and even reworked coon songs and square dance calls. He also recorded a few no-doubt-about-it blues, and these give us the clearest notion we have of what the blues must have sounded like in the late 1890s, when Thomas's musical values were formed. He sang these and his other numbers buoyantly and disarmingly, in what the British writer Giles Oakley aptly describes as a voice "neither particularly plaintive or melancholy—it is the voice of a man who perhaps doesn't really expect to be listened to, just to rather hoarsely remind the milling crowds that there's some old guy worthy of the spare change in your pocket." Never straying very far from a simple, dancelike beat on his guitar, Thomas also frequently accompanied himself on the quills, a double-reed instrument descended from African panpipes and long before abandoned by most rural black country performers. If anything, the quills should further distance contemporary listeners from Thomas, but they have the opposite effect—their eerie tonality piquing our curiosity, adding to Thomas's otherworldly aura.

A favorite of 1960s folkies and blues revivalists (Bob Dylan covered his "Allow Me One More Chance" and Canned Heat reworked his "Bull Doze Blues" into "Goin' Up the Country," a Top 40 hit for them in 1968), Thomas was occasionally spotted here and there in the years following his last recording session, in 1929—though someone thought to be him could have been any old hobo with a guitar. He seems such a figment of myth that it's always something of a shock to slap the one CD reissue of his work into the player, hit a button, and hear his voice, guitar, and quills.

O F the black songsters who first recorded in the late 1920s, Gus Cannon was arguably the most versatile and Walter "Furry" Lewis the most indefatigable. Both are indelibly associated with Memphis; Mississippi natives who had a hand in making Beale Street black music's main drag in the decade after World War I. Both wound up working for the Memphis sanitation department in later years, pushing brooms along the same street their music once enlivened.

Furry Lewis's recording career paralleled the ebb and flow of commercial interest in rural black music. He recorded for both Vocalion and RCA Victor

in Memphis and Chicago from 1927 to 1929, after which nothing else was heard from him until the blues revival of the early 1960s. After being rediscovered by Sam Charters, Lewis recorded prolifically for a decade or so, then sporadically until his death in 1981. That Lewis's best-known number was a version of "Casey Jones," the tale of an engineer who races the Devil,[3] is grimly ironic in view of the fact that he lost a leg when he caught his foot in a railroad coupling while attempting to hop a locomotive in 1916. Lewis favored traditional narratives along the lines of "Casey Jones" and "Stager Lee," and as contradictory as it sounds, his greatest strength was as a storyteller and his greatest charm was his inability to just tell the goddamn story. He was forever interjecting personal boasts, verses from other songs, and periodic reports on his own state of mind and that of everyone else mentioned in the song—and bless him for it. My favorite moment on his "Kassie Jones" is when somebody (Furry? Mrs. Jones? the train's passengers?) warns the hero that he's risking an "occulusion" with another freight.

Though he frequently worked solo in the medicine shows and first recorded as Blind Blake's duet partner, Gus Cannon's name will forever be

3. Furry pronounced the man's name "Kassie," and that's the way his version was spelled: "Kassie Jones."

Cannon's Jug Stompers— Gus Cannon, Ashley Thompson, Noah Lewis (COURTESY SHELDON HARRIS COLLECTION) linked to jug bands. His Jug Stompers, sparked by Noah Lewis's crazed harmonica and Cannon's own blues-influenced banjo and vocals, were Beale Street's best in the 1920s, when the competition included Will Shade's Memphis Jug Band and the various outfits fronted by Jack Kelly and Charlie Bourse (the original pelvis twister, still active on Beale Street well into the fifties—as were Cannon and most of the others—and said to have made an impression on the young Elvis Presley). In 1963, long after Cannon had fallen into obscurity, a remake of his "Walk Right In" by a white group called the Rooftop Singers (led by Erik Darling, of the Weavers) reached number one and started a college jug band revival.

In common with the bands led by Cannon's rivals, the Jug Stompers recorded a wide range of material and probably treated their live audiences to an even wider range. "Money Never Runs Out," which the Jug Stompers recorded in 1928, was a latterday version of a number by Irving T. Jones, a black turn-of-the-century composer of ragtime and coon songs. Cannon's was also the most blues-savvy of its era's jug bands, and such Stompers numbers as "Minglewood Blues," "Noah's Blues," and "Viola Lee Blues" (later revived by the Grateful Dead) were blues in structure and feeling, not just name.

Jug bands differed in size and instrumentation, though they invariably included either a harmonica or a kazoo as a lead melodic voice, a variety of string instruments, and at least one band member providing a bass line by blowing rhythmically across the top of a jug—a poor man's tuba, as it were. Like the rural fife-and-drum bands of which we have regrettably few recorded examples, jug bands can be heard as a missing link between the blues and the music of West Africa: the buzzing textures produced by the jug, especially when used as a melody instrument, are likely to remind us of Robert Palmer's comments about the mouthpieces built into African ceremonial masks. Along with the washboard bands in which a simple laundry device was transformed into a percussion instrument, the jug bands were a tribute to the ingenuity shown by impoverished rural blacks in expressing themselves musically on whatever they found at hand. For that matter, Cannon fashioned his first banjo out of a bread pan and a broom handle. And there are obvious parallels to be drawn between the use of such homemade or "nonmusical" instruments then and similar practices in hip-hop, most notably "scratching."

THESE, however, are points of interest mainly to musicologists or sociologists. They don't really explain why records by bands like Cannon's sound so seductive to anyone who chances to hear them now. Beyond the attractive juxtaposition of rumble and twitter, the earthy and the levitational, it's the contagious appeal of music at once so structured and so wild—so obviously archaic but fresh to the individuals making it. The jug bands of Memphis enjoyed a reputation as the roughest of their kind; the most sophisticated were supposed to be those from Louisville, where the tradition is believed to have started. In this context, "sophisticated" means jazz-influenced, by which standard the most sophisticated jug band of all was Clifford Hayes and the Dixieland Jug Blowers, which usually included trombone and alto saxophone, and often dispensed with the jug. Hayes was a violinist with jazz aspirations who even snared Earl "Fatha" Hines to play piano on one of his dates.

This was in 1929, by which time Hines—the first pianist to take a hornlike approach on the keys—was already revered in jazz circles. A few years later, Stanley Dance tells us in *The World of Earl Hines*, Hines was sharing a booth in a Chicago restaurant with Louis Armstrong and the drummer Zutty Singleton when one of the records he'd made with Hayes came on the radio. Armstrong and Singleton recognized Hines's piano style right away, but Hines went on insisting that it couldn't possibly be him even after realizing that it was. Describing Hayes's band as a "hillbilly group," Hines explained to Dance that "if [Armstrong] had seen that band, I would never have heard the end of it. The trombone player's slide was bent up so it looked like he was playing around a corner, and the violinist held his violin down where his chest was."

Armstrong was more appreciative of many kinds of music—and more rustic in his own background—than this anecdote indicates. But that's not the point, nor is it Hines's greater musical sophistication. The story reminds me of W. C. Handy's bewildered reaction to the guitarist at Tutwiler Station, only here the difference between the two men boils down to geography, not class. Hines was born and raised in Pittsburgh, and to a Northern-born musician like him, even a band as refined as Hayes's sounded hopelessly "country," not to mention old hat. But who knows? By the late 1920s, jug bands may have sounded like a relic from another day even to those people who enjoyed them—country people to whom jazz was a city folks' dicty glide. Black America was in flux as the 1920s rolled on. So was black music, and the fledgling record industry's perception of it. Jug bands, songsters, and blues-singing black vaudevillians, though still relatively new on record, were about to be displaced by big bands from Chicago and Harlem, but not just by them. On record at least, the blues was about to become the property of loners from Mississippi, Texas, and the Piedmonts—discographical phantoms with guitars for whom the blues wasn't just an approach to music, but a state of mind.

CHAPTER 3

DELTA TRANSCENDENTALISTS, TEXAS TROUBADOURS, AND EAST COAST FINGERPICKERS

b*lind Lemon Jefferson* was born on a farm in Couchman, Texas, around 1897, but lived nowhere in particular. He was a vagabond singer and guitarist likely to turn up in the Delta at harvest time or wherever else black workers found themselves with enough spare change in their pockets to indulge their passion for music and good times. It's surprising that Jefferson interrupted

Blind Lemon Jefferson
(COURTESY BLUES ARCHIVE, UNIVERSITY OF MISSISSIPPI)

his rambles long enough to record, but he did—close to one hundred sides for Paramount over a three-year period beginning in 1926. These recordings outsold those of any other black male country performer up to that point, establishing Jefferson as a star of the magnitude of Ma Rainey or Bessie Smith.

Despite his stardom, Jefferson went on playing country picnics and urban house parties right up to 1930, when he froze to death during a Chicago blizzard (according to some sources, he died after being abandoned on the street by an unnamed man who was serving as both his driver and his eyes). Also despite his stardom, Jefferson was photographed only once that anyone knows of: a Paramount publicity shot of him seated with his guitar on his lap. "Cordially yours, Blind Lemon Jefferson," reads the inscription at the bottom, though both the signature and the cordiality are assumed to be a publicist's forgeries. As incredible as it seems, Jefferson was once a wrestler, which would tend to support the contention of many of those who knew him that he was only partially blind ("he darn sure could *feel* his way around," Victoria Spivey once quipped). In his lone photograph, he looks hulking enough to have wrestled, but he also has round, thick spectacles and eyes no larger than slits.

So Jefferson was big and he was blind; or losing his sight, at the very least. He had close-cropped hair, a medium-dark complexion, a broad nose, and thick lips. But everything else we might deduce from his one photo turns out to be false. Jefferson looks extremely uncomfortable, his erect posture presumably feigned to go along with a suit and tie to which he is also unaccustomed. Yet according to Spivey and others, this is the way he normally carried himself, the manner in which he usually dressed—perhaps to distance himself from the coveralled land serfs and wage slaves he entertained. This was a man whose guitar was his echo, a second voice. Yet the guitar on his lap in the photo looks like a prop, or a hoax played on a blind man who realized it was there just a split second before the shutter closed. He fingers it gingerly, as if trying to figure out exactly what it is; the strap from which it dangles looks absurdly long. You can't imagine this man tapping out a rhythm on a string or bending one to complete a vocal phrase, the way that Jefferson did on his records. This man could be a colleague of Booker T. Washington, a black country schoolmaster fond of lecturing to his pupils that the way for them to prove that they're as good as anybody else is to be *better* than anybody else, by God. Owlish and high-buttoned, this is a man so resolute that he interprets his own sightlessness as a moral challenge. No songs about deceitful brownskins, 'lectric chairs, or being broke and hungry from this upstanding citizen—no.

There's a photo from 1929 or '30—not far removed from a Daguerreotype—of Memphis Minnie standing next to the seated Kansas Joe McCoy, the first of her three husbands and duet partners. Neither of them is smiling.

McCoy, who's strumming a guitar and simulating relaxation with an ankle over one knee, merely looks wary. Without *her* guitar as an anchor, Memphis Minnie looks nervous enough to levitate; she's touching her husband's shoulder in what's undoubtedly supposed to be a display of marital affection, though you imagine she's holding on to him to prevent herself from floating out of the frame. A publicity photo from the late 1930s in which she smiles incandescently shows her with her guitar, her legs crossed, large hoop earrings dangling from her lobes, and her hair fixed in a flattering off-face style. In another shot from around the same time, she might be a big-boned, high-heeled, guitar-toting showgirl, her slit dress exposing one shapely leg almost to the loin. In the ten years separating these two photos from the one with Kansas Joe, Memphis Minnie had gotten used to being photographed—as had most of the rest of America.

Eastman Kodak introduced the box camera and roll film in 1888, and flash photography was introduced in 1925. But it took several decades more for portable cameras to become everyday objects in most people's lives. In the late twenties, especially for country people, having a picture taken required a visit to a photographer's studio, and you dressed for the occasion in your Sunday best, as you would for a visit to any professional. You also wore a serious demeanor, because the people in paintings rarely smiled (photography still meant portraiture, not candids), and because it could be hard work sitting still for the length of time it took a photographer to set the proper lighting and reload his plates. I doubt that many people consciously recognized their photographs as artifacts that would outlive them. To the contrary, the modest goal was to look in a photograph as you wished to look in your coffin, which is to say prosperous and respected. A session with a photographer was a dress rehearsal for eternity.

Ma Rainey and Bessie Smith took to the camera right away, but they were experienced stage performers for whom the lens must have seemed one more pair of eyes, not the diabolical contraption that drifters like Blind Lemon Jefferson and Charley Patton must have regarded it as. Without their recordings, such men would be phantoms who lived and died without a trace, names on yellowed birth certificates, marriage licenses, or death certificates—rarely all three. Which is more remarkable? That Jefferson, Patton, and Blind Blake each was photographed only once? Or that these men-on-the-run, who lived at a time when an appointment with a photographer was a badge of bourgeois propriety, sat in one spot long enough to be photographed at all?

We want the few photographs of such men to combine with their recordings to put flesh on their legends, to tell us as much about their daily lives as Walker Evans's photographs tell us about the lives of white migrant sharecroppers. But this may be asking too much. The one known photograph of Charley Patton barely establishes his corporeal being; he hardly shows up in it. One of the few things it does suggest, oddly, is that Patton was very short: the smallness of his head is accentuated by his comically large ears, and he looks up at us as though out of habit. His light complexion and "good" hair suggest not very distant white or Native American ancestry.[1] What else? Nothing. Some people who look at this photo think they see madness or fear or a bad hangover in Patton's dazed stare and slightly parted lips. But this is probably discomfort at being photographed—nothing more. Other people read cool menace into Patton's expressionless mug, but this is a deduction based on the gravel of his recorded voice and on his reputation as a woman-beater and braggart. (He was once expelled from Dockery Farms for using a bullwhip on one of his many common-law wives; Patton's own version of the story was that he was banished for keeping the plantation's women up all night with his music and sexual prowess, rendering them useless in the fields the next day.) No, Charley Patton appears to have been some piece of work, but the man in the picture is unfinished, a blank. We're told that some African tribes used to fear that the camera would steal their souls. Patton's photograph suggests that this fear was not unfounded.

FOR all his vitality, the man in Patton's songs is something of a blank, too. To a greater extent than any of his contemporaries, Patton drew on personal experience, reshaping verses in common usage to his own ends. But his lyrics were observational rather than autobiographical. In his two-part "High Water Everywhere," for example, we learn more about the havoc wreaked by the Great Flood of 1927 than we do about the singer. "High Sheriff Blues" and "Tom Rushen Blues" likewise tell us much about the power wielded over blacks by small-town Mississippi law enforcement officers, but nothing about what provoked Patton's run-ins with them.

Yet the rhythmic weave of Patton's voice and guitar is so compelling, so primeval, that even the most level-headed of blues scholars yield to the temptation to conjecture a mythic past for him. Sam Charters speculates that Patton may have been one of the unschooled local musicians who upstaged Handy's men at that dance in Cleveland, Mississippi, where it rained silver and gold coins. And David Evans writes, "It is even possible that the singer [encountered by W.C. Handy at the Tutwiler railroad station in 1902] was the young Charley Patton, who was able to play knife-style

1. According to David Evans's research, Patton was "at least one-quarter Caucasian, probably one-quarter to one-half Indian, and the remainder African," which qualified him as Negro by Mississippi law. Stephen Calt and Gayle Wardlow's *King of the Delta Blues* shows a heavily retouched photograph from 1908 of a young man of uncertain race with a thick mustache whom the authors believe to be Patton. If it is him (and the large ears certainly look like his), you can see why Howlin' Wolf described him as looking like a Puerto Rican. Patton must have looked "light" to blacks, and "dark" to whites.

guitar and who recorded that very stanza ["Goin' where the Southern cross the dog"] twenty-five years later in his 'Green River Blues.'" Maybe so, but Patton is believed to have born in Edwards, Mississippi, no earlier than 1881 and no later than 1891, which means that he was probably in his early teens or younger in 1902. You'd think that Handy would have mentioned it if his anonymous singer and guitarist had been a child. But such is Patton's legend, such is his grip on the imagination, that we want him to have been there in Tutwiler and Cleveland, for our knowledge of the blues to *begin* with him.

If the world was the creation of E. L. Doctorow, a novelist for whom history amounts to name-dropping and literature to rotogravure, Patton would have crossed paths with William Faulkner. The singer would have been the model for the "young, black, lean-hipped man" who, still strumming his guitar, boards a skiff full of blacks rescued from the flood in *Old Man*, Faulkner's novella about the 1927 flood to which Patton himself bore eloquent witness in "High Water Everywhere."

"I saw that launch and them boats come up and they never had no room for me," complains one of Faulkner's white characters.

> Full of bastard niggers and one of them setting there playing a guitar but there wasn't no room for me. "A guitar!" he cried; now he began to scream, trembling, slavering, his face twitching and jerking. "Room for a bastard nigger guitar but not for me—"

Patton's point of view in "High Water Everywhere," though by no means "literary," is comparable to that of a novelist. Especially in part two, he shifts perspective from verse to verse, so that even though we already know the general drift of the story, we're never quite sure what's coming next. In telling of his own trial by water, his tone is one of ironic exaggeration: the icy floodwaters roll through his door and rise up over his bed, and he sings, "I thought I would take a trip, Lord, / Out on that big ice sled." He also gives us a sense of the flood's widespread devastation, in images whose precision is in counterpoint to his slurred delivery:

> The water was rising
> Up in my friend's door
> The water was rising
> Up in my friend's door
> The man said to his women folk
> Lord, we'd better go . . .

> Ohhhhhh-ah the water rising
> Families sinking down
> Say now, the water was rising
> At places all around
>   (Boy, they's all around)[2]
> It was fifty men and children
> Come to sink and drown.

"High Water Everywhere" is the most vivid of the many blues songs to tell of the 1927 flood; it's not going too far to say that it rivals Faulkner's novella in detail. Yet despite his being the subject of perhaps the most extensive biography of any early blues musician, Stephen Calt and Gayle Wardlow's *King of the Delta Blues: The Life and Music of Charlie Patton*, the author of "High Water Everywhere" is such a riddle that he might himself be a fiction, a Faulkner creation, a Joe Christmas. Everything we think we know about him, beginning with his birthdate and including the revisionist assessment of him as *the* key figure in the evolution of the blues, turns out to be an educated guess or a matter of opinion.

In listening to Patton, you never doubt for a second that you're hearing a performer who left his own imprint on what was probably traditional material. The heart of Patton's style was its polyrhythmic complexity—though all of the numbers he recorded were in conventional quadruple meter, he generated tension and ensured variety with high tunings, chimed and choked guitar runs, tapped bass notes, omitted words and spoken asides, and a tricky way of accenting the first beat in the measure with his guitar and the fourth beat with his voice, so that the two would coincide only fleetingly. As many observers have noted, rhythm isn't simply one component of a Charley Patton song—it *is* the song, and it's what pulls you in. Though he may not have been the first Delta guitarist to use a bottleneck, or the first singer from the area to bellow his lyrics in what we now characterize as a Delta growl, he may have been the first Delta *bluesman*—the performer who codified these and other elements into the blues, and established the blues as a vehicle for personal commentary. Robert Johnson's name might be more familiar, but Patton came first and Johnson used his recordings as a kind of source book. (Patton's "Down the Dirt Road Blues" and "Tom

2. The parenthesis indicates a spoken interjection—one of many on Patton's records. These asides sometimes come from Patton himself, sometimes from Willie Brown or someone else from Patton's circle; it's usually difficult to say which. Also, be warned that reading a Patton transcription is a different matter than actually listening to him. The hiss and crackle on his recordings combine with his Mississippi dialect to render him all but unintelligible to anyone hearing him for the first time. A good place to "read" Patton is in the chapter on him in Samuel Charters's *The Blues Makers*, or in Eric Sackheim's *The Blues Line*, a kind of *Norton Anthology* of the blues.

Rushen Blues" became Johnson's "Crossroads Blues" and "From Four Till Late," respectively.) That famous guitar riff on Johnson's "If I Had Possession Over Judgment Day," itself the source of Elmore James's "Dust My Broom" and countless other postwar blues, can be traced to "Roll and Tumble Blues," a 1929 recording by the otherwise forgotten Hambone Willie Newbern, but also to Patton's "Screamin' and Hollerin' the Blues," from the same year.

A good possibility exists that these melodies and chord progressions were commonplace in Mississippi long before Patton got hold of them. Patton probably thought of himself as a songster, and perhaps he was essentially a transitional figure—a bluester, if you will. Of the sixty-odd numbers he recorded, only about half were blues by the most generous definition. Most of the remainder were personalized versions of uptempo country tunes long enjoyed by both rural blacks and whites. Given that Patton often played for whites and that he began his recording career in 1929, fairly late in the game, when blues were already much in demand by record company executives, it seems reasonable to assume that blues accounted for *less* than half of his live repertoire. Though he wasn't particularly religious, he even recorded a goodly number of sacred songs, some under the pseudonym Elder J. J. Hadley.[3] In "On Death," one of the more than two dozen numbers he recorded for Vocalion in New York City in 1934, just a few months before his own death, he even broke into an impromptu sermon.

PATTON probably learned these hymns from Bill C. Patton, the man who raised him. If so, he seems to have learned little else from Bill C., a church elder who was married to Charley's mother but might not have been his biological father. In his own time, legend had it that Charley was actually the son of one of his mother's earlier suitors, Henderson Chatmon, the fiddler-patriarch of a musical family that included the members of the Mississippi Sheiks, a black string band that performed mostly for whites and recorded for Bluebird in the 1920s and 1930s. Patton apparently spent as much of his adolescence with the Chatmons as with his own family, and in speaking of him to blues researchers, Sam Chatmon of the Sheiks always referred to him as "my half brother." It seems somehow fitting, doesn't it, that even Charley Patton's lineage should be ambiguous. And fitting that, according to David Evans, one of Bill Patton's names for Charley was "X."

In any case, Bill C. Patton moved his large family, including Charley, to Will Dockery's 10,000-acre plantation five miles southeast of Cleveland,

3. "Charley knew all those religious songs from boyhood and sang them later 'cause they're good songs, I guess," Viola Cannon, Patton's sister, told Gayle Wardlow and Bernard Klatzko. Though Patton apparently had a brief career as a preacher as a young man, Cannon seemed amused at Wardlow's suggestion that her brother might have been religious.

Mississippi, in Sunflower County, around 1897. More than any other Delta plantation, Dockery's was a self-sufficient town, with its own cotton gins, dry goods and furniture stores, infirmary, cemetery, post office, train depot (celebrated by Patton in "Pea Vine Blues"), and even its own currency. No juke houses, though, because Will Dockery—the son of a Confederate general killed at the Battle of Bull Run—had no ear for what whites of that day were apt to call "nigger" music.

In this and many other ways, Dockery was the opposite of many of his fellow plantation owners. According to Calt and Wardlow, the Mississippi Sheiks were for a long time "personal minstrels" to Dockery's close friend, William Howard Stovall. Following Patton's expulsion from Dockery's, he was taken in by George Kirkland, the owner of a smaller plantation a few miles away, who initially exempted him from field work, putting him to work strictly as a musician. Despite Dockery's aversion toward, or simple lack of interest in, the music of his croppers and field hands, however, the picture of him that emerges from the literature on Patton is that of an extremely decent man given the time and place, and given that what might appear to be humane behavior on his part was probably just smart business from his own point of view. Dockery's best black workers tended to stay with him for life. He had a reputation for paying relatively high wages, and for not shorting his tenant families during the season-ending weigh-ins. On land that had only recently been swamp, malaria-carrying mosquitoes were still enough of a threat to keep most white laborers away.[4] The black farmers and sharecroppers who flocked to Dockery's from all over Mississippi after its founding in 1895 were followed by itinerant musicians, many of whom wound up working for Dockery as day laborers and nearly all of whom supplemented their incomes by performing on weekends in the jukes in surrounding towns. One of these musicians was Henry Sloan, an unrecorded songster who took the young Charley Patton under his wing, and presumably taught him a song or two.

Patton seems to have learned more from Sloan and Henderson Chatmon than from the man whose surname he took. Though he was illiterate, Bill C. Patton was an industrious man who knew how to save money. Even while working for Dockery, he operated his own lumber-hauling wagons. He later bought 100-plus acres of his own in Mound Bayou, an all-black Delta town where he also ran a general store. In a culture where "honest" work meant manual labor, his son (or stepson) was infamous for never having done an honest day's work in his life, at least not by choice.

4. Blacks were thought by Southern whites to be more resistant to malaria, a belief perhaps rooted in the knowledge that a particularly deadly strain of the disease had been carried to America on the slave ships. In any case, when a vaccine was finally developed during one of the worst epidemics of the 1920s, the blacks on Dockery Farms were among the first Southerners to be inoculated, at the owner's personal expense.

"Charley could have helped his father in [his] enterprises, eventually inheriting them and perhaps building them into something even more grandiose," David Evans observes in *Nothing But the Blues*. "This, however, would have involved the acceptance of the social status quo in the Delta, one which was driven by rampant racism that assigned an inferior caste role to all people of African ancestry, no matter what their accomplishments. Charley wanted a greater degree of freedom than his father had."

This is a valid way of looking at Charley Patton's life, though it's based on the dubious assumption that *freedom* was something a young Southern black man of Patton's generation would have allowed himself to think about. The status quo in Mississippi in the early nineteenth century may have been onerous for black sharecroppers and farmers, but it was the only reality they knew. Deprived of any knowledge of Africa, their only ready ancestral memory was of slavery. Another way of looking at Charley Patton and the choices he made was Bill C. Patton's way, which was also Will Dockery's: that Charley was no damn good. And maybe these men had a point. Patton possessed, or was possessed by, what would now be euphemistically called "an artistic temperament" and understood to be as much a curse as a blessing. Fellow musicians, though they tended to gravitate to him, seemed not to like him very much. According to Son House—a frequent companion of Patton's, who made his recording debut in 1930, when Patton took him and several other members of his entourage along to a session for Paramount in Grafton, Wisconsin—Patton was a blowhard, especially on the subject of his sexual conquests. "You could hardly get a word in edgeways yourself, not when Charley [was] around," Son House once complained. "His woman yesterday, the day before yesterday, all what he done to the woman. . . . He'd be talkin' about all the time he's 'with' her, they goin' to bed, and how long they can 'stay,' and all that. . . . Oh, I [used to get] *sick* of that son of a bitch!"[5]

House apparently didn't think much of Patton as a musician, either; following his own rediscovery in 1963, he often accused Patton of "breaking" time—that is, not keeping a steady beat. Many of Patton's contemporaries resented his showboating. "He be in there putting his guitar all between his legs, carry it behind his head, lay down on the floor, and never stop picking," Sam Chatmon once told a British interviewer from the BBC. This would make Patton a spiritual ancestor to Chuck Berry and Jimi Hendrix, as well as heir to an African tradition in which (as Alan Lomax explains it) "musicians are constantly shifting the position of their rattles and stringed instruments, tossing drums in the air between strokes and the like, playing *with* them," as opposed to just playing them (italics added). But this failed to impress

5. The quote from House is in Calt and Wardlow, who fail to give a source.

Chatmon, who once complained to Lomax that Patton "could clown better than he could pick."

It needs to be remembered that Patton was in a line of work in which a man's best friends are likely to be his fiercest rivals. His guitar twirling no doubt went over big in the juke houses, and men such as Sam Chatmon and Son House were probably envious of his popularity. But professional envy doesn't completely explain the personal animosity many of Patton's competitors harbored toward him. Talking about him years after his death, they inevitably characterized him as indolent, dishonest, sexually wanton, prone to violence, and drunk more often than not—negative characteristics frequently attributed by whites to blacks in general. What makes this ironic is that their reminiscences also suggest—as do certain of Patton's verses— that he considered himself genetically superior to blacks darker in complexion than himself. "Brownskin woman like something fit to eat," he sang in "Pony Blues." "But a jet-black woman, don't put your hands on me."

On the other hand, many of the performers of Patton's day responded to him the same way that many of us do now, as much for the figure he cut and the ethos he embodied as for his music. "I always wanted to be like old Charley Patton . . . and play them numbers about 'Hitch up my buggy

Sam Chatman, Mariposa Folk Festival, 1974
(DOUG FULTON)

and saddle up my black mare,' " Bukka White told Ed Denson and John Fahey. "I'd say 'I wants to come to be a great man like Charley Patton,' but I didn't want to be killed like he did, the way he had to go . . . one of them old sandfoot womens coming up and cut my throat or do something that's unnecessary."

Such was Patton's legend that long after his death in 1934, many of those who had known him continued to believe that he was the victim of a woman with a razor. It's easy to understand how that story got started. He did have his throat cut (though probably not by a woman) in a barroom brawl in the early 1930s, and perhaps as a result of this injury, his voice does sound constricted on some of his final recordings, including the aforementioned "On Death." But in fact, Patton died in bed, in the arms of Berth Lee Pate, his final wife and a blues singer herself, in Indianola, Mississippi, not twenty miles from Dockery Farms, a few weeks after collapsing on his way home from performing at a white dance. What felled him was an infection caused by a simple heart murmur. He suffered from what would today be diagnosed as a mitric valvic prolapse, a condition which is usually congenital but sometimes a result of childhood rheumatic fever. Such a condition would be treated with antibiotics not yet in existence in 1934. In something of an unintended joke, his death certificate listed his occupation as "farmer."

LONG after his own time, Patton has gained such a hold on the thinking of blues scholars that they tend to work backward in tracing his influence on his contemporaries—that is, they start from the premise that he was influential, then go to their record collections to find proof.

Tommy Johnson
(COURTESY SHELDON HARRIS COLLECTION)

One of the first Mississippi bluesmen touched by Patton is supposed to have been Tommy Johnson, a performer originally from the southern part of the state approximately five years younger who's said to have emulated Patton's guitar twirling after migrating to the Delta in the late teens. The problem with branding Johnson a Patton disciple is that by the late 1920s, when he made his handful of recordings for Bluebird and Paramount, Johnson was already a mature performer who had left Patton far behind, along with any other role models he may once have had. There was no trace of the songster in Johnson. Though his blues didn't always conform to twelve-bar convention, they were as undiluted as the genre ever gets. He may or may not have been the first Delta bluesman to ask for water and be given gasoline, and he may or not have been the first to inquire of a stationmaster how long the evening train taking his woman away from him was gone. These lyrical conceits are believed to have been in general circulation long before their appearance in Johnson's February 1928 recording of "Cool Drink of Water Blues." The provenance of Johnson's lyrics hardly matters, however, because the manner in which he sang them rendered them practically unintelligible, and the story they tell isn't what pulls you into the performance anyway—what does is Johnson's vocal hula and the voodoo bass drone of his and Charlie McCoy's guitars. Intricate only in its synergism, this guitar part gives the impression that these two men have been strumming long before the record begins and will go on strumming long after the fade. It's one of those recorded performances that supports the view of the blues as mankind's eternal music, without beginning or end.

But what's likely to strike a contemporary listener as original about "Cool Drink of Water Blues," for all its obvious nods to tradition, is Johnson's falsetto, a lupine yodel that's something of a shock the first time you hear it and thereafter a puzzle. Is it an African retention, a melodicized field holler, an adaptation of a Scots-Irish croon, a wolf imitation, something Johnson learned from a medicine show songster, or (like steel guitar) a memento of the Hawaiian music craze of the early years of the twentieth century? All of the above; none of the above? It's likely to remind anyone coming to Johnson's music armed with a knowledge of modern jazz of a John Coltrane or Pharaoh Sanders saxophone scream. Despite Johnson's musicality and self-control, that yodel of his seems as natural as speech, *rooted* in speech: specifically, black male voices at their most excited.

Johnson's yodel was the ur-falsetto, and it wasn't all that started with him. At least a decade before his younger, unrelated namesake Robert, this Johnson was supposed to have sold his soul to the Devil at a crossroads. "If you want to learn to play anything you want to play and learn how to make songs yourself, you take your guitar and you go to where a crossroads is," LeDell Johnson told David Evans, no doubt repeating the story as his brother Tommy had told it to him. "A big black man will walk up there [at the stroke of midnight] and take your guitar, and he'll tune it."

This "big black man" was one of many shapes assumed by an African deity called Èsù by the Yoruba and Légba by the Dahomey, guardian of the crossroads, "the mystical barrier," as Henry Louis Gates, Jr., explains it, "that separates the divine from the profane world." A cosmic prankster, Èsù/Légba "interprets the will of the gods to man and carries the desires of man to the gods." Gates notes that Christian missionaries to Africa made the mistake of confusing this trickster figure with their own Satan. They weren't the only ones: in black Delta folklore, the literal crossroads formed by two highways or railroad lines was one of the areas in which African and Christian beliefs converged. Did Johnson's peers believe that Satan owned deed to his soul? No doubt some of them did. More important, did Johnson? He was a chronic alcoholic, whose songs (including "Canned Heat Blues," about Sterno, and "Alcohol and Jake Blues," named for a Prohibition-era homebrew cut with ingredients used in paint and lacquers) suggest that he would swallow anything in a pinch. That he lived to be almost sixty in spite of these habits may have been taken by some, possibly including Johnson himself, as evidence of diabolical intervention. It could be how the story got started.

If instrumental prowess was part of what Tommy Johnson was hoping for in striking his Faustian bargain, he was tricked but good: his guitar technique was no better than rudimentary. But that voice—changing contour as it rises in pitch, it's the voice of a mesmerist, a master of disguise, a man both possessed and self-possessed, himself a trickster.

HERE is the folklorist Alan Lomax describing the music of Eddie James, Jr., a singer and guitarist originally from Riverton, Mississippi, who was better known as Son House:

> "Hitch up my black pony, saddle up my bay maare," he sang, his words conjuring up nights of coupling in the tropical heat of Mississippi. His voice, guttural and hoarse with passion, ripping apart the surface of the music like his tractor-driven deep plow ripped apart the wet black earth in the springtime, making the sap of the earth song run, while his powerful, work-hard hands snatched strange chords out of the steel strings the way they had snatched so many tons of cotton out of brown thorny cotton bolls in the fall. And with him the sorrow of the blues was not tentative, or retiring, or ironic. Son's whole body wept, as with his eyes closed, the tendons in his powerful neck standing out with the violence of his feeling and his brown face flushing, he sang in an awesome voice the *Death Letter Blues*.

The passage—in which Son House, his music, and the Mississippi soil are a similar hue—is from Lomax's 1993 memoir *The Land Where the Blues Began*, which recounts, among other fascinating stories, how Lomax recorded House and a handful of his buddies for the Library of Congress in a country store near Lake Coromont, Mississippi, in the summer of 1941. Distrustful of commercial recordings, Lomax was apparently unaware that House, who was by then almost forty, had made eight sides for Paramount in Grafton, Wisconsin, eleven years earlier, as a member of Charley Patton's posse. The lyric Lomax quotes is from House's Library of Congress recording of "Pony Blues," which Lomax failed to recognize as Patton's first regional hit and signature song. Nevertheless, Lomax's heated poetry captures that of his subject, even though the equation of House with the earth, and of his music with field labor, is facile and a touch misleading. The implication is that Son House, though possessed by something approaching genius, was in most ways a typical specimen of his culture. In reality, he was unique even among Mississippi singers and guitar players of his generation—not an exception to the rule that says that the Delta bluesmen of the 1930s were soul searchers who confided only in their guitars, but the extreme case.

House was a paradox in any number of ways. First of all, there is the question of his stylistic relationship to Charley Patton. House was born in 1902, which means that he was at least a decade Patton's junior, and suggests that Patton was something of a mentor to him. Patton's influence is certainly discernable in House's repertoire, his gravel singing, his stinging slide. Yet if there was little trace of the songster in Tommy Johnson, there was absolutely none in Son House. Though he was a less artful guitarist than Patton, House was a much more passionate singer, and a bluesman to the core—a direct influence on Robert Johnson and Muddy Waters, both of whom

Son House,
1964
(DICK WATERMAN)

learned much of what they knew about Patton secondhand, through House.

The blues came naturally to Son House. Yet many who saw House play in the 1960s, and many who interviewed him then, say that he gave the impression that he was less at peace with himself performing the blues than he would have been driving a tractor or punching a timecard. His sporadic recording career was a happy accident in which he seemed to take little interest. He first recorded as a result of tagging along to a session with Patton and Willie Brown. Then Lomax stumbled upon him while looking for Robert Johnson, and twice recorded him "in the field," in 1941 and again the following year. (He'd been paid $5 a side by Paramount, $40 in all, which he later told interviewers was more than the annual salary of the average plantation worker back then. Lomax, working on a small budget from the Library of Congress, bought him a Coke—in telling the story decades later, House would get a laugh by noting that at least the soda was ice cold.)

After recording for Lomax, House drifted back into obscurity for twenty years. He moved to upstate New York and worked as a railroad porter and barbecue chef, giving up music entirely until his rediscovery in the summer of 1964. Less than a year later, he was in the studio for Columbia Records and staring out at crowds of young, white festival goers who outnumbered the entire populations of the towns in which he'd spent his youth. His was the most significant rediscovery of those years, and not just because he was able to perform with something approaching his old power despite two decades of inactivity. By virtue of having survived most of his Delta contemporaries, he became a stand-in for all of them, a living link to the holiest blues tradition, Jesus and Lazarus and the twelve apostles all rolled into one. Yet he never attempted to capitalize on the adoration of that era's blues fans. He performed only when nudged to do so until falling ill in 1971, and then kept his silence until his death in 1988.

During those years, he was frequently visited by John Mooney, a white singer and guitarist with whom he would discuss philosophy or religion around the kitchen table—though if they wanted to play the blues, they had to go outdoors. "That was [his wife] Evie's rule, that we couldn't play the blues in the house," Mooney told Eleanor Ellis, for her article on him in *Blues Revue Quarterly*.

I T probably wasn't just Evie, though. House's own songs suggest that he thought of the blues as wicked, and of his talent for them as grim fate. This is what gives his work its drenching intensity: the suspicion that he recognized the blues as both his only means of self-expression and a form of blasphemy. On his 1930 Paramount session, he recorded a two-part song called "Preachin' the Blues" in which he sang that he was going to get himself religion and join the Baptist Church:

> I'm gonna be a Baptist preacher,
> And I sure won't have to work.

These lyrics look lighthearted on paper, where they can be taken as gentle mockery of the black clergy. Implicit in the title—and in the singer's brimstone delivery—is the point that the Delta's blues singers and its black preachers had more in common than was first apparent. They were the only members of their community who didn't work for the white man—unless you count the white men at record companies and the White Man Upstairs.

In performance, however, with House clipping his words and whacking his guitar, the same lyrics tell a different story. The atmosphere is one of self-flagellation. It's the song of a man in spiritual free fall, preparing himself for hell.

Son House was, in fact, a fallen evangelist, the teenage pastor of his own church who became a prison inmate ten years later, a pious young man who cringed at the sight of a drifter with a guitar before becoming one himself. His downfall was a woman considerably older than himself and probably married, with whom he ran away to Louisiana, leaving his congregation behind. But if it hadn't been a woman, it would have been something else—whiskey, perhaps, or his temper (in 1928, he was sentenced to fifteen years of hard labor for shooting a man in a barroom brawl, though he served only two). His was the kind of faith that sets a man up for a fall.

One of House's happiest songs was "My Black Mama," a declaration of love for a dark, dark woman somehow more affecting than any of soul's tributes to Nubian princesses of the 1960s and 1970s:

> Well,
> My black mama's face shine
> Like the sun,
> Oh, lipstick and powder sure won't
> Help her none.

But even here, when not comparing the relative virtues of brown- and black-skinned women, asking his milk cow to hurry home, going to the race track to see his pony run, or receiving a letter telling him that the woman he loves is dead, House muses about his own time on earth, and his ultimate fate:

> It ain't no heaven now, and it ain't no
> Burning hell,
> Said I,
> Where I'm going when I die, can't no
> Body tell.[6]

6. "My Black Mama" was one of the most influential of all early blues songs, a template for Kokomo Arnold's "Milk Cow Blues," Robert Johnson's "Milkcow Calf's Blues," and John Lee Hooker's "Burning Hell," among others.

•

IT was fitting, in a way, that House rematerialized on the same day as Nehemiah "Skip" James, a performer of exactly the same age whose songs also addressed the issue of sin and redemption, and were used as models by Robert Johnson. But James had practically nothing else in common with House or any other Delta bluesman. He was the Delta's odd man out, both geographically and stylistically. A preacher's son and a high school graduate from Bentonia, a small town on the Delta's southern periphery, James sang in a falsetto not at all like Tommy Johnson's—his was more serene, and yet eerily disembodied—and the antithesis of the typical low-throated Delta growl. Instead of taking a slide to his guitar, he relied on a sophisticated fingerpicking technique. He also played piano, and though he had been given lessons as part of his schooling, he jabbed at the keys in a nervous, insistent fashion that smacked of the barrelhouse, albeit with a sense of rhythmic construction that recalls nobody so much as Thelonious Monk. Until his rediscovery in 1964, James's entire recorded output consisted of the eighteen numbers that he recorded for Paramount in 1931, just before the label went out of business, a casualty of the Depression. These were commercial failures for which James—who was proud of his musicianship, and had every right to be—was apparently never paid. Embittered, he put

Skip James
(RAY AVERY'S JAZZ
ARCHIVES)

the blues aside, entered the ministry, and formed a gospel group in Dallas. He settled for a time in Birmingham, where he led a church choir and worked for his father, who was by then the director of a Baptist seminary. For whatever reason, he eventually drifted back to Mississippi and a life as a sharecropper, before spending the last five years of his life on the sixties college and coffeehouse circuit.

Despite their poor sales to black audiences in the early thirties, James's Paramounts struck those white collectors who eventually came upon them as so different from anything else recorded in that era—not just unique, but downright *supernatural*—that an entire mythology formed around them. James is still believed by some to have been an exponent of "the Bentonia school" of singing and guitar playing, though only a few other exponents of this so-called school have ever emerged (Jack Owens, for example), and odds are that they were merely imitating James. Musicians in Bentonia in the 1930s, including James, were supposed to have played "special" guitars not manufactured anywhere else and discontinued soon after his early recording sessions. This turned out not to have been the case, nor did James favor esoteric tunings, as many believed he did (unless you consider E minor esoteric).

James was a complete original, right down to that melismatic falsetto, which was intense but curiously detached—an upper register shiver of the kind that we today associate with love's rapture or the soul's deliverance, though in James's case it signified something else, something so chilling that you're certain that a plummeting economy and a belly-up label weren't the only reasons his records failed to find a ready audience in 1931. Despite their light textures, James's songs were dark stuff, musically adventurous and morally unforgiving. If Son House's music was a veritable battlefield between sin and redemption, the battle is already lost in James's "Devil Got My Woman," in which the singer seems to take between-the-lines comfort from the knowledge that his was one of very few souls not slated to burn. Unlike House, he saw the larger picture: he had the blues for the human race.

UNABLE to shake their Eurocentric frame of reference, early writers on the blues heard in the songs of the men from Mississippi something bardic, Homeric. Times change, as they say, and the curious thing is that the past seems to change right along with them. Now that Westerners know more about African culture, the Delta's singers and guitarists are frequently likened to *griots*. But this fashionable Afrocentric view of African-African culture may be no less simplistic. In traditional African societies, *griots* were as much oral historians as musicians: "*Griots* in Senegambian society sang the praises of their social leaders, committed to memory epic genealogies which became the oral history of their culture, sang and played in groups to set rhythms for farmers and others at their work." The passage is from James Sallis's *The Long-Legged Fly*, a recent crime novel narrated by Lew Griffin, a black New Orleans private eye and Canal Street existentialist who (unfortunately, in this instance) doesn't reveal his sources.

Blues singers in the Delta and elsewhere did serve as oral historians, conveyers of local myths. But their similarity to *griots* ended there. Blues songs contained no "epic genealogies," nor could they, because slavery had erased whatever sense of extended family history the performers and their audiences might otherwise have had. Unlike many Northern cities, where there were black chapters of Masons, Elks, and Knights of Pythias, there was no acknowledged African-American leadership in the Deep South after Reconstruction. Such leadership as there was consisted of preachers, under-takers, and field bosses—hardly figures whose exploits begged to be docu-mented in song. If a Delta bluesman sang anybody's praises, it was likely to be his own, often in songs in which he itemized his travels or boasted of his way with women. And though the blues had evolved from the shouts and chants of men and women at work in the fields, it was the goal of most blues performers to stay as far away from such work as possible.

There is, however, one way in which the Delta bluesmen of Son House and Skip James's generation did resemble *griots*, though full recognition of this entails rethinking our view of *griots* as well as our view of bluesmen. In *Music 1961*, one of those thick, reflective extra editions *Down Beat* used to publish annually, Alan P. Merriam (identified only as a "noted scholar") wrote that his field research into the music of the Basongye people of the eastern Kasai region of the Congo had yielded evidence that musicians there were negatively stereotyped as habitual drunkards and men of loose morals, much as jazz musicians were in the United States at that time. And what prompts Lew Griffin's observations about *griots* in *The Long-Legged Fly* (and my reason for quoting a work of fiction rather than one of ethnomusicology) is the memory of the town drunk of his Delta youth, a man talked about "almost as though [being town drunk] were an elected, honorary position, or something like the African *griots*, mavericks central to their culture yet reviled . . . when the *griot* died he could not be buried among his society's respectable folk. His body, instead, was left to rot in a hollow tree."

Even when the song in question amounts to little more than a random assortment of traditional verses, the tone of early recorded country blues performances tends to be *personal* in a way that doesn't seem African or European, but peculiarly American. Despite the great deal that an early country blues can tell us about the common beliefs and values of black Southerners of Son House and Skip James's generation, the singer usually emerges as someone with a sense of himself as an outsider—central to his culture but reviled, in Sallis's phrase.[7]

This was especially true of the Delta blues, given its frequent tone of self-revulsion—the air of spiritual disquiet and the preoccupation with morbidity in songs such as Son House's "My Black Mama," Skip James's "Devil Got My Woman" and "Hard-Time Killin' Floor Blues," Bukka White's "Fixin' to Die Blues," and (ultimately, as we shall see) Robert Johnson's "Hell Hound on My Trail" and "Me and the Devil Blues."

Not every Delta guitar slinger was a rustic transcendentalist, nor did all of them except for Skip James sing in a deep growl which they imitated with a slide. Ishman Bracey, whose voice was rough and who did use a slide, was a journeyman with no special gift for lyrics, though many of the records he made were rhythmically infectious. Bo Carter, despite specializing in penis songs such as "Banana in Your Fruit Basket," "Ram Rod Daddy," and "Please Warm My Wiener," seems to have led a quiet, uneventful life, until going blind and becoming a street singer in Memphis. He was a member of the Mississippi Sheiks, as was Walter Vincson, whose solo records were notable for his high level of musicianship, rather than his singing ability or insights into the human condition. "Crying" Sam Collins was generally upbeat on his recordings; the nominative referred to his high-pitched vocals and the plaintive sound of his slide.

Ishmon Bracey
(COURTESY SHELDON HARRIS COLLECTION)

One performer who seemed to fit the popular image of the Delta bluesman as a troubled soul caught between conjure and the cross was Robert Wilkins, though in truth he was different from most of his contemporaries in every conceivable way. Originally from Hernando, Mississippi, and a veteran of World War I, Wilkins was a fixture in Memphis in the late twenties and early thirties, before being ordained as a minister in the Church of God in Christ and becoming a practitioner of herbal medicine. He was a lifelong

7. It should be noted that both *The Long-Legged Fly* (1992) and Sallis's second novel, *Moth* (1994), are peppered with blues references. His alter ego Griffin is as likely to invoke Robert Johnson as he is Dashiell Hammett or Albert Camus.

teetotaler, scornful of much of the loose behavior he witnessed in the juke houses, and apparently shaken by the frequent outbursts of violence that occurred in them. What made him an even greater oddity among Delta musicians, however, was that he was a better guitarist and songwriter than singer. Before Wilkins abandoned secular music, his songs were those of a man wondering if he was on the right path. They were also such polished little gems that it's surprising that so few of them have been reinterpreted by other performers—especially in light of the fact that the Rolling Stones covered his "That's No Way to Get Along" as "Prodigal Son" on *Beggar's Banquet* (for what it's worth, Wilkins recorded a two-part blues called "Rollin' Stone" in 1928). Wilkins was one of the many elderly performers unearthed by revivalists in the 1960s, but when persuaded to record again, he insisted on making an album of gospel songs—no blues.

On face value, Booker Washington White—who hated the name "Bukka" but was stuck with it on account of a record company executive who had never heard of Booker T. Washington and was thrown by *this* Booker's Mississippi drawl—was a virtual stereotype of the sort of Delta bluesman we've been talking about here. White, an older cousin to B. B. King, recorded his most indelible sides in 1940, long after the demand for solo country blues had waned (companies attempted to "modernize" him by enlisting the then-popular Washboard Sam as his accompanist). Among these 1940 sides for Decca were the sorrowful "How Long Before I Change My Clothes" and several others telling of White's despair during his two years of hard labor in Mississippi for shooting and wounding a man in a 1937 juke house brawl (he'd jumped bail and fled to Chicago just long enough to record "Shake 'Em On Down," a song later covered by Led Zeppelin, before his extradition). The 1940 session also yielded "Fixing to Die Blues," in which White mourned (or gloated at) the fact that everyone living was, like him, "born to die."

Add to this the information that White doubled on record as Washington White, the Singing Preacher, and you might jump to the conclusion that his music was pretty grim. Not so. It was salty and shambling, its contagious animation belying the mordant lyrics and suggesting that what seemed like an undue emphasis on the trials of the soul and the mortification of the flesh was simply a nod to Delta conventions. White was frequently described as bull-necked and barrel-chested, and this also describes his music. No fool, he recorded a couple of numbers for Alan Lomax while in the penitentiary at Parchman Farm, but saved what he considered to be his strongest material for his first commercial session after his release. He was one of the stars of the sixties blues revival, though the extended playing time afforded on LP worked to his disadvantage—he called his numbers "sky songs," boasting that he could pull verses out of thin air; his resourcefulness was impressive, but he did tend to ramble on.

•

THE female blues vaudevillians had orchestras of brass and reeds; the Mississippi transcendentalists, Texas troubadours, and Georgia and Carolina pickers usually had just their guitars. In performance, the guitar took the place of horns and piano, serving as a responsorial voice; a relationship much like that between a preacher and his congregation. In the case of the men from Mississippi—if only in our imaginations—the guitar also took the place of an audience, the testifying singer's only witness. Anyone who's read even a fraction of the literature on the blues knows that the Delta bluesmen entertained rowdy crowds in juke houses and at country picnics—that the same song that might strike us as almost embarrassingly personal on record probably sounded very different in a setting where self-expression took a back seat to getting a crowd up on its feet and dancing. What sounds sullen and anguished to us may have been interpreted as humorous by the audiences to whom it was originally addressed—and *intended* as humorous, too, or as ironic. Given that it was such romantic mental images that drew many of us to the blues in the first place, it's difficult for us to shake the illusion of the bluesman of the twenties as a man alone, with only his guitar for succor, and of the blues itself as a cross on his shoulders, or a noose around his neck.

And though only blues historians are likely to make such a distinction, it's usually the Delta blues we're thinking of when such images come to mind. This is the style in which the relationship between voice and guitar is most symbiotic. The most lucid description of this relationship was in an unsigned liner note to *The Mississippi Blues 1927–1940*, an anthology released some thirty years ago by Origin Jazz Library:

> The guitar is conspicuous here, often harshly and stridently pulsive with work rhythms, taking over emphatically, almost impatiently, at the end of a vocal line. Lyrically, [Delta] blues are kin to field hollers with the mainly familiar verses or variations on same strung informally together. The intoned sounds of monosyllables frequently carry more "meaning" than whatever signification the words may have. . . . Rarely is any really connected narrative unfolded. *What organic form there is depends on the development of the extraordinary expressive guitar playing to which the words stand pretty much as chorus.* [Emphasis added]

In other words, the guitar part contributed as much as the vocal (and more than the literal words) to the sound and mood of a typical Delta blues, and therefore to its perceived *meaning*.

There was a similar balance between voice and guitar in Delta, Texas, and

East Coast blues, but the guitar lines themselves were different in character in each of these regions, as were the singing styles. As a general rule, guitarists in Texas (starting with Blind Lemon Jefferson) delivered their lyrics more clearly, singing in a higher register than their Delta counterparts. Their guitar lines were leaner and less harsh, and more melodic than percussive—lighter and freer in the rhythmic patterns behind the vocals, with linear embellishments that frequently suggested the influence of both jazz and flamenco. This latter may have been the result of proximity to Mexican *vaquero*, who introduced the guitar to the United States. Even after the discovery of oil in Spindletop, Texas, in 1901, the state's economy remained more diverse than that of Mississippi, and this contributed to a greater diversity of musical styles. The same was true of Georgia and the Carolinas, where there were fewer restrictions on black mobility than in either Mississippi or Texas, and consequently, a greater degree of interplay between black and white musicians. The songs of such Atlantic Seaboard fingerpickers as Blind Blake, Blind Willie McTell, and Blind Boy Fuller were more genuinely songlike than their contemporaries in the Delta and the Southwest. These guitarists were relative sophisticates, with an intuitive grasp of passing chords offsetting a rhythmic conception anchored in older ragtime and minstrel songs.

These three styles provided the foundation for modern folk music and blues. A direct line can be traced from the Delta to Chicago, from Charley Patton and Son House to Howlin' Wolf and Muddy Waters. Jefferson's influence and that of other early Texans lived on in the jazzlike improvisations of T-Bone Walker and B. B. King. And there was hardly a folk guitarist of the 1960s who didn't emulate the picking style of the blind street singers of Georgia and the Carolinas.

THESE are, of course, general rules to which almost every blues performer of any lasting significance can be named as an exception. And it should go without saying that the widespread availability of country blues records quickly blurred regional distinctions that were fuzzy to begin with, on account of the nomadic existence of most blues performers.

Generalities are especially suspect in the case of Texas performers of the 1920s and early 1930s, who must have cultivated what each saw as his individualism to gain an edge over the competition. B. K. Turner, who performed under the name "Black Ace," is a case in point. Though many performers, black and white, sought to emulate the *sound* of Hawaiian guitar, Turner was one of only a handful of mainlanders who adopted the most characteristic technique of the islanders—that is, one of very few to hold the guitar flat on his knees while moving a glass slide across its strings.

If his nickname didn't tell us otherwise, we might assume that Algier "Texas" Alexander was from deep in the Delta. Mississippi is where the blues

Blind Blake
(FRANK DRIGGS COLLECTION)

*Cordially Yours
Blind Blake*

**Blind Willie
McTell**
(COURTESY BLUES ARCHIVE,
UNIVERSITY OF MISSISSIPPI)

Texas Alexander
(COURTESY BLUES ARCHIVE, UNIVERSITY
OF MISSISSIPPI)

is supposed to have existed *in utero* well into the late twenties, yet there was no bluesman rawer or more primitive than Alexander, an older cousin of Lightnin' Hopkins whose bellow was only a step or two removed from a field holler or work song (indeed, farm and prison labor were his most frequent themes). Alexander was also nicknamed "The Voice of Texas," the implication being that the voice was as big and wide open as the state. He was the only major male blues singer of his era not to play an instrument, and as Sam Charters has pointed out, the remnant of work song in Alexander's blues may have resulted from his singing mostly unaccompanied on his travels around the South. As if to underscore Alexander's own lack of evolution, his producers at Okeh Records enlisted such polished musicians as Lonnie Johnson, Eddie Lang, King Oliver, Clarence Williams, and Eddie Haywood to accompany him. Johnson, in particular, did a heroic job of keeping up with Alexander, anticipating him beautifully and never being thrown by his irregular melodic and rhythmic patterns. The most satisfying of Alexander's more than sixty commercial recordings tend to be those featuring Johnson, especially the first few sides they made together in the late twenties. Alexander started off sounding like an untamed force of nature, but by 1934, the year of his final session for Okeh, he was imitating other blues singers, including Blind Lemon Jefferson and a few others whose work he presumably knew only from records.

The singing evangelist Blind Willie Johnson was another Texan who might be mistaken for a Mississippian, and not merely because he slurred and croaked his lyrics and had few equals as a slide guitarist (like the guitarist at Tutwiler Station, he used a pocketknife in lieu of a bottleneck). To an even greater extent than Son House's, Johnson's music was charred with purgatorial fire—more than sixty years later, you can still smell the smoke on it. He was a man of God, perhaps even a religious fanatic, but he ranted like a man possessed by demons. His life was tragic, even by the cruel standards of his day. Born just after the turn of the century and blinded as a child by lye thrown at him by an unfaithful stepmother who had just taken a beating from his father, Johnson died of pneumonia after putting out a fire in his cabin and wearing his wet nightgown to bed. As near as anyone can figure, this was in 1947, long after his brief recording career had come to a end. With his wife Angeline serving as his eyes (she also sang on many of his records, her eerie falsetto doubling his demented bass), he made his living by playing on Texas street corners—a blind man with a guitar and a tin cup shaking the faith of passers-by with the absolute certainty of his.

Were Johnson alive today, he might be livid to find his name in so many books on the blues. He performed mostly traditional hymns, hardly any secular material. Yet his style had more in common with those of the blues performers of his day than that of any of his fellow guitar evangelists, and no one was more original. In terms of its intensity alone—its spiritual *ache*—there is nothing else from the period to compare with Johnson's 1927 recording of "Dark Was the Night, Cold Was the Ground," on which his guitar takes the part of a preacher and his wordless voice the part of a rapt congregation. It's one of those performances that makes you realize that the aspect of Christianity to which the African-Americans who had it forced on them most responded was the value it placed on suffering—His and (if only in their own minds) theirs.

THE most striking characteristics of the blues from Georgia and the Carolinas were its wistfulness and instrumental virtuosity. Atlanta, in particular, wasn't merely an urban center but a

Blind Willie
Johnson
(FRANK DRIGGS
COLLECTION)

Columbia

BLIND WILLIE JOHNSON

This new and exclusive Columbia artist, Blind Willie Johnson, sings sacred selections in a way that you have never heard before. Be sure to hear his first record and listen close to that guitar accompaniment. Nothing like it anywhere else.

Record No. 14276-D, 10-Inch, 75c
I Know His Blood Can Make Me Whole
Jesus Make Up My Dying Bed

Ask Your Dealer for Latest Race Record Catalog
Columbia Phonograph Company, 1819 Broadway, New York City

Columbia
NEW PROCESS RECORDS
Made the New Way - Electrically
Viva-tonal Recording - The Records without Scratch

Peg Leg Howell
(FRANK DRIGGS COLLECTION)

pipeline to the North. This resulted in a style that mixed black and white, and rural and urban, influences. For whatever reason, the Atlantic Seaboard singer/guitarists who became nationally known via their recordings were blind men judged unqualified for farm or factory work and forced to earn their livings by performing on street corners. The only significant exception was Peg Leg Howell, who was an amputee, and Robert Hicks, an Atlanta barbecue chef and waiter who—roughly equivalent to Bo Carter in Mississippi—recorded several dozen rollicking, mostly filthy, songs as "Barbecue Bob." (Some of these were with his brother, Charlie, who also recorded under the name Charlie Lincoln.)

Blind Blake, whose real name is variously given as Arthur Blake or Arthur Phelps, was the most elegant and technically accomplished of the East Coast fingerpickers, though a rather stilted singer whose precise enunciation suggests the influence of female vaudevillians like Sara Martin and Mamie Smith (though not Bessie Smith or Ma Rainey). Blake himself was a major influence on a number of white folk and country fingerpickers, beginning with Merle Travis. Little is known for sure about Blake's background. Though most standard sources have it that he was born in Jacksonville, Florida, in the early 1890s, he may have been as much as a decade older, and (to judge from his comfort with a Geechee dialect on his recording of "Southern Rag") there's a good chance that he was born or raised in the Georgia South Sea Islands. In any case, he seems to have passed most of his youth in or near Atlanta, settling in Chicago shortly after traveling there to make his first records for Paramount in the summer of 1926. He was one of the most prolific of his era's recording artists, making close to a hundred titles between

1926 and 1932, when Paramount's demise halted his career (a heavy drinker, he died the following year, according to most sources). Paramount's ads for him touted his "famous piano-sounding guitar," and this is as good a description of his style as any. His figures were based on those of ragtime pianists—a nice bit of turnabout, given that ragtime owed much to the music of country banjo players—and his accents were so sharp and true that many contemporary guitarists suspect he used a pick.

Blind Boy Fuller (Fulton Allen) was at least a decade younger than Blake, and didn't begin his recording career until 1935. But his music sounded older and less urban—more directly linked to country traditions, especially in its emphasis on thumbed bass notes and Fuller's occasional use of a bottleneck. Fuller, who was a more expressive singer than Blake, if not quite his equal as a guitarist, was based in Durham, North Carolina. This was tobacco country, spared the worst of the Depression by virtue of America's undiminished craving for cigarettes; and Fuller's normal base of operations—even after being discovered by J. B. Long, a Durham record-store owner, and becoming a prolific recording artist—was a street corner outside a Durham cigarette factory. He was such an inveterate street performer that—the story goes—on being taken to New York by Long to record for ARC in 1935, he set up shop on a busy Manhattan street corner immediately after the session. (It's tempting to speculate that he probably made more in spare change than he was paid for the recordings he made that day. But Long, who was also Fuller's manager, is said to have seen to it that he was treated fairly.) Fuller was so popular with black record buyers that after his death from what is believed to have been pneumonia in 1941, Brownie McGhee (soon to emerge as an important figure in his own right) was rushed into the studio as Blind Boy Fuller #2.

In the long run, the greatest of the ragtime-influenced East Coast guitarists proved to be Reverend Gary Davis, a close friend of Fuller's who recorded only a handful of sides in the 1930s, but whose time finally came in the 1960s. His career will be discussed in a later chapter, but suffice it to say for now that even though he started off as a bluesman and wound up as a singing preacher, his versions of sacred tunes were relatively lighthearted, with little of the spiritual tension—the brimstone—of the Mississippi performers whose careers followed a similar path. There's a strong emotional content in the East Coast blues of the twenties and thirties, an undercurrent of longing no amount of wistfulness can disguise. But it stays well below the surface, becoming fully apparent only here and there, most notably in the few solo recordings of Peg Leg Howell and the many by Blind Willie McTell.

Howell was an Atlanta bootlegger whose most famous recordings were issued as the work of "Peg Leg Howell and His Gang," an enjoyably ragtag outfit usually featuring Eddie Anthony on fiddle and Henry Williams on second guitar. But the four self-accompanied numbers with which he began his recording career in 1926 revealed a different side of Howell, one that he never again explored on records, or was never again allowed to explore. They have the charm of a man singing almost to himself, strictly for his own amusement.

The same quality pervades the best recordings of McTell, who was born in rural Georgia in 1901 and died there as a whiskey-soaked Atlanta street performer in 1959, just before the widespread rediscovery of elder blues performers got underway. In his prime, McTell was a marvel. As a guitarist, he was nothing if not versatile, handling a twelve-string as well as he did a conventional model, and manipulating a slide as deftly as he picked— indeed, as deftly as any of the men from Mississippi, although rather more delicately. A performer with medicine shows and traveling carnivals as a young man, McTell recorded for a bewildering variety of commercial labels, not to mention the Library of Congress. He seems to have been content to supply each company with what he assumed it wanted from him: sorrowful blues in some instances, and frolicking rags and songster material in others. This makes him tough to get a fix on, yet few performers of his generation are as instantly identifiable. He was an incandescent singer with a high-pitched warble that's difficult to forget once you've heard it. More than one blues historian has remarked that McTell's careful enunciation often made him sound like a white man emulating a black vocal style. On his earliest recordings, from the late twenties, he also occasionally sounded like a woman, so much so that you suspect some listeners of the period probably mistook him for one, before seeing the name "Willie" on the label. His best recorded performances are downright irresistible, thanks to the tension between his guitar virtuosity and the touching modesty of his voice.

IN the end, it all comes back to Blind Lemon Jefferson, without whose success we might never have heard any of the others, including Charley Patton. Think what Jefferson's first records must have sounded like to those black country people who heard them in 1926—what a shock it must have been, what a *delight*, to hear what amounted to musical documentation of their own lives. What's amazing is that something of that shock still registers on hearing Jefferson today. When he sings "That's all right, mama; that's all right for you" on "That Black Snake Moan," it isn't just that we suddenly know where both Arthur "Big Boy" Crudup and Elvis Presley came from, any more than Jefferson's "Match Box Blues" is important just for disclosing the origins of Carl Perkins's seminal 1955 rockabilly hit. With just a little imagination, you can hear a world opening up in Jefferson's records, a social order shifting, hitherto suppressed voices making themselves heard, the oldest black traditions feeding into something new, a mass culture in which blacks would play a dominant rather than a submissive part.

Jefferson was an inimitable performer whose guitar lines alone were evidence of an intuitive genius, and whose voice was one of the most supple and melismatic ever captured on record. To be sure, many of his melodies, as well as many of his verses, were probably older than he was—*learned* rather than created. His songs about women troubles and homelessness and prison were more from the point of view of his audience than from his own. He sang about experiences common to black Southerners in the first quarter of this century, revealing very little about his own life in the process. Yet the originality of certain of his songs, certain of his verses, certain of his inflections, probably stopped record buyers of the late 1920s dead in their tracks, much as they're likely to stop us today:

> Uum, better find my mama soon
> Uum, better find my mama soon.
> I woke up this morning, black snake was
>   makin' such a ruckus in my room.
>
> Black snake is evil, black snake is all I see,
> Black snake is evil, black snake is all I see,
> I woke up this morning he was moved in on me.

The lines are from "That Black Snake Moan," the first of Jefferson's recordings to cause a stir. Though tumescent members have always been plentiful in the blues, there have been few expressions of naked sexual *need* as urgent as this—certainly not before 1926. "The woman rocks the cradle, and I swear she rules the home," Jefferson sang in "That Crawling Baby Blues" (1929), "Many [a] man rocks some other man's baby, and the fool thinks he's rocking his own." It would be difficult to find as forceful an expression of male anxiety over female sexual infidelity.

In the final analysis, Jefferson was a contradiction in terms, a voice of tradition and a harbinger of change. His success not only enabled other rural male performers to record, but challenged them to compete for the dollars of record buyers with songs and vocal and guitar styles as striking and original as his. The blues was then still largely a folk tradition, so it would be foolish to overestimate the impact of Jefferson's Paramount recordings. But it would be even more foolish to ignore their impact completely. These recordings were studied—*internalized*—by performers all over the South, including Mississippi. It could be that the responsorial role played by the guitar in the Delta blues (supposedly a regional trademark) was shaped by Jefferson and the Victrola, not local tradition. In the absence of a good number of country blues recordings before his, it's impossible to say. This is why the history of the blues occasionally reads more like a mystery.

· ·

R O B E R T   J O H N S O N ' S
S A T A N I C   V E R S E S

I've saved the greatest of the Delta transcendentalists for last, because that's where he fell within the continuum, and because he warrants individual consideration as a mystery as enduring as the blues itself.

Here are two consecutive verses from Robert Johnson's 1937 recording of "From Four Till Late":

> From Memphis to Norfolk is a thirty-six
>   hours' ride.
>   (*repeat*)
> A man is like a prisoner, and he's never satisfied.
>
> A woman is just like a dresser, some man
>   always ramblin' [through] its drawers.
>   (*repeat*)
> It cause so many men [to] wear an apron
>   overall.

That's Johnson for you: an expression of angst that sends a chill from his soul straight to yours, followed by a double entendre unworthy of an adolescent (and probably swiped from another recording—most likely Roosevelt Sykes's "44 Blues," from eight years earlier). If the first verse is an artist's pronouncement on life as a life sentence, the second is an example of the sort of verbal moonshine that Johnson—a Delta bluesman of the 1930s who presumably never read Jean-Paul Sartre or Albert Camus—must have routinely served up in the Mississippi juke houses in which he practiced his art.

"From Four Till Late" can be found on *Robert Johnson: The Complete*

Robert
Johnson
(COPYRIGHT © 1989
MIMOSA RECORDS
PRODUCTIONS, INC.)

Recordings, the most unlikely pop phenomenon of the 1990s. Presumably appealing to record buyers who aren't usually interested in new blues releases or reissues or any sort, Johnson's *Complete Recordings* sold in excess of 400,000 copies within six months of its release in August 1990—enough for it to be certified gold. In contrast, Johnson's raunchy "Terraplane Blues," recorded in 1936 and his most popular record during his lifetime, sold just 4,000 copies upon its initial release and was distributed only in the South.

Johnson's sales were part of a reawakened interest in "roots music"—or, as I like to call it, "handmade" music, an adult alternative to rap, metal, techno, and other forms of pop seen as mass-produced for kids. Still gathering momentum, this was a trend of the early 1990s that made semistars of Robert Cray and Los Lobos, revived the careers of the Neville Brothers, Eric Clapton, Etta James, and Bonnie Raitt, and filled the stores with reissues by Muddy Waters and Howlin' Wolf. But Johnson's unexpected success can also be seen as the latest chapter in a mystery that has resisted easy resolution for over half a century. The literature on Johnson, already voluminous and still piling up, reads like an ongoing detective novel, with Johnson—who is believed to have been born in Hazelhurst, Mississippi, in 1911, and to have been fatally poisoned by a jealous husband after playing a country dance in Three Forks, near Greenwood, Mississippi, in 1938—as the missing person whose trail leads everywhere but to himself.

In the 1940s, for example, the search for information about Johnson, conducted by early blues historians going door to door asking black Mississippians what they knew about him, led to the discovery of Muddy Waters, who was still working as a field hand on Stovall's Farms when he made his first recordings, for the Library of Congress, and to the rediscovery of Son House, one of the elder bluesmen assumed to have influenced Johnson. But Johnson himself seemed to have died without leaving a trace. The historians couldn't even be sure of the name of the man they were asking about. They eventually discovered that Johnson had been born out of wedlock to a woman whose first husband (the father of her ten other children), after narrowly escaping a lynch mob in Hazelhurst, had changed his last name from Dodds to Spencer and started a new life for himself and his family in Memphis. Johnson went by both of those names at various times, as well as that of his natural father, but never that of his mother (Major) or of her second husband (Willis).

To further complicate matters, Don Law, Johnson's record producer, misinterpreting Johnson's guardedness around white people as naivete, spread the story that Johnson had spent his entire life on a Mississippi plantation, leaving it only to record sixteen of his songs in a makeshift studio in San Antonio, Texas, in November 1936, and another thirteen of them in Dallas the following June. In fact, Johnson was a nomad, "no good," to his stepfather's way of thinking, "because he wouldn't get behind that mule in the mornin' [and] plow." (We've heard that complaint before, about Charley Patton.) By the time he recorded, Johnson had hopped boxcars or thumbed his way all around the Delta and to cities as far away as Chicago and New York, earning his living solely through music. Twice legally married, Johnson was a ladies' man to whom "women were like hotel rooms," in the words of Johnny Shines, another blues performer, who frequently traveled with him. Immediately upon arriving in a new town, Shines said, Johnson would attach himself to an older woman who figured to be grateful for the attention, or to a homely young girl for whom there would likely be no competition.

He must have chosen the wrong woman in Three Forks. His death certificate, finally discovered by Gayle Dean Wardlow in 1968, lists no cause of death, but supposed eyewitnesses have told that Johnson died after drinking whiskey laced with strychnine. Some have said that Johnson crawled on his hands and knees and barked like a dog before he died; others that the cause of death was "a douche tablet" that "dried up" Johnson's blood.[1]

But these stories and others like them have become part of the legend. Two photographs located years after Johnson's death show us what he looked like. In one of them, used as the cover for *Robert Johnson: The Complete Recordings*, he looks young and eager-to-please in a natty pinstripe suit and a hat tilted at a jaunty angle, his pitchfork fingers forming chords on his guitar. The other photograph, which is cropped for inclusion in the accompanying booklet, shows him hatless, with a cigarette dangling from his mouth. He looks heavy-lidded, ageless, and hard: someone you wouldn't want to tangle with.

W E now have a sense of the broad outlines of Johnson's life, thanks to the combined efforts of Wardlow and others, including Alan Lomax, Sam Charters, David Evans, Robert Palmer, Stephen Calt, and Stephen LaVere (a co-producer of the Columbia reissue). The list also includes Mack McCormick, whose unpublished "Biography of a Phantom" Peter Guralnick admits to drawing on freely for his own *Searching for Robert Johnson*, currently the most reliable Johnson primer. Despite the valuable findings of these men, we still lack an explanation for Johnson's art.

With most blues performers of Johnson's era, it's enough to acknowledge a folk tradition in which verses and even entire songs, including the guitar parts, reappear so frequently that the question of individual authorship sometimes becomes moot. Most of Johnson's songs can be traced to sources

---

1. The singer David "Honeyboy" Edwards told Stephen LaVere that Johnson was "in terrific pain" the day before he died. Edwards suggested that Johnson may have been slipped "passagreen," which a physician subsequently told LaVere was an odorless, tasteless backwoods poison extracted from mothballs. According to LaVere, victims of "passagreen" were known "to crawl on their hands and knees and bark like a dog."

such as Tommy and Lonnie Johnson (no relation to each other, or to Robert), Charley Patton, Son House, Skip James, Big Bill Broonzy, Leroy Carr, Texas Alexander, Hambone Willie Newbern, Kokomo Arnold, and Peetie Wheatstraw, all of whom Johnson conceivably heard in person or on record (see the table below). But Johnson so successfully made even his slightest and most derivative songs sound like personal emanations that it becomes necessary to speculate on his inner life, and this is where we draw a blank.

ROBERT JOHNSON'S PROBABLE SOURCES

(PARTIAL LIST)

• •

JOHNSON SONG	PROBABLE SOURCE(S)
"Sweet Home Chicago"	Kokomo Arnold's "Old Original Kokomo Blues" (1934)
"Milkcow Calf's Blues"	Son House's "My Black Mama" (1930); Kokomo Arnold's "Milkcow Blues" (1934)
"If I Had Possession Over Judgment Day"	Charley Patton's "Screamin' and Hollerin' the Blues" (1929); Hambone Willie Newbern's "Roll and Tumble Blues" (1929); Sleepy John Estes's "The Girl I Love, She Got Long Curly Hair" (1929)
"Malted Milk; Drunken Hearted Man"	Lonnie Johnson's work in general
"Love in Vain"	Leroy Carr's "How Long—How Long Blues" (1928); Texas Alexander's "No More Woman Blues," with Lonnie Johnson on guitar (1928)
"32–20 Blues"	Skip James's "22–20 Blues" (1931)
"Hell Hound on My Trail"	Skip James's "Devil Got My Woman" (1931)
"Me and the Devil Blues"	Peetie Wheatstraw's "Six Weeks Old Blues" (1931)
"Preachin' Blues"	Son House's "Preachin' the Blues" (1930)
"Crossroads Blues"	Charley Patton's "Down the Dirt Road Blues" (1929)
"From Four Till Late"	Charley Patton's "Tom Rushen Blues" (1929)

On a strictly musical level, Johnson's appeal lies in the tension between his raw vocals and a sophisticated guitar technique that enabled him to make good on his boast (to Johnny Shines) of being able to play anything a pianist could, including boogie-woogie bass lines. "His guitar seemed to talk—repeat and say words with him like no one else in the world could," Shines once marveled, and there is an especially lucid example of Johnson doing just that—utilizing his guitar as an equal, contrapuntal voice—in "Come On in My Kitchen," a seduction blues in which sex is understood to equal shelter both for Johnson and for the woman he's trying to cajole in from the rain.

But Johnson's lyrics are the real source of his power to transcend his own time and place, and so much has been read into them over the decades that it's now virtually impossible to listen to his songs, whether for the first time or the thousandth, without hearing Johnson's legend singing and playing guitar along with him. The crux of that legend—apparently accepted as gospel by some of Johnson's contemporaries, and by Johnson himself, according to some accounts—is that he sold his soul to the Devil, presumably at the stroke of midnight at the crossroads of two highways, in exchange for speed and agility on guitar. This is supposed to be the subject matter of Johnson's "Cross Road Blues," in which he begs "the Lord above" to "have mercy now, save poor Bob if You please," apparently to no avail.

In a black folk culture in which Christian and voodoo superstitions reinforced one another, Johnson had a number of traits that might have been seen as demonic: he had a cataract in one eye; he often played with his back turned to other musicians, which some of them took as proof that he had something to hide (he probably just wanted to prevent them from copying his fingerings); and he favored unusual guitar tunings (remember what LeDell Johnson told David Evans about his brother Tommy's unholy pact: "You go to where . . . a crossroads is. . . . A big black man will walk up there and take your guitar and tune it").

Devil imagery abounded in the blues of Johnson's contemporaries and forebears, and the enormously popular Peetie Wheatstraw (real name: William Bunch) even billed himself as "The Devil's Son-in-Law" or as "The High Sheriff from Hell." Wheatstraw was a potato-headed pianist and singer, who delivered his lyrics in a slightly tipsy fashion and punctuated his verses with annoying crys of "Ohh, well, well," a mannerism copied by many black singers of the 1970s who were probably unaware of him as its source. Originally from Ripley, Tennessee (a rural town elegized in a recent Arrested Development hit), he was a central figure in the thriving blues scene that sprang up in St. Louis in the early thirties as a result of black migration to that Midwestern city. Despite his diabolical sobriquets, Wheatstraw's most common themes were the wiles of women, unemployment, public assistance,

129

and makeshift jobs created by the New Deal. In common with Delta blues-men, he occasionally sang of death and the supernatural, but did so more from the point of view of a ghetto bon vivant. There was nothing tortured or menacing about his music. He was essentially a merrymaker, which Robert Johnson most definitely was not.[2]

Maybe the notion that a performer was evil incarnate titillated juke joint revelers in the thirties as much as it does the audiences for rap and heavy metal today. Or maybe the belief that a man was one of Satan's minions amounted to an insurance policy against some of the rough customers who assembled in the backwoods gambling dens in which the blues used to be played, many of whom regarded musicians as pampered dandies out to steal their women.

Still, Johnson's lyrics can't be completely explained away, because the intensity with which he delivers them can give you an existential migraine. Because the passage of time compresses decades into a one-dimensional entity we call "history," Johnson is frequently spoken of these days as one of the founders of Delta blues, even by people who should know better. Hardly the prototypal Delta country bluesman, he was actually the last of the breed—the last *great* performer, anyway, to sing and play the blues in the style originated by Tommy Johnson or Son House or Charley Patton or Big Bill Broonzy (more about him once we move on to Chicago) or someone else whose name has been lost to us, along with his music: Johnson's only rival among the Delta performers of his own generation (and the competition wasn't very close) was Tommy McClennan, a rough-voiced singer and guitar-ist from Yazoo City only three years Johnson's elder who relocated to Chicago after first going there to record for Bluebird in 1939.

McClennan's most popular recording was "Bottle Up and Go," his adapta-tion of an old folk song about a game of craps between a white man and a black man. In most versions of the song, the black man wins but is afraid to pick up his winnings. Though McClennan soft-pedaled this aspect of the song, his use of the word "nigger" offended many Northern blacks. Along with McClennan's drawl, the word in question is all that identifies the record as Southern; we might otherwise hear it today as a proto-urban blues. So the blues was changing by the time Robert Johnson recorded—it was already citified and on the verge of plugging in. As a self-accompanied country performer, he was a throwback, almost an anachronism.

What was unprecedented about Johnson, however, were his lyrics, which in placing as much emphasis on intention and desire as on actual deeds, were "new" in the same way that the New Testament was in relationship to

2. Wheatstraw—or Peter Wheatstraw, a blues-singing street peddler much like him, a trickster figure of a man, "who could whistle a three-toned chord"—makes a cameo appearance in Ralph Ellison's *Invisible Man*.

the Old, "new" in the way that Freudian psychoanalysis was in relationship to Judeo-Christian law. "You well's to kill me," he tells a lover in "Kindhearted Woman Blues," "as to have it on your mind." About himself, he tells us (in "Ramblin' on My Mind") that he's got "mean things all on my mind," and in "When You Got a Good Friend," gives us an idea of what some of those mean things were:

> I mistreated my baby
> and I can't see no reason why
>> (*repeat*)
>
> Everytime I think about it,
> I just wring my hands and cry

Here's someone who would have understood what Jimmy Carter was talking about when he confessed to lusting after women in his heart. Damned if you do and damned if you don't: the sum and substance of Christianity.

I N *Shining Trumpets*, published in 1949, more than a decade before the first LP collection of Johnson's work and almost three before the publication of his photographs, Rudi Blesh imagined Johnson to be "a lonely, bedeviled figure, bent to the wind, with his *easy rider* [guitar] held by one arm as it swings from its cord around his neck," and described Johnson's "Hell Hound on My Trail" as "full of evil, surcharged with the terror of one alone among the moving, unseen shapes of the night."

More recently, Charles Shaar Murray, in *Crosstown Traffic*, an entertainingly discursive biography of Jimi Hendrix, wrote of Johnson: "His songs dwell in realms of existential terror where he and the devil walk side by side [in "Me and the Devil Blues," in which he vows "to beat my woman until I get satisfied"], where stones are forever in his pathway ["Stones in My Passway"], where he is both consumed by lust and stricken with impotence ["Dead Shrimp Blues," for example, although he's just temporarily sidelined on account of too much "barbecuin' the bone"], where the blues comes walking like a man ["Preaching Blues (Up Jumped the Devil)"] or falling down like hail ["Hell Hound on My Trail"]."

I don't quote Blesh and Murray to mock them; such overheated prose captures the exact temperature of Johnson's Satanic verses. But this was only one side of Johnson. Listening to him sing any of the above-mentioned songs—or "If I Had Possession Over Judgment Day," in which he declares that if he did, "the little woman I'm lovin' wouldn't have no right to pray," a wish you might expect to hear from one of the psychotic narrators of Jim

Thompson's brutal 1950s pulp novels—it's difficult to imagine the same man boasting that "the stuff I got'll bust your brains out . . . it'll make you lose your mind" (in "Stop Breakin' Down Blues") or ebulliently telling his woman that she "can squeeze my lemon . . . 'til the juice runs down my leg" (in "Traveling Riverside Blues"—and yes, this is where Led Zeppelin got the conceit).

It's also difficult to imagine Johnson stretching out his songs, adding verses to them on the spur of the moment, to the delight of the crapshooters and belly-rubbing dancers in the jukes. But those who were there say that he did. And Johnny Shines tells us that Johnson, when playing for money on Southern street corners, was as likely to honor a request for "Tumbling Tumbleweeds" or a Bing Crosby number or a current jazz hit as he was to sing one of his own songs. The *Complete Recordings* gives us a hint of what he must have sounded like doing this, in "They're Red Hot," an amiable piece of jive that Johnson reportedly learned from his brother, although it could pass for a Fats Waller tune. It's an anomaly which many of the blues fans I know disdain. But it fascinates me, maybe because I like Waller so much, or maybe because it's another piece of the puzzle that just doesn't fit.

Another point worth considering in reference to Johnson's driven imagery was raised by Vernon Reid, the guitarist in the black hard rock band Living Colour, who said, in a 1991 issue of *Musician* with a spread on Johnson, "People look at the dread in Robert Johnson as existential, but you've got to look at it in social terms, too." *Blues in the Mississippi Night*, a 1946 session produced by Alan Lomax and reissued a month or so before Johnson's *Complete Recordings*, features Big Bill Broonzy, Sonny Boy Williamson, and Memphis Slim's sometimes comic but more often chilling recollections of what life was like for Southern blacks in the first half of this century on the lumber and levee camps, the prison farms, and the plantations on which, as Broonzy observes, "a Negro didn't mean no more to a white man than a mule." It reinforces Reid's contention that the hounds that Johnson was trying to stay one step ahead of may not always have been metaphorical, while perhaps also explaining why no one was ever charged with Johnson's murder. "If you were a good worker, you could kill anyone down there, so long as he's colored," Memphis Slim explains at one point, "[Just] don't kill a good worker."

THERE is disagreement over where Johnson is buried: in an unmarked plot in the far corner of the graveyard of Mt. Zion Baptist Church in Morgan City, near Three Forks, as suggested by his death certificate; or in another unmarked grave, next to a jagged tree stump, in the churchyard of Payne Chapel in Quito, Mississippi. There is disagreement about Johnson's legacy, too. Billed as *The King of the Delta Blues Singers* on the 1961 LP collection that made my generation aware of him, he was hailed as "The Father of Rock and Roll" on the cover of the same issue of *Musician* in which Reid was quoted, presumably because Cream and the Rolling Stones recorded famous versions of his "Cross Roads Blues" and "Love in Vain," respectively, and because his walking bass lines show up, several times removed, in most boogie guitar shuffles.

But to call Johnson a progenitor of rock 'n' roll is as meaningless as to compare him with Sartre and Camus, as some writers in fact have. Both amount to cultural gerrymandering that inadvertently relegates Johnson's own cultural milieu to second-class status. (When are rock critics going to stop announcing to the world that the likes of Johnson, Mozart, and Cole Porter were rock 'n' rollers but didn't know it?) In a 1990 issue of *Living Blues* almost exclusively devoted to the question of Johnson's exact role in the evolution of the blues, Ron Weinstock correctly observes that "the frequency with which rock artists have recorded Johnson songs . . . lacks relevance to [his] place in blues history. . . . It doesn't mean Johnson was a significant influence on blues performers."

Among the outlandish claims made for Johnson is that he was the first blues performer to develop coherent themes in his songs—to think of them as songs or as *records*, rather than as tossed-together blues verses. But so had Skip James and Blind Lemon Jefferson, among others. And so did Lonnie Johnson, whom Robert Johnson idolized to the point of virtually imitating his delivery (slightly careworn even when he was young) on songs like "Malted Milk" and "Drunken Hearted Man," and of telling people that they were cousins. Though commonly acknowledged to have been Robert Johnson's primary model as a guitarist, the elder Johnson—more about him in the next chapter—is rarely mentioned as an influence on the younger's lyrics, though Robert probably learned a good deal from studying such sustained narratives as "Blues for Murder Only" and "She's Making Whoopee in Hell Tonight," songs of Lonnie's full of playfully misanthropic imagery which the younger Johnson took to crazed extremes in his own songs.

In the end, though, artistic primacy is one thing, and artistic power another. Regardless of who he may have learned from or who he influenced, Robert Johnson doesn't really sound like anyone else, past or present. In our own era, when the mass media force-feeds us more than we want to know about the personal lives of pop stars, the mystery that continues to shroud Robert Johnson only strengthens his grip on our imagination.

. . . .

T H E   T H I R T I E S   A N D   F O R T I E S :   R U R A L ,   U R B A N ,   A N D   M I D W A Y   B E T W E E N

robert Johnson's recordings initially went on sale in the late 1930s, when the United States was still reeling from the worst financial disaster in its history, and bracing for its entry into a European war that everyone sensed would soon be global. This was a period of enormous change for America, a period fraught with the anxiety that comes with change—perhaps especially for those black Americans who had fled a history of servitude in the rural South but remained uncertain of what life held in store for them as menial laborers in the large cities of the North. Bearing in mind that the U.S. Census has always been suspected of undercounting blacks, the figures tell a dramatic story. At the turn of the century, just under nine out of ten of this country's nearly 9 million blacks lived in the South, and only 20 percent of these approximately 8 million Southern blacks lived in cities; the rest of them, the overwhelming majority of America's total black population, lived in country towns and villages. Twenty years later, the black population of the United States numbered just under 10.5 million, with almost 9 million still living in the South. But in the wake of industrial manpower shortages during World War I and the *Chicago Defender*'s Great Northern Drive of 1917 (the paper likened migration from the South to the biblical exodus from Egypt), a fundamental shift in the country's black population had already begun to occur: one third of black Americans now lived in cities. By 1940, there were nearly 13 million blacks in the United States, and although 10 million remained in the South, a full half of the country's total black population was urban, with the most dramatic shift set to happen during World War II, when an estimated half-million Southern blacks would depart for what they hoped would be a better life in the North—almost as many as had migrated during the previous forty years. By 1970, the transformation of African-American culture from essentially rural to essentially urban would be complete, with over half of the black population of the United States living in the North and nearly 80 percent making their homes in cities.

Hoped-for freedom from Jim Crow was just one of many factors behind this shift in black population. Except for tobacco and textiles, most of the country's emerging industries—most of its steel mills, auto assembly lines, packing houses, stockyards—were located in the North, and the combination of World War I and the tighter restrictions on foreign immigration imposed as a result had created opportunities for black workers, opportunities that proved, in most cases, to be temporary. And in something of a cruel irony, the mechanization of Southern cotton farming in the 1940s meant fewer plantation jobs for blacks, not more.[1]

Life was far short of paradise for most Southern blacks who heeded the call north. They paid a heavy price for their limited wartime acceptance in packing plants and on assembly lines: the enmity of unskilled whites competing for the same jobs, an ironic consequence of their escape to cities in which the "place" of blacks wasn't as rigidly defined as in the rural South. We think of what we call "race riots" as a by-product of civil rights–era frustration, and the image conjured up by the phrase—and reinforced by the events in South Central Los Angeles in the spring of 1992—is that of blacks destroying their own neighborhoods. But so-called race riots were endemic in the U.S. in the years just after World War I, and almost without exception took the form of white mobs roaming city streets with torches, in search of black victims. There were at least two dozen such riots in 1919 alone, the bloodiest in Chicago, where twenty-three blacks were killed, six hundred wounded, and as many as a thousand burned out of their homes.

By 1930, there were large numbers of blacks in most major Northern cities and factory towns. Their presence was a fact of life, but whites continued to regard them warily. In 1915, valorized by the success of D. W. Griffith's *Birth of a Nation*, the Ku Klux Klan reemerged as a force in American politics. By 1930, the Klan's largest chapters were in Indiana, not Alabama or Mississippi. Granting that a good many Klansmen were more riled by what they perceived as the threat of a papal takeover of the United States on account of the immigration of large numbers of Irish and Italian Catholics than they were by the presumption of equality on the part of an increasing number of blacks, this suggests the extent to which race (or "color," to use the language of the time) had become a national, rather than an exclusively Southern, obsession.

It almost goes without saying that when the market crashed in 1929,

---

1. Beginning less than half a century later, in yet another cruel irony, demand for unskilled labor would steadily decrease, as technology overtook industry and jobs moved to the Sunbelt. What unused country fields overgrown with weeds were to the blues, warehouses with conveyor belts stilled and windows broken are to rap.

blacks were the ones pinched hardest by the faltering economy, and the last to recover. But in common with those friends and relatives left behind in the South, émigrés to the north experienced hard times long before Black Tuesday, October 29. To a large extent, the promise of greater social mobility proved to be a myth; in terms of housing, the black population in most big cities was restricted to neighborhoods that soon became overcrowded with the steady influx from the South. For most of the immigrants who arrived in this country during the later decades of the nineteenth century and the early decades of the twentieth, the American Dream became as much one of assimilation as of abundance. When neither came quickly or easily, these Irish and Italians and Eastern European Jews relied on the customs, idioms, and lore of their mother countries to buffer their cultural dislocation. Color made assimilation a virtual impossibility for Southern blacks funneling into Chicago and other Northern cities. They, too, clung to their old ways, but—ancestral memories negated by slavery, and Africa not signifying what it does today—their old country was the American South, their mother tongue the blues.

Blacks enjoyed one advantage over foreign immigrants, though it must not have been much consolation at the time. No matter how unattractive a prospect it might have been, when things failed to work out as well as planned in the North, a former sharecropper could always run "home"—to Mississippi or Georgia or wherever. This was difficult if not impossible for European immigrants whose "homes" no longer existed, at least not as remembered, in the wake of the Bolshevik Revolution and two world wars.

As a people, black Americans found themselves torn between the country and the city; and this is reflected in the blues of the thirties and forties—especially if we agree to recognize decades as ideological constructs rather than finite units of time, in order to begin our discussion of the thirties with a pair of recordings from 1928 that immediately caught on with black audiences, and whose echoes can still be heard in much of the music that has followed.

THE irresistible "It's Tight Like That," recorded in September of that year, featured Tampa Red, a transplanted Floridian who had been born in Georgia and whose real name was Hudson Whittaker or Hudson Woodbridge, on guitar and vocals, with the tune's composer, "Georgia Tom" Dorsey (Thomas A. Dorsey, better remembered today as the composer of "Peace in the Valley" and "Precious Lord, Take My Hand") playing piano and mirthfully singing "re-doo-dee-dum" at the end of every verse. The song caused a sensation, its popularity best measured by the slew of cover versions it spawned and the number of times Tampa Red himself had to re-record it. Even Louis

Thomas Dorsey
(FRANK DRIGGS COLLECTION)

Tampa Red (RAY AVERY'S JAZZ ARCHIVES)

Armstrong got into the act, recording a sound-alike ditty he called "Tight Like This" three months later.

"We didn't want to call ourselves blues singers, and we didn't want to call ourselves popular singers," Dorsey told an interviewer for the BBC decades later, explaining how his and Tampa Red's music came to be called "hokum." "I don't know what the word 'hokum' means . . . if there is such a word in the dictionary. But it was a good word to carry, for nobody knew what it meant." He and Tampa Red were quickly dubbed the Hokum Boys. During the same interview, Dorsey also observed that the song in question had "live beats" to it. This was his way of saying that the bass rhythm was more pronounced—lighter but somehow heavier, too—than was usually characteristic of blues recordings up to that point.

"It's Tight Like That" was one of the first "city" blues, its beat anticipating much of the music recorded in Chicago by Bluebird Records in the late 1930s and early 1940s (a subject of the next chapter). Yet for all that was prescient about this recording, it's easier for a modern-day commentator to pinpoint what was old about it, which in this context means "rural." Tampa Red delivered one slightly risqué witticism after another, and the impression he gave of being able to go on in such manner all night is what gives the performance its charm. His rhymes (or Dorsey's) already had whiskers on them in 1928, and weren't especially funny to begin with: "You got a dollar, I got a dime/Let's go down the alley, buy some wine." Yet this is what's so captivating about the song. You feel like you're eavesdropping on a back-woods picnic where everybody already knows the performer's jokes, and *that's* somehow what makes them so funny (it's like being in the Catskills). And the jokes aren't the only old-fashioned touch. In some ways, "It's Tight Like That" is an updated coon song. There's a hint of ragtime banjo in Tampa Red's clean guitar lines (though he was a wizard with a bottleneck, he shows no evidence of that here). And Dorsey's "re-doo-dee-dums" could be the sound of a man blowing into a jug.

Despite its Chicago postmark, "It's Tight Like That" sounds country, and this must have been reassuring to many of those who bought it in 1928—people with one foot in the city and one foot back home, like Tampa Red himself. It's neither rural nor urban, but midway between.

THE same is true, but more poetically so, of the moody and reflective "How Long—How Long Blues," recorded in Indianapolis in June 1928 by its composer, the singer and pianist Leroy Carr, with Francis "Scrapper" Blackwell on guitar.

> I've been sitting here thinking
> with my mind a million miles away

These lines are from Carr's "Blues Before Sunrise," which he recorded in 1934, just a few months before his death at the age of thirty, probably from cirrhosis of the liver. But they're typical of the introspective temperament of all of Carr's best songs, including "How Long."

"A million miles away" might have been a small town in the South, a familiar way of life left behind, fled in disgust but turned idyllic in recollection. Or at least that's how Carr's imagery must have struck many of his listeners. He himself was an urbanite, a native of Nashville (where his father had worked as a porter at Vanderbilt University and owned his own home) and a resident of Indianapolis by the time he recorded. But he sang as though from the point of view of his nostalgic-for-the-country audiences, and this must have been part of what endeared him to them.

In formal terms, what was innovative about "How Long" was its understatement—the sense Carr gave of holding technique in reserve in backing Blackwell's stinging guitar lines so simply and efficiently. (Blackwell was a virtuoso who made no bones about it, a former moonshiner who more or less gave up music following Carr's death but who lived long enough to be rediscovered in the early 1960s.) Introspection wasn't exactly a new quality in the blues, but before Carr, it had mostly taken the form of soul-searching lyrics. Carr also *played* introspectively, and by his example, encouraged Blackwell to do likewise.

In a way, we owe the very concept of urban blues to Carr and Blackwell, the commercial success of whose duets sent record company representatives in search of talent in cities, not just in rural outposts. "How Long" departs from the norm in structure: its individual verses are eight bars long, instead of twelve, and Carr doesn't repeat the first line of any of them. Just as he wastes not a single note, he wastes not a single word. But I doubt this was what black buyers responded to in 1928, just as I doubt that they responded to the elegant communication between the two instruments on anything but a subconscious level. They probably responded to what we still respond to today, on hearing this evocative record for the first time: Carr's description of the faraway whistle of the evening train as heard by someone left behind, which somehow also captures the anxiety of those on board. Was the train bound north?

A case need hardly be made for "How Long—How Long Blues" as a great record, one of a handful that reconfigured the blues into an urban form. Its greatness envelops it, becoming part of what we hear. By comparison, "It's Tight Like That" sounds like a novelty record. But the blues was already a form of popular music by 1928, and we're talking about a field in which novelty and innovation frequently amount to the same thing. The commercial success of these two guitar-and-piano duos—Tampa Red and Tom Dorsey, and Leroy Carr and Scrapper Blackwell—nudged the blues away from self-accompanied performance and toward a *band* sound. Amplification is usually seen as the characteristic that most clearly distinguishes urban blues from its rural antecedent. But pick-ups and amps came later. The first step was the formation of ensembles, with these two duos showing the way.

Carr and Tampa Red became two of the most popular blues recording artists of their day, and the key phrase is *recording artists*. Records may have been incidental to Charley Patton or even to Blind Lemon Jefferson, who probably considered them a lucrative sideline to his performances at country picnics and urban rent parties. A country bluesman's primary audience was the people in his community. Carr's primary audience, and that of Tampa

Red, was people who bought records, regardless of where they lived.

Remember Rudi Blesh's image of Robert Johnson as "a lonely, bedeviled figure, bent to the wind, with his *easy rider* held by one arm as it swings from its cord around his neck"? Something's missing from this description, and in a passage from *Searching for Robert Johnson*, Peter Guralnick tells us what it is. "It makes a curious picture," Guralnick writes. "The neat, always impeccable bluesman walking down a dusty road, shoulders high and hunched a little bit forward, his guitar in one hand, his latest record in the other."

Wholesale recording of blues performers had started before radio, before record stores as such, before anyone had a sense of the American public as a mass market. Record companies offered one catalogue to buyers in the North, another to those in the South. They assumed that Jewish immigrants wanted to hear klezmers and cantors, that Italians wanted Caruso, that the Irish wanted John McCormick, that white Southerners wanted hillbilly, that rural blacks wanted sermons and blues (pop, as such, meant show tunes and jazz). A happy side effect of this inability of record companies to think big was a wider diversity of music on major labels than at any time since, though what a record buyer could find depended to a large extent on where he or she lived.

The Depression changed all of this, but only temporarily and only slightly. What ultimately rescued the record industry was the repeal of Prohibition in 1933, and the opening of thousands of taverns equipped with coin-operated jukeboxes. The jukebox quickly became ubiquitous. By 1939, there were as many as a quarter of a million such machines in the United States, in every manner of commercial establishment. Back in Mississippi, Muddy Waters had one installed in his shack, which was by then doubling as a still (neither Prohibition nor its repeal having had much effect on the consumption of moonshine).

Most musicians, however, saw the jukebox as second only to radio as a threat to their livelihood. In August 1942, the American Federation of Musicians ordered its members to refrain from recording until a new royalty arrangement could be negotiated with record companies. The stand-off lasted over two years, and the union imposed another ban in 1948, this time lasting only a few months. Today, the jukebox is an object of nostalgia. When introduced, it was an affirmation of the centrality of music in people's lives. It was also a force for diversity, in that the songs that enticed regulars to part with their coins in a New York soda shop might not do the trick in a Mississippi roadside café. The jukebox brought recorded music to where people congregated, and people were themselves increasingly on the move in the thirties and forties, blacks especially. This mobility means that there's little point in drawing a hard-and-fast distinction between "rural" and "urban" blues styles after 1928 or thereabouts (a mere two years after Blind

Lemon Jefferson's first session, and less than a decade after "Crazy Blues"), and no point at all in discussing the work of individual performers from the vantage point of where they grew up or happened to spend most of their adult lives.

In Robert Johnson's "Phonograph Blues," he tells a woman that he wants to "wind" her Victrola, "just to hear your little motor moan." Johnson apparently did a lot of winding, not all of it sexual. It's true that he was essentially a country performer, heir to the rich Delta tradition. But in addition to Charley Patton and Son House, his influences included performers whose work he would have known only from records, most notably Peetie Wheatstraw and Lonnie Johnson, both of whom were associated with

Peetie
Wheatstraw
(COURTESY SHELDON
HARRIS COLLECTION)

St. Louis in the 1930s, when they would have made the greatest impact on him. We take it for granted that the music of rural performers such as Robert Johnson was a cornerstone of what ultimately became identified as urban blues. But Johnson's own recordings, and those of many of his contemporaries, confirm that the blues traveled both ways. The music made by blacks in cities in the 1930s altered forever the shape of country blues, once it was transported to rural areas on phonograph records.

SLEEPY John Estes, the wiry-voiced singer and guitarist who was the poet laureate of Brownsville, Tennessee, was an exception to this rule. One of sixteen children, Estes was born into a family of sharecroppers in 1904—that, anyway, is the date usually given, though his repertoire and strum were those of a man born well before the turn of the century. After making his first recordings in 1929, he lived the vagabond life we associate with the country blues performers of the early part of this century, wandering back and forth between his hometown and Chicago, where he occasionally performed for Al Capone. (Big Al was "crazy" about the blues, according to Sleepy John, even though he expected black performers "to cut up and act a fool.") Estes toured with the Rabbit Foot Minstrels in 1939, and turned up in Memphis just long enough to record for Sun in the early fifties. Advancing age and failing eyesight finally took him off the road, and when he was rediscovered by Bob Koester in 1961, Estes was living in a two-room shack amid abandoned farms on a back road in Brownsville, a rural town not far from Memphis. Despite becoming a popular coffeehouse attraction, this is where he made his home until his death in 1977, often putting on front-porch concerts with his longtime running partner, the jug and harmonica player Hammie Nixon.

Estes clung to the country in his music, too. As a storyteller, he was essentially a local colorist; the musician with whom he enjoyed the greatest rapport was the mandolinist Yank Rachell, and their records together from the thirties conjure up images of a much earlier day.

BUT as noted, Estes was the exception. Memphis Minnie was far more typical of the blues performers of her generation, even if her gender made her something of a novelty at a time when the blues was increasingly becoming a male preserve.

Was she rural or urban? She delivered her songs in a strident twang, and you can easily imagine her shouting over the voices of carousers without the assistance of amplification in backwoods honky tonks. Sam Charters once pointed out that "the modesty of her accompaniments kept the feeling of shabby poverty that was the social context of what she sang."

Yet Minnie was a city girl. She was born Lizzie Douglas just outside of New Orleans in 1897 and was singing on the streets of Memphis before she was in her teens (she also toured with the Ringling Brothers Circus in some undisclosed capacity around the same time). Eyewitness accounts have her playing electric guitar as early as 1942; even before that, her riffs had the toughness and energy, the get-out-of-my-way jostle we identify with urban life. She played as decisive a role as anyone in shaping the sound of Chicago blues; her 1929 "Bumble Bee," one of the songs that made her a star, was the direct source of Muddy Waters's "Honey Bee."

As for "shabby poverty," Memphis Minnie's lyrics were one thing and her wardrobe quite another. Though an important part of her appeal to her audiences was as a woman who played guitar and sang as powerfully as any man (there is a famous story, perhaps apocryphal, of her besting Big Bill Broonzy in a blues contest in Chicago in the early thirties), she seems to have consciously modeled her stage image on that of the glamorous women vaudeville stars of the 1920s. She and her succession of husband/duet partners (Casey Bill Weldon, Kansas Joe McCoy, and Ernest "Little Son Joe" Lawlar) traveled from job to job in new-model luxury cars. Money was her "trademark," according to the Chicago guitarist Jimmy Rogers. "She wore a bracelet around each wrist, made out of silver dollars, and then she had a set of earrings with two silver dimes [on them]," Rogers told Jim O'Neal—shades of Ma Rainey's eagle. Like Rainey, Minnie didn't so much worship the dollar as offer it up for worship. Surrounding herself with luxury was a way of surrounding her audience with luxury, too; not just her secret, but that of any number of black performers past and present.

•

MEMPHIS Minnie died virtually forgotten in a Memphis nursing home in 1977. Paul and Beth Garon's *Woman with Guitar*, a full-length biography of her, includes quite a find: a handwritten list of the two dozen tunes she performed during one of her sets in a nightclub. Though the year is unspecified, the list is probably from the late 1940s: it includes "I Want to Be Loved," a hit for Savannah Churchills in 1947 and far from the most unlikely number Minnie performed that night. In addition to several blues, she did George Gershwin's "Summertime" and "Oh, Lady Be Good." She also did "When My Dreamboat Comes Home," "For Sentimental Reasons," "How High the Moon," "Exactly Like You," "It's the Talk of the Town," "That's My Desire" (which she or whoever took down the request misspelled "That My Descrer"), and "The Woody Woodpecker Song."

She didn't record any of these, of course, or anything remotely like them. But think of it this way, because she and her fellow performers probably did: by the late 1940s, it wasn't as though the jukebox was taking the place of live musicians, but the other way around. A performer had to be prepared

Memphis
Minnie
(RAY AVERY'S JAZZ
ARCHIVES)

to deliver anything the audience might want to hear, because a jukebox certainly could. On record, someone like Memphis Minnie was a blues singer. In performance, she was a mechanical-age songster. Many blues performers prided themselves on their versatility—and on their ability to gauge an audience's desires. They aimed to please. If a blues was called for, fine. A recent pop tune? No problem. It was what being a professional entertainer was all about, and evidence suggests that this was how blues performers were beginning to think of themselves, even when (as in the case of Leadbelly and several others discussed later in this section) appearing before white audiences that regarded them as folk musicians.

No doubt many of them resented being forced by their labels to record only blues. Chris Albertson, whom I mentioned earlier as the author of the definitive biography of Bessie Smith, once told me a funny but revealing story about Lonnie Johnson's days on the revival circuit in the 1960s. Albertson was then managing Johnson, having relocated him working as a porter in the Benjamin Franklin Hotel in Philadelphia and gotten him a contract with Bluesville Records, a subsidiary of the jazz label Prestige. Johnson had made a handful of records for Bluesville on which he sang and played vintage pop tunes such as "My Mother's Eyes" and "Prisoner of Love," as well as the blues. No one's idea of a folk musician—this, after all, was a man who had recorded duets with the white jazz guitarist Eddie Lang and as a sideman with the Duke Ellington Orchestra and Louis Armstrong's Hot Five in the late 1920s, and topped the rhythm-'n'-blues charts with a song called "Tomorrow Night" in 1948—Johnson regarded the young white folk blues enthusiasts of the sixties with skepticism, and they in turn hardly knew what to make of him.

Somewhere in the middle of all this, Johnson was signed to do two numbers at an all-star benefit concert at Town Hall in New York, the lone "blues" performer on a bill otherwise filled with white folkies. "Remember, Lonnie, this is a folk audience," Albertson cautioned in the wings. "They want the blues, so give them the blues."

Johnson nodded his understanding. Then he went out and sang "Red Sails in the Sunset," following that with his version of Frank Sinatra's "This Love of Mine."

"I thought you said to give them my best," Johnson later told the chagrined Albertson, who doesn't know to this day whether Johnson *deliberately* misunderstood him.

JOHNSON—who was born in New Orleans in 1894 and got his start in music as a violinist in a string band led by his father there—probably sang those two songs beautifully, in that fluttering way of his, marking the ends of choruses with elegant, flatpicked arpeggios, phrasing his guitar one jump ahead of the beat, or one step behind. Had his career worked out differently, he might have become a celebrated crooner, the black Crosby. Then again, had he followed up his work with Lang, Armstrong, and Ellington, he might today be regarded as a forerunner to Django Reinhardt and Charlie Christian. His rhythm and harmonic sense were fanciful and unerring, and he was probably the first improvising guitarist to base his style on cleanly articulated single-string lines rather than heavily strummed chords—the first guitarist to phrase like a horn, in other words, a full decade before Christian.

But Johnson's fate was decided for him when he won first prize in a blues contest staged by Okeh Records in a St. Louis vaudeville theater in 1925. Signed to Okeh and then to Bluebird, he recorded well over a hundred sides for these labels during the next five years, outselling every male blues performer with the exception of Blind Lemon Jefferson. His most popular records tended to be those on which he traded racy banter with Victoria Spivey or Clara Smith. But it was his more contemplative numbers that showed him off to best advantage as a singer and instrumentalist—in particular, "Careless Love," which he first recorded in 1928 and last recorded at his final session almost forty years later. Johnson so succeeded in making the mother of all public domain blues songs his own that you don't even do a double take on seeing it listed under his name in *The Blues Line*, Eric Sackheim's 1969 anthology of blues lyrics.[2]

2. This is the ballad W. C. Handy copyrighted as "Loveless Love" in 1921, though it's at least three decades older. In *Folk Song U.S.A* (1947), John and Alan Lomax cite it as "one of the earliest, if not actually the first, blues," guessing it to be a song of white origin that "has changed hands across the race line so frequently that it has acquired a pleasant coffee color." In *Negro Folk Music U.S.A.* (1963), Harold Courlander notes: "Among the many blues versions of 'Careless Love' there are some which are hard to classify as true blues, and some which are nothing more than pop songs in disguise. The singer Lonnie Johnson, for example, turned 'Careless Love' into maudlin doggerel." Courlander's reaction is an example of what happens when ideology stands in the way of hearing.

Lonnie Johnson
(FRANK DRIGGS COLLECTION)

Personifying careless love, addressing it directly as "you," Johnson attributes to it powers of the sort attributed to the blues by countless other singers. The scourge of his life, it causes him to weep and moan, robs him of his money, chases him from the comfort of his bed and out into the rain and snow. It drives his father insane and sends his mother to her grave. The song ends with Johnson vowing to shoot his supernatural assailant and to stand watch over it until it dies. But you know, as he seems to, that this is one chill he's never going to shake. What's traditionally been a song about prostitution becomes the lament of a man dogged by misfortune most of his life, beginning with the death of his entire family except for himself and a brother in the influenza epidemic of 1919.

Johnson's troubles included an acrimonious divorce from the singer Mary Johnson (for a time, he and she squabbled on their individual records), and lengthy interruptions in his career on account of the changing tastes of record buyers and his own dissatisfaction with record companies. He was already in his fifties when he scored his one big R&B hit (a song Elvis Presley later covered in loving imitation of him), and this was in an era in which pop was increasingly becoming a young man's game. In *The Blues Line*, Sackheim includes Johnson's "Careless Love" among a selection of blues from St. Louis. But Johnson, who was a resident of Toronto when he died in 1970, was a blues performer who resisted classification by region or even style. "I played everything that was playable," he once said, referring to types of venues, though he might very well have said the same thing about his mastery of so many different musical genres. He had a genuine knack for the blues, but he would have preferred not to limit himself to them. Though largely uncelebrated today, he was one of the most influential figures in American music—the inspiration Robert Johnson and Elvis Presley had in common (to say nothing of Charlie Christian and B. B. King). He even figures indirectly in Beatles lore: Lonnie Donegan, the British skiffle-band leader who was an early idol of Paul McCartney's, took the name "Lonnie" in honor of him, much as Robert Johnson had decided on the surname "Johnson."

THOUGH there would continue to be room in the blues for musical primitives, expert guitarists such as Johnson, Scrapper Blackwell, and Kokomo Arnold were beginning to set a high professional standard. Arnold—born in rural Georgia in 1908, but a longtime resident of Chicago, where he died in 1968—was the most enigmatic of these guitarists of the thirties, in that he might never have recorded if given his own choice. He was a bootlegger for whom music seems to have remained a sideline even after the commercial success of his "Milk Cow Blues" and "Original Old Kokomo Blues" in 1934. Like Black Ace in Texas, Arnold played a steel guitar Hawaiian style, holding

Scrapper Blackwell
(FRANK DRIGGS COLLECTION)

James "Kokomo" Arnold
(FRANK DRIGGS COLLECTION)

it flat across his knees while he ran a glass flask over the strings. Everything about his music was fast and high-pitched, from the tremolos he coaxed out of the strings to the falsetto wail of his vocals. Rediscovered in the early 1960s, he made the rounds of blues and folk festivals but declined offers to resume his recording career, which had apparently never meant that much to him to begin with.

THE piano has traditionally meant different things to different people. An orchestra in miniature, the tempered scale in a box, it can also be a drum,

Memphis Slim (Peter Chatman)
(FRANK DRIGGS COLLECTION)

should one be inclined to beat on it. In a turn-of-the-century parlor, it was a symbol of bourgeois propriety. But it was also a fixture in that era's brothels and beer joints (barrelhouses), and itinerant piano players usually supplied the entertainment in the dining halls provided for the bruisers employed in the lumber and turpentine camps in Mississippi's Piney Woods.

You know the cliché about "tickling" the ivories? Such veterans of the work camps and barrelhouses as Memphis Slim, Champion Jack Dupree, Eurreal "Little Brother" Montgomery, Roosevelt Sykes, Sunnyland Slim, and Speckled Red didn't tickle the keys—they *crushed* them. The trick was to make yourself heard, and the best way to do that was to play and sing loud; to hammer out the beat with your left hand and not try anything fancy with your right; to put the beat in front where it belonged *and keep it there all night*.

Because their instrument requires them to be sedentary, we're prone to think of piano players themselves as stationary, unable to hit the road as

Sunnyland Slim
(RAY AVERY'S JAZZ ARCHIVES)

easily as guitarists and harmonica players. But think about it. The barrelhouse crushers named above traveled lighter than any other bluesmen of their era. They didn't even have to stick their harmonicas in their front shirt pocket, or steady their guitars on the floor of a moving boxcar before scrambling aboard. All they needed to do on arriving in a new town was to look for a dump with beer on tap and sawdust on the floor—odds were there would also be a splintered upright.

As it did for Dupree, the road ultimately led to Europe for Memphis Slim (Peter Chatman), a pianist and singer more associated with Chicago than with the city that gave him his nickname. In Paris in the late 1960s, Slim was worshipped as a blues demigod, his great height and regal bearing adding to the drama of his slow, atmospheric piano blues.

In contrast to Speckled Red and Sunnyland Slim, both of whom were shouters who made do with limited keyboard technique, the most sophisticated of the barrelhouse crushers—though a somewhat hesitant singer—was Little Brother Montgomery, whose rolling bass and chiming melodic lines earmarked a highly personal synthesis of blues and jazz. (The only blues pianist of his generation whose work showed a keener understanding of jazz harmony was the versatile Sammy Price, a Texan who ultimately made a name for himself in New York jazz circles, even recording with Lester Young. He was also a much-in-demand R&B session pianist in the 1950s.) Born near New Orleans in 1906, where he played in jazz bands as a young man, Montgomery was a favorite of Chicago blues fans from his arrival in that city in the early thirties to his death in 1985.

In terms of combining a powerful voice and piano style, few could match Roosevelt Sykes, a good-natured bear of a man who was born in rural Arkansas in 1906, and was active in and around St. Louis in the thirties and forties (when he was the primary influence on the elusive pianist and

Big Mama Thornton with Roosevelt Sykes, Ann Arbor Blues Festival, 1969
(DOUG FULTON)

guitarist Henry Townsend). A resident of New Orleans from 1952 until his death in 1984, and the composer of a song called "Night Time Is the Right Time" (not to be confused with the similarly named Ray Charles anthem), Sykes was nicknamed "The Honeydripper" in honor of his way with women. Though he was a splendid band pianist, his style was so dichotomous as to be practically self-sufficient, his left hand tethered to the beat while his right enjoyed the run of the keyboard.

TWO other piano players should be mentioned before we close the book on barrelhouse for now, one of them arguably the greatest practitioner of the style, the other a man who had the potential to be until Jesus intervened.

We've already met Tom Dorsey, Tampa Red's partner on "It's Tight Like That" and the father of modern gospel music (he was, in fact, the first to call it "gospel"). Unlike most blues pianists of his era—indeed, unlike most of that day's black musicians, including those in jazz—Dorsey had studied music on a collegiate level, having first arrived in Chicago from his native Georgia in order to attend school there. In addition to serving as musical director for both Ma Rainey and Bessie Smith, he wrote arrangements for the jazz bands of King Oliver and Les Hite. The son of a revivalist preacher, he himself entered the fold in 1929, soon after the success of "It's Tight Like That," thereafter devoting himself exclusively to sacred music until his death in 1993.

Major Merriweather (Big Maceo) (COURTESY SHELDON HARRIS COLLECTION)

You're probably thinking that this is a familiar story. But the details are a little surprising. Dorsey was "saved" at a Billy Sunday revival meeting in 1921, seven years before writing "It's Tight Like That." He published "If You See My Savior, Tell Him That You Saw Me," his first gospel composition, in 1926, not abandoning the blues until the orders from church choirs began to trickle in. His conversion to Christ wasn't accompanied by any of the manic-depressive mood swings we associate with the Delta. He never renounced his more earthly music. "Blues is [still] a part of the way I play [and] the way I write," he told Anthony Heilbut, the author of *The Gospel Sound*, in the early 1970s. Like Lonnie Johnson, Dorsey was a consummate professional who left his mark on every kind of music he tried.

By contrast, it's difficult to imagine Major Merriweather, the force of nature recruited by Tampa Red as Dorsey's replacement, playing

anything but the blues. "Big Maceo," as he was known professionally, was born in Atlanta in 1905 and died in Chicago in 1953, seven years after being chased from the piano bench by a massive stroke (always a drowsy-voiced singer, he continued to perform in that capacity until his death). Maceo was the man who modernized barrelhouse and pointed the way to Otis Spann, and he pulled this off not by elaborating on the style or embellishing it, but by trimming it even leaner—by pounding the treble as hard as the bass, with every ounce of his two hundred and fifty pounds, and reducing whatever song he happened to be playing into unmoderated rhythm with the clap of thunder. In a style in which heavyhandedness was a virtue, Big Maceo's were the heaviest hands of all.

SOMEWHERE along the way—no one knows for sure exactly when—barrelhouse forked into boogie-woogie, an urban style characterized by eight insistent beats to the measure in the bass, and right-hand melodies that were essentially rhythmic variations on this bass line. Boogie-woogie is assumed to have come into being in the rural South around the turn of the century, more or less simultaneously with the blues. But the style perhaps owed more to ragtime than to the blues. The late Eubie Blake used to tell interviewers that he first heard boogie-woogie played by a ragtime pianist from Baltimore named William Turk. At any rate, the word "boogie" apparently once described what men paid prostitutes to do with them in the Southern "boogie" houses where the style was first played.

The first recorded example of boogie-woogie that anyone is aware of was "The Rocks" by Clay Cluster (a pseudonym for George Thomas, the brother of Sippie Wallace), in 1923. This was followed by a number of records in the same vein over the next few years, most notably Cow Cow Davenport's "Cow Cow Blues" and Meade Lux Lewis's many versions of his "Honky Tonk Train Blues."[3] But the style's commercial breakthrough came in 1929, with the release of "Pine Top's Boogie Woogie" by Clarence "Pine Top" Smith, one of the biggest selling and most widely imitated race hits of the period (a pop crossover hit, in fact). "Pine Top's Boogie Woogie" started such a craze that Davenport and Lewis were rushed into the studios to re-record their signature tunes. As crazes go, the initial one for boogie-woogie was short-lived. But two unrelated events in the waning days of 1938 sparked a revival that was to prove more long-lasting and far-reaching than the original vogue. Two days before Christmas, a trio of boogie-woogie pian-

3. You'll notice that practically every title mentioned in this and the previous chapter ends with the word "blues." This was the record companies' way of targeting releases to black audiences. The word seems to have been routinely added to the titles the performers themselves gave their songs. That is, Robert Johnson probably wrote a song called "Crossroads," Leroy Carr a song called "How Long," and Meade Lux Lewis a song called "Honky Tonk Train."

ists—Lewis; his fellow Chicago cabdriver and roommate Albert Ammons; and Pete Johnson, from Kansas City—participated in the first "From Spirituals to Swing" concert at Carnegie Hall.[4] Lewis, Ammons, and Johnson became regulars on the bill at Café Society, a fashionable New York nightclub that was adamantly interracial in both its bookings and its admission policies. By then, Tommy Dorsey had already climbed the charts with a cleverly orchestrated version of "Pine Top's Boogie Woogie," retitled simply "Boogie Woogie." Thanks to Dorsey, boogie-woogie was no longer regarded as just a piano style, but as a beat to end all beats. The style went pop with a vengeance during World War II, yielding such chart hits as Freddie Slack and Ella Mae Morse's "Cow Cow Boogie" and Will Bradley's "Beat Me, Daddy, Eight to the Bar," before reaching its nadir with the Andrews Sisters' "Boogie Woogie Bugle Boy."

F O R all of this, the man acknowledged by most boogie-woogie pianists as the greatest exponent of the form toiled in relative obscurity, his musical career never more than a sideline to his regular job as a groundskeeper at Comiskey Park, the home of the Chicago White Sox. Jimmy Yancey, a native of Chicago who started out as a singer and tap dancer in vaudeville and was rumored to have played professional baseball himself with an unspecified black team as a young man, was over forty when he made his recording debut in the spring of 1939. But his name had appeared on a label three years earlier, when Meade Lux Lewis recorded "Yancey Special" as a kind of homage to him.

Yancey was such a dazzling pianist that to call him the greatest of the boogie-woogie men hardly does him justice. In contrast to most of his competitors, whose philosophy might have been "the faster the better," Yancey favored restrained tempos; the slower he played, the more blues feeling he wrung out of every note. You hear the rudiments of fifties rock 'n' roll in his bass lines, as you do in those of the other boogie-woogie players. But in his lines, you also hear a pre-echo of sixties soul. Though he never recorded with horns, a case could be made for him as a jazz musician strictly in terms of his rhythmic sense, the odd angle of his stuttering

4. Organized by John Hammond as an attempt to trace the evolution of black American music from its beginnings in Africa, the first "From Spirituals to Swing" concert opened with Hammond playing African field recordings, then featured performances by the Mitchell Christian Singers, Sonny Terry, Big Bill Broonzy, Count Basie's big band, the New Orleans Footwarmers with Sidney Bechet, Ruby Smith (a niece of Bessie Smith's, singing her songs), Big Joe Turner, and the three boogie-woogie pianists. Broonzy was on the bill as a substitute for Robert Johnson, who had been murdered four months earlier or would have been Hammond's first choice to represent the country blues. An encore concert the following Christmas Eve included commentary by the poet Sterling A. Brown, as well as performances by Benny Goodman, Lester Young, Charlie Christian and the Golden Gate Quartet.

Meade "Lux" Lewis
(FRANK DRIGGS COLLECTION)

Jimmy Yancey
(RAY AVERY'S JAZZ ARCHIVES)

and elongated phrases to the beat. Yancey *teased* at notes, attacking them sharp or flat and giving them a Latin accent, often pausing for suspense before bouncing a sequence of them like so many rubber balls off the hard wall of his left-hand bass lines. An unsuspecting listener hearing Yancey for the first time could be hoodwinked into believing that he was hearing Thelonious Monk.

Yancey wasn't much of a singer, but many of his best recordings featured penetrating vocals by his wife, Estelle "Mama" Yancey. He died in 1951, by which time boogie-woogie had run out of steam and most of Yancey's contemporaries were back beating out eight bass notes to the bar in dank neighborhood taverns and lounges. Any number of recordings by Meade Lux Lewis and Albert Ammons show what was originally so exhilarating about the style. But only Yancey's show the depth of invention that was possible in the name of boogie-woogie.

THE exact nature of the relationship between the blues and jazz is a tricky question that could be the subject of a complete volume. Suffice it to say that jazz occasionally shares with the blues a structure, an approach to tonality, and a mood. The two musics no doubt shared similar origins; both take an ironic stance toward popular song. But this hardly makes them the same music. What are we really saying when we say that jazz "evolved" from the blues, if not that the blues is a vestigial musical form whose main purpose since the early 1920s has been to chasten jazz musicians from going too far out?

Jazz musicians assign such a high value to being able to play the blues in a "natural" and convincing fashion that it's often said that any jazz impro- viser worth his salt is also a superlative blues player. This simply isn't true. Louis Armstrong was a great blues player, but Coleman Hawkins wasn't. Lester Young and Charlie Parker were, but not Art Tatum or Bud Powell. Were Hawkins, Tatum, and Powell not great jazz improvisers?

When jazz musicians speak of "playing the blues," they mean using a tune twelve-bars-long and in the key of B flat as a springboard for harmonic improvisation. This is quite different from what Robert Johnson took the phrase to mean, and different from what John Lee Hooker still takes it to mean close to sixty years after Armstrong more or less set the guidelines for jazz improvisation with his solo on "West End Blues." And for what it's worth, blues musicians have long favored the keys of A and E, not B flat.

Even so, no one would dispute the *presence* of the blues in jazz, and that presence would never again be as audible as it was in the late 1930s. Nor would it ever again be the source of as much ideological buttonholing, which is my point in bringing up the subject here. Like the blues, jazz was fewer than two decades old as a form of recorded music in the late thirties, but its origins were assumed to date back to the end of the previous century and to be part (along with the blues and gospel) of the "missing" Negro past, a source of fascination to both black and white liberal intellectuals since the 1920s. Flush with nationalistic pride following their country's victory in World War I, Americans became obsessed with the question of what it meant to be an American. This created a climate in which Negroes were seen to actually enjoy an advantage of sorts in being more American than anyone else by virtue of having no traceable links to Europe. On the other hand, there was a sense among intellectuals of the Negro past as a largely undocumented story. These two seemingly contradictory impulses triggered the Harlem Renaissance of the 1920s, and also resulted in the publication during that era of such collections as Abbe Niles and W. C. Handy's *Blues*, Howard W. Odum and Guy B. Johnson's *The Negro and His Songs*, and James Weldon Johnson and J. Rosamond Johnson's *The First Book of Negro Spirituals* (as well as their *The Book of American Negro Poetry*). Even then, black music was thought to be the race's greatest contribution to American culture, and a key not just to blacks' own identity as a people but to America's. The 1930s witnessed the publication, in French or English, of such books as Hugues Panassié's *Le Jazz Hot*, Robert Goffin's *Aux Frontières du Jazz*, Winthrop Sargeant's *Jazz, Hot & Hybrid*, and Wilder Hobson's *American Jazz Music*, all of which traced jazz to African-derived work songs, field hollers, and the blues. Along with Gershwin's *Porgy and Bess*, yet another manifestation of this preoccupation with the musical identity of the Negro was the "From Spirituals to Swing" concerts of 1938 and 1939, the philosophical rationale for which was the conviction that jazz, blues, and gospel had sprung from the same roots.

Such an argument would meet with little resistance today, and probably no one disputed it in 1938. It was just that no one had given the matter much thought before then, the rapid evolution of jazz having left musicians and their followers little time to reflect on the music's origins. By the late 1930s, this rapid evolution had itself become cause for alarm to some, along with the increasing role played by virtuoso soloists in what had originally been a vehicle for collective improvisation. Even though bebop was still several years in the future, there were those who felt that jazz had already strayed too far from its folk origins—that it had lost its innocence, so to speak.

In 1938, William Russell and Frederick Ramsey tracked down a cornetist named Bunk Johnson working as a field hand in a rice field in New Iberia, Louisiana. Then nearing fifty or sixty, depending on which of the two birthdates usually given for him you trust, Johnson had supposedly begun his musical career in New Orleans in the early 1900s as an associate of Buddy Bolden, the legendary, unrecorded trumpeter believed to have set the standard for Freddie Keppard, King Oliver, and Louis Armstrong. At the time of his rediscovery, Johnson had been musically inactive for several years. This was seen as an advantage by those who rallied behind him once he was outfitted with dentures and a new horn. It meant that he was presumably oblivious to the new directions jazz had taken in its pursuit of harmonic sophistication. From the point of view of those traditionalists who decried as the erosion of folk traditions what others saw as natural evolution in jazz, Johnson was "uncontaminated"—a word we shall encounter again in discussing Leadbelly.

Johnson's discovery ultimately triggered the New Orleans (or "Dixieland")

155

revival of the 1940s, a movement of interest to us here largely for what it tells us about the unfortunate equation of "authenticity" in black music with primitivism by a good number of that day's otherwise racially enlightened white intellectuals. From a half century's vantage point, perhaps the most curious aspect of this New Orleans revival was its timing. The same musicians who were then setting the stage for bebop—Count Basie, Lester Young, Charlie Christian, and a handful of others, mostly from the Southwestern United States—were also putting jazz back in touch with the blues. As has often been true since, the period's most innovative jazz echoed its rural past.

Christian, an Oklahoman who took the world by storm on joining Benny Goodman in the summer of 1939, wasn't the first electric guitarist—merely the first who mattered. So much has been written about this aspect of his music—how he employed amplification to elevate what had been a rhythm instrument to equal footing with horns—that his eloquence as a blues player often goes overlooked. Though still most celebrated for his work with Goodman's small groups, Christian's crowning moment on record was probably his wistful and loamy solo on "Profoundly Blue" from a 1941 date issued under the clarinetist Edmond Hall's name, and featuring Meade Lux Lewis on celeste. No matter the harmonic complexity of his solos, Christian's point of departure was usually a simple blues riff. He was a virtuoso with red clay under his fingernails.

His only match for lyricism, harmonic invention, and earthiness was Lester Young, the star soloist in Basie's band. It would be an exaggeration to say that big bands were essentially the domain of composers and arrangers before

Count Basie
(FRANK DRIGGS COLLECTION)

Jimmy
Rushing
(RAY AVERY'S JAZZ
ARCHIVES)

Basie's arrival in New York from Kansas City in 1936. There were charismatic improvisers in such "composer's" bands as Duke Ellington's, Fletcher Henderson's, even Paul Whiteman's. Still, by encouraging his men to blow the blues as freely in performance as they might during informal jams, Basie (who was originally from New Jersey) deflated some of the pomposity that had attached itself to the big band idiom. He deployed a full complement of horns not so much to frame his soloists as to goad them on. Band and soloist would play call-and-response, with a spirit of big band camaraderie infusing the unrefined ensemble passages, and a sense of jam session rivalry fueling the solos. And as if this didn't amount to excitement enough, there was Jimmy Rushing to holler the blues as though trying to outshout the entire aggregation.

SUCH women singers as Ma Rainey, Bessie Smith, and Ida Cox had tightened the bonds between jazz and blues in the 1920s. The most notable of their few successors in the two decades that followed was the delightful Lil Green, whose teasing 1943 smash "Why Don't You Do Right?" was made into an even bigger hit by Peggy Lee and Benny Goodman a year later. In addition to Christian and the men in Basie's band, there were numerous other instrumentalists who drew an exceedingly fine line between jazz and the blues. Among the most gifted of them was the pianist Avery Parrish, whose introductory solo on the Erskine Hawkins 1940 recording of "After Hours" was as funky as anything ever recorded by Sunnyland Slim or Otis Spann.

Meanwhile, the tradition initiated by the women blues vaudevillians—that of the jazz and blues double header, as it were—was carried on by the men who sang with the big swing orchestras of the 1930s and 1940s, including Rushing. Though "Mr. Five by Five," as he was called, swung the blues harder than anyone had before (or has since), his beery croak was suited to practically any kind of song. *The You and Me That Used to Be*, his final album, released just a few months before his death in 1971, featured his sparkling interpretations of all manner of pop and jump tunes, including "I Surrender, Dear" (he rolled his "r"s as shamelessly as any dowager) and "Bei Mir Bist Du Schöen." He was one of the greatest American singers, period.

Walter Brown and then Jimmy Witherspoon were Rushing's counterparts with Jay McShann's big band, an outfit important to jazz history as the Basie band's only serious rival on its home turf of Kansas City, and as the band that introduced the world to Charlie Parker. Among Rushing's successors with Basie was Joe Williams, who will forever be identified with the band's 1955 hit of Memphis Slim's "Everyday I Have the Blues," though he, too, is a well-rounded singer perhaps most admired, at this point, for his graceful interpretations of pop ballads. One of the most exciting of the big band shouters was Eddie "Cleanhead" Vinson, who also played alto saxophone in Cootie Williams's big band in the 1940s, and was one of the first musicians outside of bebop's inner circle to absorb the innovations of Charlie Parker (in the early fifties, the depilated shouter toured with a small band of his own, featuring the young John Coltrane). Following the lead of Basie, who at one point offered audiences the thrill of hearing Rushing *and* Billie Holiday, most black bands of the 1940s featured both male and female vocalists. The roles of these singers tended to be rigidly defined: the men growled the blues and the women sang the pretty love songs. But the shouter with Lionel Hampton's band of the mid-1940s was Dinah Washington, then in her prime and still free of the mannerisms she would embrace on trying her hand at pop standards.

The most powerful and mesmerizing of the male shouters was Big Joe Turner, who sang with Basie for a brief time in the 1940s and subsequently straddled the worlds of jazz and pop like a colossus.

Turner, another Kansas City import, first made people sit up and take notice when he sang "Roll 'Em Pete" with Pete Johnson at that initial "From Spirituals to Swing" concert, in 1938. Three years later, he played a major role in the original Los Angeles production of Duke Ellington's topical revue *Jump for Joy*. In the early fifties, he cracked the pop charts with a string of singles that helped to set America's metronome to rock 'n' roll ("a different name for the same music I had been singing all my life," he once said). These included "Shake, Rattle and Roll," later covered by spit-curled mayo-boy Bill Haley, who probably had no inkling of what anatomical parts were

Eddie "Cleanhead" Vinson
(COURTESY SHELDON HARRIS COLLECTION)

Joe Turner
(COURTESY SHELDON HARRIS COLLECTION)

being referred to in the line about "a one-eyed jack peeping in a seafood store" (just think about it, just think about it). Turner recorded prolifically over a nearly fifty-year career, and if I had to choose just one album by him, it would be *The Boss of the Blues*, a late fifties reunion with Johnson featuring zesty updates of some of their early successes, including "Roll 'Em Pete," "Piney Brown Blues," and "Cherry Red."

Still, Big Joe was one of those performers you had to hear live, and I feel sorry for future generations who won't have the opportunity. I saw him perform live only once, at a New York club called Tramps during the Christmas holidays in 1981, four years before his death from a heart attack at the age of seventy-four. Though he was a good thirty years past his prime then, he gave a powerful exhibition I will never forget.

The show didn't start off very promisingly. Big Joe sat at the bar downing a roast beef sandwich and a fifth as his backup group vamped its way through an aimless opening set. Always mountainous, he had ballooned to grotesque proportions, and when he hobbled down the narrow aisle to the stage on his crutches, he almost toppled my chair with me in it. In a slurred voice like Moms Mabley's, he told a long, meandering story with no punch line about how he had addressed his Christmas cards but forgotten to mail them. When he finally got around to singing, he was miked at such an ear-splitting volume that one of my companions rushed to the sound man to plead with him to turn it down.

Big Joe saw what was happening, and didn't like it one bit.

"Stop fiddling with them dials, boy!" he roared between choruses of "Cherry Red." "You just leave them where they was."

The intimidated sound man obeyed.

If Big Joe was worried that his voice had lost some of its capacity, he had no reason to be. Amplification wasn't something he had needed when he was a singing bartender in Kansas City in the 1920s, and it was superfluous that night at Tramps. Once he got down to business, his voice filled the room and then some, vibrating the floor and caroming off the ceiling and walls. When he began "Shake, Rattle and Roll," the beer bottles and shot glasses on the tabletops looked and felt like they were about to.

I had never heard anything like it before, and I don't expect to hear anything like it again. Though the lyrics he sang were the standard doggerel about cheating women and troubled times, they weren't as important as what a poststructuralist would call the "grain" of Turner's voice—the rub of his entire weight in every syllable.

He looked like the whale that swallowed Jonah, and sounded like Jonah bellowing to get out. He was an indomitable force of nature, an overweight old man whose singing and stage presence had been described as "godlike" by more than one observer, and it was awe-inspiring to imagine what it must have been like to hear him three or four decades earlier, before the years exacted their toll on him. There was no one else like him, and no one has come along to take his place. They don't make them that big any more.

THE music ultimately called rhythm 'n' blues—not just an urban offshoot of country blues, but an inevitable reaction to the faster pace and looser rhythms of city life—began to take shape during World War II and just after, though black audiences of that day were likelier to call this sound "jump" or "jive," and possibly to hear it as nothing more than an updated example of twenties hokum. The father of rhythm 'n' blues and one of the biggest selling recording artists of the 1940s (almost as popular among whites as he was among blacks) was Louis Jordan, an alto saxophonist and vocalist once with Chick Webb's big band, whose own Tympany Five combined a polished style of musicianship and presentation with downhome lyrics that said more to Jordan's black audiences than they seemed to say on face value—poking gentle fun at the "country" ways that betrayed some blacks as recent arrivals in Northern cities even as they cushioned the frustrations of longtime city dwellers with nostalgic reminders of "home." Among Jordan's nineteen chart hits between 1944 and 1949, "Ain't Nobody Here But Us Chickens" and "Saturday Night Fish Fry" should suffice as examples. But the best example of all might be a song of his from 1954, long after the hits had stopped coming: "If I Had Any Sense, I'd Go Back Home."

EVEN though he borrowed his beat from boogie-woogie, there was something new going on rhythmically in Jordan's music, something both frantic and chic. He was born in Arkansas, but his home base was New York. Black music increasingly became an urban phenomenon in the 1940s, and something of a national phenomenon as well. Trends no longer originated in the South, or in a handful of Midwestern destination cities such as St. Louis and Chicago.

Louis Jordan
(FRANK DRIGGS COLLECTION)

Los Angeles and the San Francisco Bay area became blues focal points second only to Chicago as blacks fought what amounted to a war within a war, a battle for equality both in the armed services and in the homefront labor force. In the summer of 1941, with Pearl Harbor still months away but America already gearing for war, A. Philip Randolph—then president of the Brotherhood of Sleeping Car Porters, one of the first black labor unions—called for a march on Washington to demand more jobs for blacks in the burgeoning defense industries. Though the threat of war had produced jobs for millions of unemployed whites, effectively ending the Depression for them, untold numbers of blacks remained out of work. A blueprint of sorts for the 1963 gathering at the Lincoln Memorial during which Martin

Luther King, Jr., delivered his "I have a dream" speech, this first march on Washington never actually happened. It was called off days before it was scheduled to occur, when FDR met with Randolph and agreed to issue an executive order making it illegal for industries receiving government contracts (and for the government itself) to refuse to hire workers on account of "race, creed, color or national origin."

Executive Order 8802—the strongest civil rights action by the federal government since Reconstruction—opened the way to California for hundreds of thousands of blacks from Texas and elsewhere in the Southwest who streamed there to take jobs in shipyards and munitions plants. California's black population quadrupled in the forties, to just under a quarter of a million by the end of the decade.

As they always had, musicians emigrated with the rest of the black population. If there was a difference in this case, it was that the musicians who journeyed to California tended, to a much greater extent than those who settled elsewhere, to be full-time entertainers, not just men supplementing their income by playing and singing in clubs. Even so, records such as T-Bone Walker's "Stormy Monday Blues," Pee Wee Crayton's "Blues After Hours," and Lowell Fulson's "Three O'Clock Blues" (later B. B. King's first big hit) suggest that the blues played in California clubs in the forties was workingman's music, as gritty as anything from Chicago. It differed from the blues elsewhere, however, in being more flamboyant in presentation and in bearing a more direct resemblance to jazz, especially in the case of Walker, who was usually backed by riffing horns.

Walker—as imposing a singer as he was a guitarist—was the most charis-

T-Bone Walker 1969 (DOUG FULTON)

162

matic and durable of the West Coast bluesmen. Born Aaron Thibeaux "T-Bone" Walker in Linden, Texas, in 1910 and an active performer until his death in 1975, he had roots going back almost as far as the blues itself, though he labored in semiobscurity until 1947, when his "Call It Stormy Monday" hit the country like a hurricane. As a child, Walker had guided Blind Lemon Jefferson around the streets of Dallas, holding Jefferson's tin cup for him and picking up a trick or two on guitar. Before making his recording debut as Oak Cliff T-Bone in 1929, Walker had traveled the Southwest as a tap dancer in a medicine show. But he also had a foot in jazz, having played banjo with Cab Calloway's band in 1930 (the gig was his prize for winning a Dallas talent contest) and acoustic guitar with a variety of Los Angeles–based bands in the early 1930s (he beat the rush to the West Coast by about ten years).

Though Walker didn't record on amplified guitar until 1939, several years after he began to experiment with a prototype, the blues was never the same once he plugged in. It wasn't just his instrument that was electric; it was his cutting tone and supple dynamics, his very *conception*. In addition to being a jaw-dropping instrumentalist, Walker was a devastating showman whose little jump bands, usually including only a rhythm section and one or two horns, swung as forcefully as a jazz orchestra. Playing substitute chords and doubling up on the shuffle beat, he would bend his knees and execute a tricky split, leaping across the stage as though he himself were plugged in. On record, T-Bone faltered only when forced to record teen bait such as "Bobby Sox Baby" in the early 1950s. He would hold himself back, as though fearful of sounding like a middle-aged lech. But even these boasted sinuous guitar lines that show up reconfigured in the solos in every important blues and rock electric guitarist, including B. B. King, Jimi Hendrix, and Stevie Ray Vaughan.

SOME Southern California blues, epitomized by Jimmy Liggins's "Cadillac Boogie" and his brother Joe's "The Honeydripper," was virtually indistinguishable from R&B. In Percy Mayfield, Charles Brown, and Ivory Joe Hunter, Los Angeles also had its share of poets, crooners, and dreamers, most of them painists as well as singers, and all of them influenced to some degree by Nat "King" Cole—not a bluesman by any stretch of the imagination, but a performer who epitomized masculine *smooth*, and whose ascendancy from jazz to pop was seen by blacks as an advance for the entire race. In the lingo of that day, Nat was "clean": this was a large part of his appeal to men and women who dirtied their hands on jobs all day, and to the performers who serenaded them in squalid dives at night, both groups lulled by wartime and postwar posterity into thinking that it wouldn't always be so.

CHAPTER 6

L E A D B E L L Y ' S   B L A C K   B O D Y

the last chapter began in Chicago, with Tampa Red and Georgia Tom. Before returning there for an extended stay, let's recap. If you buy the theory of blues evolution that goes straight from the Delta to Chicago—from Charley Patton to Muddy Waters with Robert Johnson as the only stop along the way—the 1930s and 1940s were just passing scenery, the nebulous time "between." In reality, these may have been the most productive decades of all for the blues, those in which the music began to take on a distinctly urban identity. Against a backdrop of war and economic calamity the blues began to develop its own standards of professionalism and instrumental virtuosity, becoming less a form of folk expression and more a style of popular music. Jazz and the blues continually renewed their familial ties; most vividly, perhaps, in Illinois Jacquet's honking tenor saxophone solo on the Lionel Hampton Orchestra's original recording of "Flying Home," a tune credited to Hampton but said to be based on one of Charlie Christian's endless supply of riffs. Rhythm 'n' blues, first hinted at in the recordings of Louis Jordan, Tiny Grimes, Tiny Bradshaw, and a handful of rogue jazzmen, emerged full blown in the late 1940s, assisted by the jukebox, the growing popularity of radio, a 1940 music-publishing war between the entrenched American Society of Composers, Authors, and Publishers (ASCAP) and the upstart Broadcast Music Industries, a proliferation of small labels after the war, and several other factors that broke the stranglehold of Tin Pan Alley and a handful of major record companies.

Most of the performers discussed in the last chapter found immediate success with black audiences. This doesn't reflect an ideological bias on my part in favor of such performers. It's just that those blues records that found the largest audiences in the thirties and forties tend to hold up as the finest of their period some fifty or sixty years later—not always the case, regardless of the race of the audience in question.

An obvious exception to this rule was Robert Johnson, whose records initially failed to find their way into many homes, black or white. Another exception is a man whose booming voice and potent, if elementary, twelve-string guitar style were synonymous with the blues for most Americans, but who had no black following to speak of. Before Hudie Ledbetter—the larger-than-life performer known as "Leadbelly"—no black folk or blues performer had ever won a sizable white audience without first appealing to his own race. At risk of doing a grave injustice to the man who kept the songster tradition alive into the 1940s and whose repertoire—songs from before the turn of the century that might otherwise have been forgotten, including "Cotton Fields," "Rock Island Line," "The Midnight Special," and "Goodnight Irene"—laid the cornerstone of the folk revival of the early 1960s, Leadbelly's unprecedented appeal to white intellectuals may have been the most significant thing about him. If ever a performer truly was a legend in his own time, it was Leadbelly—so much so that he's almost a mythical character to us today, practically indistinguishable from John Henry, the muscular steel-driving man he sang about in "Take This Hammer."

Everybody knows the story of how Leadbelly sang his way to freedom,

Leadbelly
(RAY AVERY'S JAZZ ARCHIVES)

even if the specifics are sometimes vague. He was born near Shiloh, Louisiana, in 1888, the only surviving child of sharecropper parents who tended the land for a wealthy black man and saved enough money to buy a small spread of their own in Lake Caddo, near the Texas border, in 1900. By the age of sixteen, Ledbetter was playing piano in Shreveport brothels. He spent a good deal of time in Dallas as a young man, occasionally serving as "lead man" for Blind Lemon Jefferson, much as T-Bone Walker would do a decade or so later.

But Leadbelly (at what point he acquired the nickname is unclear) seems to have put as much effort into becoming a felon as he did into becoming a folk singer, though felony probably came naturally to someone with his explosive temper. Doted on by his parents as a young man, he had a habit of using a pistol given to him for his sixteenth birthday to settle arguments. His first brush with the law was in 1903, when he pistol-whipped another youth in an argument over a girl, firing several shots at him for good measure. Because the local sheriff knew and respected the elder Ledbetter, Hudie got off with a $25 fine.

In 1917, while going under the alias Walter Boyd, and having acquired an ear-to-ear scar somewhere along the way, Leadbelly got into serious trouble with the law, fatally shooting a rival for a woman with whom they had both been keeping company. He was sentenced to thirty years of hard labor in a Texas prison farm, with another six years added on in punishment for an unsuccessful escape attempt. Making good use of his musical ability, he avoided work detail by entertaining the prison's guards and his fellow prisoners. He won a pardon by unusual means in 1925, addressing a musical plea for freedom to Pat Neff, then governor of Texas. Maybe Neff was flattered to hear his name mentioned in a song. In any event, this ought to give you some idea of what a persuasive singer Leadbelly could be.

He didn't remain a free man for very long. He was jailed again and sentenced to the notorious Angola State Prison in Louisiana, this time for assault with intent to kill; because his intended victim was white, he narrowly escaped being lynched.

Enter the folklorist John A. Lomax, a Southern-born former banker and college professor whose paternalistic manner toward the black singers he recorded on his travels through the South bothered even his son Alan, who served as his aide. The elder Lomax wasn't scouting for talent when he set up his portable recording equipment inside Angola prison in 1933. He was collecting authorless folk songs, much as he had in Texas earlier in the century, before publishing *Cowboy Songs and Other Frontier Ballads* in 1910, and *Songs of the Cattle Trail and Cow Camp* in 1917. Now representing the Library of Congress and working on a book called *American Ballads and Folksongs* (published the following year), Lomax liked to record in state prisons, reasoning that men serving long sentences and therefore unexposed to recent commercial recordings were ideal sources for older Negro songs. In Leadbelly, Lomax found more than he had bargained for. Here was a man whose repertoire of blues, lullabies, and cowboy songs extended back to the previous century. And he sang these songs with the force of a sledge-hammer hitting steel.

Still, songs were all that Lomax was after, and all that he left Angola with. Leadbelly stayed behind, having neglected to tell Lomax of his previous incarceration or about the exact circumstances that had sent him to jail this time (Lomax, a Southern gentleman, whatever his interest in Negro folksong, probably didn't know that Leadbelly was doing time for assaulting a white man). Among the songs Leadbelly recorded for Lomax was one in praise of Louisiana's governor, O. K. Allen, in which Leadbelly pleaded for his freedom. On hearing it, Allen reacted exactly as Neff had, giving Leadbelly a pardon in 1934.

Leadbelly hooked up with Lomax, whom he considered his benefactor, and this is the point at which the story enters the realm of both the mythic and the absurd, especially as told in a 1935 *March of Time* newsreel. The complete text of the dialogue is included in Charles Wolfe and Kip Lornell's admirable *The Life and Legend of Leadbelly* (1993). Here's a sample:

Lomax: I—you can't work for me. You're a mean boy. You killed two men.

Leadbelly: Please to don't talk thataway, boss.

Lomax: Have you got a pistol?

Leadbelly: No sir, I got a knife.

Lomax: Lemme see it.

[Leadbelly produces a short knife. Lomax examines it and hands it back.]

Lomax: What do you do with that thing?

Leadbelly: I'll use it on somebody if they bother you, boss. Please boss, take me with you. You'll never have to tie your stri—, shoe strings anymore if you'll let me, long as you keep me with you.

Lomax: All right, Leadbelly, I'll try you.

Leadbelly: Thank you, sir, boss, thank you. [Claps his hands.] I'll drive you all over the United States and I'll sing all songs for you. You be my big boss and I'll be your man. Thank you, sir, thank you, sir.

Perhaps the most embarrassing thing about this inane script is that it doesn't appear to have embarrassed either Lomax or Leadbelly.

Leadbelly signed on as Lomax's driver, the idea being that he could demonstrate to Southern blacks the kinds of songs that Lomax was looking for. Their relationship soon turned acrimonious, eventually winding up in court when Lomax attempted to forbid the singer from performing any of the songs included by Lomax in his *Negro Folk Songs as Sung by Leadbelly*, published in 1936. But this came later. Leadbelly made his professional debut, as it were, in December 1934, when he accompanied Lomax and his son to a convention of the Modern Language Association, an annual English department meat market headquartered that year in Philadelphia, at the Benjamin Franklin Hotel (the same establishment through whose corridors Lonnie Johnson would later push a broom). Billed only as "a Negro minstrel from Louisiana," Leadbelly performed his songs as part of an evening of "uncontaminated" music that also included a selection of Elizabethan airs performed by a female professor from Haverford College and a round of sea shanties performed by the entire learned assemblage. After his performance, Leadbelly passed his hat, and did so again the next day, following his part in a presentation on Negro folk songs by John Lomax. He earned just under $50 for his two appearances, not a bad take at the time.

We have no way of knowing what Leadbelly made of the sea shanties and madrigals, but it's easy to figure out what the professors made of him. They were probably titillated to be in the presence of a convicted murderer (the parallels to John Henry Abbot are obvious), though mollified by the belief that this particular con was a victim of a racist Southern legal system. ("BAD NIGGER MAKES GOOD MINSTREL," screamed the headline of a *Life* magazine article about Lomax's discovery.)

What interests me about all of this is that business about "uncontaminated" music. In physics, there's a principle called the "black body," defined by the most recent edition of *the Columbia Encyclopedia* as "an ideal black substance that absorbs all, and reflects none, of the radiant energy falling on it." An example of such an ideal substance is the lampblack once used by white minstrels. In *The Wages of Whiteness,* a book about racism and the emergence of the American working class, David R. Roediger speculates that the popularity of blackface entertainment in the aftermath of the Industrial Revolution results in part from exploited, preunionized white laborers projecting onto blacks "a pornography of their former selves." Roediger borrows the phrase from the leftist historian George Rawick, and uses it to mean that blacks were seen as indolent and sexually uninhibited to a degree no longer possible for white immigrants working their way up the social ladder. This projection was reflected in racist language, Roediger notes. In the eighteenth and nineteenth centuries, for example, "*buck*" variously meant a "dashing, virile young man," a "dandy," or a "self-proclaimed fascinator of women." By the early twentieth century, "buck" was applied almost exclusively to black men, usually followed by the word "nigger."

Though they never blackened up and would have been horrified at the very thought, Lomax and those white bohemian or Marxist intellectuals who formed the bulk of Leadbelly's audience in the decade and a half between his release from Angola and his death from arterial lateral sclerosis (Lou

Gehrig's disease) in 1949, projected quite a bit of their own emotional makeup onto him. He was acknowledged to be a unique performer, but also taken to be representative of an agrarian Negro population still in touch with nature, unburdened by the weight of intellectualism, and "uncontaminated" by the pox of mass culture—mankind's sentimentalized former self, a preindustrialized American Adam. In something of an obvious irony, a black man who had served prison terms for murder and attempted murder, and who would be sent to Riker's Island for a year on an assault conviction in 1939, was judged to possess an innocence all but lost to whites as a race. In that sense, Leadbelly's black body proved to be far more absorbent than lampblack.

SCHOLARLY interest in Negro song predated Lomax's discovery of Leadbelly by almost a century; it even predated recording. The earliest published transcriptions of black song—Allen, Ware, and Garrison's 1867 *Slave Songs of the United States*, for example—tended to be collections of spirituals. Secular song was virtually excluded, possibly because there were then only scattered examples of it, but more likely because spirituals confirmed the abolitionist preconception of rural blacks as a subjugated but morally upright people. (Writing in *Jazz* magazine nearly thirty years ago, John F. Szwed characterized early collectors of black song as "ministers, abolitionists, military officers, educationalists, and members of the Freedmen's Bureau.") Though Southern field trips by commercial record companies for the express purpose of recording rural singers on location didn't begin until 1927 (as a direct result of Blind Lemon Jefferson's huge sales), folklorists had been recording examples of black secular song since the beginning of the century. These two groups of men—the academic song hunters and the commercial talent scouts—eventually recorded many of the same singers, though apparently never crossing paths.

The record company representatives were unaware that they were following in the footsteps of such pioneering folklorists as Howard W. Odum, Lawrence Gellert, and Robert W. Gordon (John A. Lomax's predecessor with the Library of Congress). For their part, the folklorists were oblivious to the possibility that the portable recording equipment they took to be a godsend actually might signal the demise of the oral tradition they placed so much faith in. By the time of Lomax's visit to Angola, a supposedly authorless and uncopyrighted song learned by ear for generations might be in reality a song once featured in a vaudeville revue, or written and recorded by some long-forgotten professional entertainer.[1] The record company men and the folklor-

1. A case in point is "Irene," a waltz associated with Leadbelly, and (as "Goodnight, Irene") a number-one hit for the folk group the Weavers in 1950. Leadbelly told the Lomaxes that he had learned "Irene" from one of his uncles. But folklorists now believe the song to have

ists were looking for completely different things, the former sometimes overvaluing novelty and the latter overestimating the role of oral tradition. There are folklorists who still think it shameful that singers were coaxed by commercial record companies into singing hokum, instead of umpteen versions of "John Henry" and "Staggolee" that would tell us more about differences in musical and narrative approachs from region to region. But maybe the real shame is that Memphis Minnie was never permitted to do "That's My Desire" and "The Woody Woodpecker Song" in a commercial recording studio, and that without such songs we lack a true sense of her as a performer. In any case, blues singers of the thirties and forties—pragmatists, most of them, whose mother wit enabled them to roam free at a time when most Southern blacks were chained to the land—were hardened judges of character, willing to give whoever put a microphone in front of them whatever he asked for. For them, this was what being a musician was all about.

Leadbelly, though not a professional entertainer before his discovery by Lomax, was no exception. His failure to win much of a black following wasn't for lack of trying. The sides he recorded for release in ARC's race series in 1936 sold poorly, probably striking most of that day's black record buyers as hopelessly old-fashioned. Whites were a different story. As Wolfe and Lornell put it, "they did not want, it seemed, a down-home blues singer: they wanted a folk singer." You have to remember, though, that in the thirties and forties, this distinction wasn't so clear to audiences, especially when the performer in question was black. What researchers such as Lomax called "folk music" was a new marketplace commodity in the late 1930s, a midcult consumer rage. As it would be in the sixties (by which time it had metabolized into "folk," a peppy, coffeehouse generic without race, ethnicity, or flavor), folk music was perceived by many of its devotees to be "people's" music—which is to say, an outlet for social protest. Though said to be nearly apolitical in private life, Leadbelly met this demand for social relevance with original songs like "Bourgeois Blues" and "The Scottsboro Boys," the former pretty much self-explanatory, the latter about the nine young black vagrants falsely accused of raping two white women in Alabama in 1931. I know that this makes Leadbelly sound like an opportunist, but he was merely doing what songsters had always done—sizing up his audience and giving them whatever he figured they wanted. Aside from which, these political numbers occasioned some of Leadbelly's most expressive singing and guitar playing.

Leadbelly was hardly the first black country performer to appeal to whites,

been an early product of Tin Pan Alley, probably the work of a composer of Irish origin. If so (and the very sound of "Goodnight, Irene" is evidence of this theory), this is an example of how songs sometimes passed from pop to folk, rather than the other way around, with folk purists being none the wiser.

but he was the first to appeal *mostly* to whites, and to achieve stardom as a result of what started off as an academic endeavor. He didn't reach an already existing audience; he virtually defined a new one, in so doing paving the way for generations of "folk" singers ranging from Woody Guthrie, Pete Seeger, and the mannered pseudo-bluesman Josh White to Harry Belafonte, Joan Baez, and the young Bob Dylan (not folk singers, these last two, but singers of folk songs for the first "alternative" audience to think of itself that way).

AMONG the first performers to benefit from Leadbelly's success were the harmonica player Sonny Terry and the guitarist Walter "Brownie" McGhee,

Sonny Terry, Manchester, Michigan, 1977
(DOUG FULTON)

Brownie McGhee, Manchester, Michigan, 1977
(DOUG FULTON)

171

both Southerners (from North Carolina and Tennessee, respectively), who first teamed up in New York in the late 1930s, and who maintained a professional partnership for close to forty years despite having little use for each other offstage. Both were essentially folk musicians, latterday medicine show veterans steeped in the traditions of the Piedmont Mountains area. Each was an accomplished instrumentalist. Terry—whose real name was Saunders Terrell, and who died in 1986—was a homespun virtuoso, able to mimic with no hint of the sideshow the roar of a locomotive, the bay of a wolf, and the rustle of the wind through the trees. McGhee, who retired not long after his breakup with Terry in the late seventies, and who was the more ebullient singer of the two, was a Blind Boy Fuller disciple, handpicked as Fuller's successor by no less an authority on Fuller's music than J. B. Lang (Blind Boy's manager, you'll recall). Terry, meanwhile, had recorded with Fuller, which perhaps explains how he and McGhee wound up pooling their resources despite their personal animosity.

Brownie and Sonny lived by the songster ethic, defining their audience as anybody willing to listen to them and pay for the privilege. (A funny story: Brownie and Sonny were given roles as strolling blues singers in the original Broadway production of Tennessee Williams's *Cat on a Hot Tin Roof*. It was explained to them that since their songs served as cues to the actors, they would have to sing them the same way every night. They said they couldn't possibly do that, then quickly changed their minds when they found out how much they would be paid for sticking to the script.) For a stretch of about ten years beginning in the late 1930s, Brownie and Sonny performed mostly for whites at folk concerts, political rallies, and in a handful of Broadway revues. When the craze for folk music waned after World War ·II, they effortlessly made the transition to rhythm 'n' blues, recording almost exclusively for black-identified labels until the late 1950s. McGhee even played second guitar on his brother Sticks McGhee's ribald "Drinkin' Wine Spo-Dee-o-Dee," one of the biggest rhythm-'n'-blues hits of 1949. Then, just as R&B was moving in a new, more youth-oriented direction in the late fifties, the blues revival drew the attention of white college students to black performers of Brownie and Sonny's generation. Brownie and Sonny went on charming mostly youthful white audiences for the next decade and a half, keeping alive the blues traditions of the Carolinas in the bargain.

In bouncing from audience to audience the way they did, Terry and McGhee were far more typical than Leadbelly of country performers of the 1940s. But my candidate for the most "typical" black country performer of that decade—in terms of obscuring the difference between "country" and "urban" by paying it absolutely no mind—is Arthur "Big Boy" Crudup. At various times in his life, Crudup—a crude but powerful singer and guitarist who was born in rural Mississippi in 1905, and whose exuberant vocal style reflected the influence of both gospel and field hollers—was a farm hand,

Arthur Crudup, Ann Arbor, Michigan, 1971
(DOUG FULTON)

a bootlegger, a delivery boy, a short-order cook, and a factory worker. He was also a fairly successful recording artist, though according to his own testimony, he never earned a dollar in royalties.

One thing Crudup wasn't, however, was a professional entertainer. Though he lived in Chicago for a few years beginning in the late thirties, he apparently sang only in the recording studio and for spare change on street corners during that time. After returning home to Mississippi in 1945, he periodically traveled to Chicago just long enough to record, not to sing in South Side clubs. He died in rural Virginia in 1974.

Crudup's way of life hardly differed from that of Mississippi John Hurt or any of the stay-at-home songsters of the teens and twenties. Yet his recordings for Bluebird echoed the rush and wallop of the city in which they were recorded (they were among the first blues records to feature

173

drums), and we're likely to honor him today not as a songster but as one of the founding fathers of rock 'n' roll.

The reason for this is simple. At one of his sessions for Bluebird, in 1946, Crudup sang a number he had written called "That's All Right," its title recalling a line from Blind Lemon Jefferson's "That Black Snake Moan" of twenty years earlier, as did its rhythm. This was the song that would launch Elvis Presley's career in 1954, and the ironic twist is that Crudup himself might never have recorded it or anything else without a helping hand from Tampa Red.

The story goes that Crudup was singing on a Chicago street corner one afternoon in 1941 when Lester Melrose happened to pass by. Melrose, then in charge of blues recording for Bluebird, RCA Victor's race label, instantly recognized Crudup's potential. Just one problem: Bluebird recorded only original material, and Crudup was singing tunes he had learned from other singers. Come see me when you write some songs, Melrose told him, or words to that effect. As Chicago blues musicians tended to do at that time, Crudup went to Tampa Red for advice. Tampa nursed some new, or at least new-sounding, songs out of the skeptical Crudup, and the rest was history in the making.

September 6, 1946, the day that Crudup recorded "That's All Right," is one of the key dates in American music history. But as we shall see in the next chapter, it was far from the only major event to take place in Chicago in the ten years just after World War II.

CHAPTER 7

• •

HOME TRUTHS: MUDDY, B.B., AND THE LAST RACE LABELS

"I took the old-time music and brought it up to date."

Muddy Waters, quoted in James Rooney's *Bossmen*

In Clarksdale, Mississippi, one Friday afternoon in May 1943, a twenty-eight-year-old tractor driver on Stovall's Farms who had somehow eluded the draft caught the 4:00 P.M. train to Memphis. Carrying only his guitar (mail-ordered from Sears, Roebuck for $11) and a suitcase with one change of clothes, McKinley Morganfield—nick-named "Muddy Waters" from his childhood in Rolling Fork, Mississippi—switched trains in Memphis, boarding a northbound Illinois Central and taking it to Chicago, the end of the line. He probably paid $11.50 for his one-way ticket, more than some of the field hands he knew back home made in a week. The last few coaches of the train—those to which Morganfield and his fellow black passengers were restricted—were probably as crowded as they always were during the war, what with several hundred blacks a week departing Southern plantations and towns for Chicago. The car in which Morganfield sat may have smelled of chicken, dumplings, and biscuits from the box dinners consumed on board by some of his luckier fellow passen-

Muddy
Waters, 1969
(DOUG FULTON)

gers. These dinners were going-away presents of a sort, prepared for Northern-bound travelers by family and friends left behind in the South as a way of saying "good luck." The aroma could make you hungry if you weren't lucky enough to be carrying one yourself; after a while, the odor of so much grease in a poorly ventilated train could make you sick. Passengers without someone to pack dinner for them, and too poor to afford the fixings themselves, would buy a box of Ritz Crackers and eat them for both dinner and breakfast. Maybe this is what Morganfield did to quiet his belly during the long, all-night journey.

Right on schedule at 9:30 the following morning, seventeen and a half hours after he'd left Clarksdale (did he watch the sun come up from his window?), Morganfield's train finally pulled into the massive indoor terminal at Twelfth and Michigan in downtown Chicago. Aptly described by Nicholas Lemann as "the Ellis Island of the black migration," Illinois Central Station was a few miles southwest of the stockyards and just a stone's throw from the brick tenements of the black South Side. People used to joke that Chicago's entire black population would flock to the station on Saturday mornings in the 1940s. Some of them came to greet relatives, others to run various scams on the shabbily dressed arrivals. Some came just to gawk at them, or to lend a helping hand—these bedraggled country folks who had never seen so many people in one place at one time, and didn't know where in Chicago people of their race were allowed to go.

Keeping your soul together in the big city was no easy thing, as Morganfield had discovered during the few months he'd spent out of work in St. Louis a few years before. His luck was better in wartime Chicago. There were friends he could stay with on the South Side. Even better, within a few hours of his arrival, he landed a decent-paying job on the loading dock of a paper factory, starting the next day on the 3:00 P.M. to 11:00 P.M. split shift. Not the type of man to squander his earnings, he was soon able to rent his own South Side apartment.

S O much for McKinley Morganfield, success story and statistic: one of almost a quarter of a million black workers to migrate to Chicago during the 1940s. What about Muddy Waters, musician? He didn't fare too badly, either, almost immediately finding work as a sideman with Memphis Slim, Sunnyland Slim, Sonny Boy Williamson, and a host of other established Chicago musicians. He also made the transition to electric guitar rather effortlessly, reasoning that "couldn't nobody hear you with an acoustic" in South Side clubs that must have been as clamorous as the factories in which black clubgoers earned the dollars they parted with so freely by night. Clearing about $40 a week from his job and earning another $30 or so in the clubs, Muddy was doing all right. But it frustrated him to be making more money on the loading dock than from music. He felt that he wasn't making any progress as a musician, and he also felt that he knew why.

"To get a name, you got to get a record," Muddy told James Rooney years later. "People lived right up under me, they didn't know who I was until I got a record out."

Muddy had, in fact, already recorded. He just didn't have a record on the market. In 1941, Alan Lomax and John Work had gone to the Delta to search for Robert Johnson, unaware that Johnson had been fatally poisoned two years earlier. They wound up recording Son House for the Library of Congress on that trip, and they also recorded Muddy singing and playing with a few of his buddies on Stovall's Farms. Muddy was then still under Son House's thrall, not yet musically his own man. Even so, the earthy vigor of his singing and of his bottleneck guitar style so impressed Lomax that he recorded Muddy again on another field trip the following year. For his part, Muddy had been so tickled upon hearing his voice emanating from a spinning black object, just like Robert Johnson's or Son House's, that he decided right then and there that he had what it took to be a professional musician. The shoppers and sporting types on Fourth Street in Clarksdale must have thought so, too, to judge from the money they tossed his way when he set himself up there on the weekends. Some nights he walked home with as much as $40 in bills and loose change. He briefly took a job playing harmonica with the Silas Green minstrel troupe, but returned to Stovall's when it became apparent that the life of an unknown musician on the road wasn't necessarily easier than driving a tractor.

In Chicago, Muddy found a champion in Big Bill Broonzy, an earlier

Big Bill Broonzy
(RAY AVERY'S JAZZ ARCHIVES)

177

Mississippi émigré who by then rivaled Tampa Red as the city's blues potentate. Broonzy put in a word for him with Lester Melrose, the white independent record producer whose pipeline to RCA and Columbia had made him as powerful a figure in his own sphere during the thirties and early forties as any behind-the-scenes City Hall stringpuller. By 1946, however, when Melrose put Muddy in front of a microphone, the majors were beginning to concede what was essentially still a race market to upstart independents. Though Melrose retained a keen ear, his influence was on the wane. He sold Muddy's sides to Columbia, which decided against releasing them. Did Muddy's electric guitar strike Columbia's execs as too new-fangled for what they persisted in thinking of as a rural market? More likely, his songs struck them as too old-fashioned—too "country" compared with the music of Louis Jordan, T-Bone Walker, and other urban performers then riding the charts.

So Muddy had already recorded twice by 1947, when Sunnyland Slim recommended him to Aristocrat, a new Chicago-based label whose owners included the Chess brothers, Leonard and Phil, Jewish immigrants from Poland who owned several bars in black neighborhoods and for whom records were then strictly a sideline. According to the most colorful version of the story, they had decided to launch their own label when a scout from a Los Angeles–based company showed up in one of their clubs to audition a singer named Andrew Tibbs. What the hell, they must have thought, with an arrogance common to self-made men: we'll record him ourselves. Tibbs's first release almost put them out of business before they got started. "Bilbo's Dead" made the mistake of expressing glee over the death of Senator Theodore G. Bilbo, a Democrat accused of winning reelection in 1946 by systematically excluding blacks from voting. It was immediately banned in the South, then still the biggest market for the blues. To make matters worse, union truckers refused to deliver Aristocrat's debut release on account of the flip side, "Union Man Blues," which protested the exclusion of blacks from labor unions. In a few instances, angry truckers actually destroyed mass quantities of the record after learning of its lyric content.

Bouncing back from that debacle, the brothers recorded Muddy toward the end of the year, bringing Sunnyland Slim and the acoustic bass player Big Crawford into the studio to accompany him. Released early the following year, "Gypsy Woman" and "Little Anna May" proved to be a two-sided flop. But at least Muddy had a record in the stores, and what happened next probably exceeded his wildest expectations.

The Chess brothers didn't exactly have high hopes for "I Can't Be Satisfied," Muddy's second release for them, which featured just himself and Big Crawford's slap bass. "I can't understand what he's singing," Len Chess is supposed to have complained on first hearing a playback of Muddy's slurred, barrel-chested vocal. Company files list the song's recording date as April 1948; most versions of the story have the song being released that month after having been recorded six months earlier. Conjecture has long been that it was released only because the fledgling record company was in no position to absorb the cost of an unreleased master, especially after the Tibbs fiasco. What everybody agrees on is that early one Saturday morning in 1948 the initial pressing of "I Can't Be Satisfied" was loaded into the trunk of an Aristocrat employee's car and hand-delivered to 180 South Side outlets— five-and-dimes and beauty salons and barber shops as well as bona fide record stores.

In those days, records were sold practically everywhere black people conducted trade, and a new release went right on the turntable out of the box. Many stores had speakers over their doors or in their arcades, and you could tell right away if a record was a hit by the number of people it walked in the door. By mid-afternoon, it was virtually impossible to find a copy of Aristocrat 1305, and the Chess brothers were being bombarded with reorders they couldn't readily supply. Stores with copies still on hand began to limit sales to one to a customer, in an attempt to prevent Pullman porters from buying copies in quantity and reselling them at a markup on trains and in stations down south.

Singles generally sold for 79 cents each in those days, but by nightfall, "I Can't Be Satisfied" was going for twice as much. Muddy, who was by then driving a truck delivering venetian blinds and still didn't have a copy, paid $1.10 for one the following morning, then stalked away in anger when the shopkeeper refused to sell him another. He had to send his wife to buy him a second copy, and it was a good thing the man behind the counter didn't recognize her.

YOU'LL recall that McKinley Morganfield began to think of himself as a performer after hearing his voice played back on Alan Lomax's portable recording equipment. In the weeks following that fateful Saturday, his voice began to taunt him as he heard it booming out of every tenement window he passed. He wondered what he was doing still driving a truck.

"I Can't Be Satisfied" got to people as soon as they heard it, and it's easy to see why. Though Muddy went on to record any number of songs that became blues anthems before his death in 1984—"Rollin' Stone," "I'm Your Hoochie Coochie Man," "I Just Want to Make Love to You," and "Got My Mojo Workin'" for starters—not even he ever recorded another blues as catchy as this. The origins of "I Can't Be Satisfied" are difficult to trace. It might have been something Muddy made up himself, but more likely it was a variation on an old country tune passed along from singer to singer in Mississippi. Muddy had first recorded it (as "I Be's Troubled") for the Library of Congress in 1941, presumably in response to Alan Lomax's request for traditional material. It has no melody as such, just a punching and irresistible four-beat/three-note rhythmic pattern with the first note elongated over two beats. It sounds like something that could be played on jew's harp, and this was an instrument that Muddy played as a child. (For what it's worth, Thelonious Monk utilized the same rhythmic pattern in a composition he titled "Bright Mississippi," ostensibly based on the chord changes of "Sweet Georgia Brown.") Using both a slide and the simple but effective single-string technique he supposedly learned from a journeyman Chicago guitarist named Claude Smith (and nicknamed Blue Smitty), Muddy stabs at the notes as Crawford improvises a fast counterpoint behind him. What sells the song is Muddy's jolting bottleneck and slight vocal shake on the turnarounds, which make it seem as though first Muddy and then the song have been stung by a bee and swollen to twice their normal sizes. There's nothing else in the blues quite like it.

From the vantage point of South Side Chicago in 1948, however, "I Can't Be Satisfied" had more working in its favor than just its catchiness and Muddy's ebullience. The then-novel sound amplified bottleneck—the delightful *shock* of it—had much to do with the song's success. But a better clue to its power is provided by the title of the flip side: "I Feel Like Going Home."

Muddy sent those who bought the record home to Mississippi, if only symbolically, which was perhaps as close to a return trip as they desired. In point of fact, the first black émigré to Chicago was Jean Baptiste Point du Sable, a Haitian who set up a trading post near the mouth of the Chicago River in 1779. This was the beginning of Chicago as a city; to that point, the river had served mainly as an entryway to the Great Plains for fur traders and missionaries. Freed and runaway slaves began to settle there as early as the 1840s, and we are told by Robert Palmer that by the start of the Civil War, Chicago had "developed a reputation throughout the generally conservative Midwest as a 'nigger-loving town'" because of the role played by its black citizens in the antislavery movement. By that point, railroads had linked Chicago to the rest of the nation, and simultaneous Western expansion and the growth of American industry allowed the city to emerge as a vital shipping center, a midway point between coasts.

By 1917, when the *Chicago Defender* issued its call for a Great Northern Drive, Chicago was seen by Americans of all descriptions as an industrial metropolis in which a man could make a new start. But for Southern blacks, the city added up to infinitely more than just its stockyards and foundries. In *The Devil's Music*, Giles Oakley writes:

> For blacks in the South urbanization meant little escape from segregation and intimidation, so that for many the North began to assume almost mystical significance. The language used to refer to the North took on the same biblical fervor as it had during the campaign to abolish slavery—The Flight Out of

Egypt, The Promised Land, Canaan. One group of Mississippians heading for Chicago even held a ceremony when they crossed the Ohio River, stopping their watches, kneeling down in prayer and singing the gospel hymn "*I Done Come Out of the Land of Egypt with the Good News.*"

And in *Chicago Breakdown*, Mike Rowe points out that many Northern cities, including Detroit, the home of the automobile industry, rivaled Chicago in offering employment opportunities. "But Chicago enjoyed certain special advantages," Rowe observes.

> As the terminus of the Illinois Central Railroad it was the most easily accessible city for blacks from Tennessee, Mississippi, Louisiana and Arkansas. Moreover Chicago intruded into every southern black man's daily life as the home of the great crusading black newspaper, the *Defender*. . . . Another reason why Chicago was on everybody's lips was that it was the address of the great mail-order firms of Sears, Roebuck and Montgomery Ward, which supplied the special needs of all isolated rural communities in the United States. So it was natural that Chicago should become one of the first choices for blacks thinking of moving north.

Harlem may have been black America's cultural and economic center, but Chicago was second only to Mississippi as its heartland. As late as the 1950s, there were stretches of the South Side that resembled Mississippi, with chickens raised in backyard pens and hand-lettered signs on grocery stores advertising fresh fish. But an overcrowded city built largely of brick (in response to the 1871 fire) wasn't Clarksdale or Rolling Fork by any stretch of the imagination. Like rural Mississippi, Chicago was surrounded by water. But the only evidence of this during bitter South Side winters was the bone-chilling wind blowing in off Lake Michigan.

Divorced from the climate and way of life with which they were familiar, Chicago's transplanted Southerners counted on music such as Muddy's to deliver home truths. You can argue that amplification and the big beat Muddy added to his music just a few years later were necessary responses to the roar of the city, vehement attempts by him and his audiences to make themselves heard above the din. But you'll listen in vain for references to Chicago's stockyards and elevated trains in Muddy's songs of the forties and fifties, or in the songs of those who followed in his path. What you'll hear instead, over the slap of the drums, are shibboleths about black cat bones and mules kicking in their stalls. Even the singers' accents sound Southern, as though they and their listeners were still living there.

On Sundays in New Orleans before abolition, slaves used to gather by the hundreds to make music in Congo Square—ironically, also the site of slave auctions. In lieu of conventional instruments, they played "hollowed logs . . . wooden horns, calabashes, animal jawbones scraped with keys, and vials of buckshot attached to wrists and ankles," according to the historian Frederick Turner. Years later, the New Orleans saxophonist Sidney Bechet speculated that what the slaves played was a "remembering song," their music an attempt to "remember" a homeland many of them had never seen.

"I Can't Be Satisfied" was a remembering song, too, though the memory *it* conjured was Southern, and if African, only indirectly.

LET'S try to keep all of this in perspective. Muddy Waters's wasn't the most momentous rail journey in American history. That would be Abraham Lincoln's ride from Washington to Gettysburg, with connections at Baltimore and Hanover Junction, in 1863, a journey of six hours during which Lincoln is supposed to have drafted and carefully revised the most famous speech ever delivered by an American President. Unlike Muddy, whose modest goals were a job, a foothold in the Chicago clubs, and to be treated like a man, Lincoln was conscious that his ultimate destination was history. And despite the stir it caused in Chicago, "I Can't Be Satisfied" was what record business types call "a local rumble." The Chess brothers lacked the distribution to ride it into a national hit, though its B-side, "I Feel Like Going Home," briefly made *Billboard*'s R&B chart that fall. Muddy didn't break out of Chicago until 1951, when he had a string of top ten R&B hits, including "Long Distance Call" and "Honey Bee." By that time, Aristocrat had been renamed Chess.

Before going any further, we also need to remind ourselves that Chicago was a blues capital before Muddy's arrival. Long after he himself stopped having hits, the scene continued to revolve around Tampa Red, whose apartment over a pawnshop at Thirty-fifth and State was once described by the bassist and songwriter Willie Dixon as "a madhouse [of] old-time musicians," with Tampa's wife in the kitchen, making sure there was enough fried chicken to go around. On the night that Arthur Crudup showed up to seek Tampa's help in writing songs, Tampa supposedly introduced him to Lonnie Johnson, Memphis Slim, "St. Louis Jimmy" Odum, Big Maceo, Lil Green, Memphis Minnie, and Washboard Sam. Crudup was probably exaggerating the number of musicians lounging around Tampa Red's living room that night; still, you get the idea.

Lester Melrose was also there on the night in question, said Crudup. According to Dixon, Melrose was seemingly *always* there, scouting for talent and indulging his appetite for liquor and fried foods. One of the first record producers to think of himself as more than a facilitator or documentarian, Melrose—the architect of what was dubbed "the Bluebird beat"—played as large a role in early Chicago blues as did any of the musicians who recorded for him, though they apparently considered him little more than a middleman. In the manner of "It's Tight Like That," records produced by Melrose tended to be light and happy, with little of the soul searching one hears in the Delta blues of the 1930s. Though said to be stingy with royalties (most of his artists were under contract to him rather than to a particular label, which meant that he paid them for their sessions and then pocketed whatever revenues accrued from sales), Melrose kept his musicians flush by using them as sidemen on one another's records. Regardless of who was singing, this resulted in a certain sameness from record to record, as did an almost unvarying instrumentation of guitar, bass, piano, drums, and either harmonica or saxophone. There are blues collectors who complain that all of Melrose's Bluebirds sound alike, and thus misrepresent their performers. Another way of looking at it is that Melrose was the first record producer to perfect what we would now call a "house" sound, thereby setting a precedent for modern labels as diverse as Chess, Blue Note, ECM, and Motown. Melrose's methods guaranteed consistency. There's almost no such thing as an unsatisfying Bluebird.

In addition to those singers and musicians mentioned by Crudup, Melrose's stable at various times included Tommy Johnson, Big Bill Broonzy, Big Joe Williams, and the first singer and harmonica player to call himself Sonny Boy Williamson (John Lee Williamson, not to be confused with Rice Miller, who took the name *after* Williamson but confused matters by calling himself the "Original" Sonny Boy). These performers hardly sounded alike. To harp on a favorite theme, it's remarkable how *country* most of them sounded on Bluebird, just as it's worth noting that whenever Melrose wanted to add a "modern" touch to one of his productions, he would do so by enlisting Washboard Sam, whose percussive scraping was as old as Congo

Washboard Sam
(FRANK DRIGGS COLELCTION)

183

Square. (Washboard Sam, whose real name was Robert Brown, was also a popular recording artist in his own right, specializing in just-short-of-scurrilous lyrics which he delivered in a butter-wouldn't-melt-in-my-mouth monotone.)

The roughest—not to say the most primitive—of Melrose's artists was Big Joe Williams, whose churning nine-string guitar (the upper strings doubled, as on a twelve string) and dark-tempered vocals made him an anomaly on Bluebird. Originally from Crawford, Mississippi, Williams had wandered throughout the South and much of the Midwest before hitting Chicago in the mid-1930s. Given a second wind by the blues revival of the 1960s (and by his royalties from the many rock cover versions of "Baby, Please Don't Go," a song of his from 1935 which he'd had the smarts to copyright), Williams remained an active performer well into the 1970s (he died in 1982), always sounding like a misplaced Delta sharecropper. The angry power of his music was such that even at his most freewheeling, he sounded like somebody or something had just rubbed him the wrong way.

Sonny Boy Williamson #1, as we shall call him, was more typical of the performers recorded by Melrose. He was originally from Tennessee, and like Williams, with whom he often recorded, he had hoboed throughout the South before settling in Chicago. Williamson suffered from a speech impediment usually described as a "slow tongue," and legend has it that he was none too bright. But his laid-back singing style successfully exploited these seeming handicaps: he practically drools his way through his 1937 recording of "Good Morning, Little Schoolgirl," coming across as a horny critter maybe only pretending to be a country bumpkin. His real importance, though, was as the first urban blues harmonica star. Williamson took a novelty instrument, a remnant from the jug band days, and won a place for it in Chicago. A dazzling exponent of what's called "cross-harp" style (it involves using a harmonica tuned to the key of C to play in the key of G, and allows the player to "bend" notes more easily than would otherwise be possible), this Sonny Boy was especially well liked by other Chicago blues musicians, who took it hard when he was stabbed to death in 1948, at the age of thirty-four, an apparent robbery victim.

No doubt relying on hearsay, Lonnie Johnson told Paul Oliver almost two decades later:

> He had seventeen holes in his head with an ice pick. They ganged him. He was 'bout one of the finest fellers I know. They never did find out who killed him. . . . Sonny Boy—I'll tell you what he did. He worked to help the people with somethin' to eat and somethin' to drink. When pay-day come he didn't have anything—he had *no* pay day. He was just good—he bought everything they wanted to drink; everything they wanted to eat. He was good to the crowd around him. That's all he did, work for them. And why they would

Big Joe Williams, Ann Arbor,
Michigan, 1969
(DOUG FULTON)

John Lee Williamson (Sonny
Boy Williamson #1)
(COURTESY BLUES ARCHIVE, UNIVERSITY OF
MISSISSIPPI)

kill a great guy like that I don't know but they did. [*Conversations with the Blues*]

Seventeen holes? The number of ice-pick wounds probably increased with each retelling, as Williamson's murder became a reminder to Southern-born musicians of the potential danger awaiting them in a city in which every street corner could be a crossroads. The story, never substantiated, was that Sonny Boy's attackers were desperate and bloodthirsty newcomers from the South, shut out of jobs by men who had taken the Illinois Central ahead of them.

A S Tampa Red's influence waned, the man who replaced him as Chicago's blues paterfamilias was Big Bill Broonzy, another of Melrose's artists second only to Lonnie Johnson as an imitated guitarist and arguably Johnson's superior as a singer. Born to a family of sharecroppers in the tiny Delta town of Scott, Mississippi, in 1893 and raised just across the river in Arkansas (where he started off playing a homemade violin), Broonzy was not just one of the most supple and expressive of all male blues singers, but one of the most supple and expressive in any branch of American music. There was no kind of song he couldn't wrap his tenor around, from hypnotic Delta chants to lighthearted hokum to a delirious and knowing combination of the two (some of his recordings with horns from the 1930s pass muster as jazz, thanks as much to the elasticity of his phrasing as to the contrapuntal bickering of the brasses and reeds).

It wasn't only Big Bill's untutored but expert musicianship that won him the admiration of fellow Chicago musicians soon after arriving there in the early twenties and learning guitar from Papa Charlie Jackson, and that gradually allowed him to surpass Tampa Red in influence, even without a hit record as big as "It's Tight Like That": Broonzy was blessed with unmistakable star quality, to judge from the dapper figure he cuts in a suit and hat and tie on the cover of the latest reprint of *Big Bill Blues*, his fanciful 1955 autobiography ("as told to" Yannick Bruynoghe). The photo is from fifteen years earlier, when Broonzy was in his prime; ironically, when *Big Bill Blues* was published (it was the first blues autobiography), its subject was back in the sharecropper's overalls he'd ditched on joining the army during World War I.

The white audiences he was then performing for demanded such attire from a performer who had taken to touting himself as the last of the "genuine" blues singers. In the early pages of *Big Bill Blues*, Broonzy recalled playing his homemade fiddle at "two-way" picnics in the Delta around the turn of the century. By "two-way," Broonzy meant "white people's picnics" with two stages for the performers, blacks on one makeshift stage and whites on another. But I misunderstood him the first time I read the passage in question, and apparently so did Charles Edward Smith, who, in his introductory essay, describes "two-way" picnics as "picnics that were segregated but shared the same music, from the same rude platform." I prefer Smith's and my misinterpretation, even though this sort of two-way picnic may have no basis in fact. Imagine it: a small town's white population gathered on one side of the platform, and its blacks gathered on the other, dancing to the same music but otherwise keeping their distance. There you have the story of black American music. It's been a two-way picnic from the beginning, the only question being in which direction the black performers have been facing at any given moment.

At some point in the 1940s, following the success of Leadbelly and with his own music having fallen out of favor with black audiences, Big Bill Broonzy unplugged his amplified guitar, bought himself a pair of overalls, and simply *turned around*, as it were. Until his death in 1958, he would sing almost exclusively for white audiences, who heard in his music the same simplicity and nobility they thought they'd heard in Leadbelly's. You might say that Big Bill once again became what he had started off as—a folk musician, albeit with an element of self-consciousness unheard of back in the Delta, where performers and their audiences shared more in common than just their taste in music. But a better way of putting it might be to say that Broonzy was a musician doing what musicians have always done—singing and playing for whichever audiences would have him. For a few years, he even worked as a janitor at Iowa State University, after playing a concert there in 1950. Big Bill liked to feel appreciated. He liked campus life. He liked being able to say he had been to college.

"**WHEN** fame came to Big Bill, there in Chicago in the 1950's, it was a lopsided fame," Smith wrote in his introduction to *Big Bill Blues*.

> To those who had ears for country blues, he was incomparable—the others kept on drinking and talking. Though rhythm and blues singers of genuine blues calibre, such as Muddy Waters, respected him, the young and knowing (and rock and rolling) called him "down home" and the words were like shutters on the sound. There were others, many of them the middle-aged or the aging—like Bill, from the South—who breathed a sigh when the term "down home" changed from one of derision to one of warmth and belonging, almost at the flip of a coin. Those who didn't see the glint of the coin—some of them would, later—walked out on Bill—and of course he'd [have] known it, even without the chair-scraping.

Overlook Smith's hedged denigration of Muddy Waters as a "rhythm and blues singer," and of his audience as rock 'n' rollers. This is an insightful passage for what it tells us about the ambivalence of urban blacks· toward the South in the 1950s, and even more so for what it tells us about the changing dynamics of the Chicago blues scene during that time.

There was no legendary blues "contest" at Sylvio's or Theresa's or some other South Side bar in which Muddy bested Tampa Red and Big Bill and became Number One. The transfer of power was gradual, and it had more to do with the changing mood of black audiences than with the relative merits of the performers. Big Bill was one of the few blues singers of his generation to tackle social issues. "I worked on a levee camp and a chain gang, too," he sang in one of his songs, the point of which was that "a black man is a boy to a white, don't care what he can do." The song was called "When Will I Get to Be Called a Man?" Muddy Waters, every bit as much a child of the Delta in his vocal inflections and cultural references, though a full generation younger—"a man, way past twenty-one," not to mention "a son of a gun"—didn't waste any time wondering or waiting; nor was his audience in any mood to. Bo Diddley, more of a rock 'n' roller but a labelmate of Muddy's and an heir to his beat, would later spell it out, lest anyone miss the point: "I spell M . . . A . . . N."

Muddy so dominated Chicago blues in the wake of hits such as "Rolling Stone" and "Hoochie Coochie Man" that we tend to categorize other Chicago bluesmen as Muddy's forebears, Muddy's rivals, Muddy's progeny, and those from his own generation whom he completely overshadowed.

Included in this final category would be Elmore James, Johnny Shines, and Robert Lockwood, Jr., all of whom were raised in the Delta and directly influenced by Robert Johnson. James, it's said, was the man who introduced electric guitar to the Delta in 1945, though he's more remembered for his many recorded versions of Johnson's "I Believe I'll Dust My Broom" (shortened by James to "Dust My Broom"). Arguably Muddy's superior on slide, James turned up the volume on the Delta blues and the energy level along with it. His guitar style was assaultive and just short of shrill, pitched for the most part in a falsetto range he also seemed to be striving to reach with his voice (no wonder he's been a favorite of so many rock guitarists, including Stevie Ray Vaughan). For all of that, he turned in some of his most indelible recorded performances on slow, mournful numbers such as "The Sky Is Crying" and his version of Tampa Red's "It Hurts Me Too."

In addition to being overshadowed by Muddy Waters, Shines and Lockwood suffered as a result of being regarded as surrogates for Robert Johnson rather than as master musicians in their own right. Both knew Johnson personally: Shines hopped boxcars with him in the 1930s, and Lockwood was the son of one of his common-law wives. An explanation for Shines's lifelong failure to excite the imagination of blues record buyers might be his subtlety. He was something of an intellectual, not just one of the most widely traveled musicians of his generation, but perhaps the most widely read

(discouraged by his inability to reach a large audience, he became a blues photographer for a brief period in the early 1960s). Shines's verses tended to be both earthy and feverishly imaginative, and until a 1980 stroke robbed him of much of his dexterity, few combined slide and picking techniques with such quiet aplomb.

Lockwood, who was born in Arkansas in 1915 about three weeks before Muddy Waters, is still alive and quite active on the blues circuit, his career having been given a boost by the platinum success of Johnson's *The Complete Recordings* and by a 1992 reissue of his own reinterpretations of his stepfather's songs. As with Shines, an excess of subtlety has also proved to Lockwood's commercial disadvantage, though his reticence as a singer may have something to do with it. He has few equals as a guitarist, his trademark being his savvy use of jazz chord substitutions within a bare-boned blues framework. He strikes a listener as someone who would be just as happy to be a nonsinging sideman, the capacity in which he served on innumerable recording dates in the 1950s. In that sense, his counterpart among guitarists from the generation after his was the late Earl Hooker, an ill-at-ease singer whose skill with a wah-wah pedal and understanding of both black and white country idioms enabled him to make his guitar practically talk.

Meanwhile, Shines's equivalent among living guitarists and singers would be Jimmy Dawkins, a blistering stylist for whom ecstatic reviews have never translated into sales. There have been any number of Chicago bluesmen whose relative lack of commercial success has been inexplicable, among them the two J.B.'s, Lenoir and Hutto, the former a topical songwriter ("Korea Blues," "Eisenhower Blues") and leader of a semijump band in the 1950s, the latter the purveyor of a rough-hewn blend of soul and barroom blues in the late 1960s. My own choice for the most unjustly neglected Chicago bluesman is Robert Nighthawk, a.k.a. Robert Lee McCoy (or McCullum), a guitarist from Arkansas who wound up influencing both Elmore James and Earl Hooker though he himself started off as a harmonica player and supposedly didn't master the intricacies of slide until coming under Tampa Red's tutelage in Chicago in the 1940s. Nighthawk's signature number was his 1949 Chess recording of "Black Angel Blues," a song of Tampa Red's which B. B. King later covered as "Sweet Black Angel." Nighthawk's version confirms that he had it all, including unforced sensuality as a singer, a ringing tone on guitar, and a sense of timing to rival that of anyone in jazz, much less the blues. Yet a few years before his death in 1967, at the age of fifty-five, when he should have been giving Muddy Waters and B. B. King a run for their money, Nighthawk was still playing with a band for loose change in the open-air market on Chicago's Maxwell Street—traditionally the place where new arrivals to that city plied their trade until gaining a foothold in the clubs.

How could this have been? One answer might be that Nighthawk seems to have been a drifter by nature. He was forever returning to the Delta, and was never in Chicago long enough to establish his presence there. Another answer might be that something as elusive and as difficult to define as star quality became crucial as the blues continued to evolve as an urban form and took on the trappings of a pop subgenre. Nighthawk simply lacked the star quality that Muddy Waters and the most formidable of his rivals, Howlin' Wolf and Sonny Boy Williamson #2, possessed in spades.

HOWLIN' Wolf, a growling hulk of a man from West Point, Mississippi, by way of Memphis, literally saw Muddy as a rival, even though Muddy had helped to get him off on the right foot in Chicago on his arrival there in 1953. Alex Rice Miller, the second Sonny Boy Williamson, also passed through Memphis before migrating north.

Both recorded for Chess, and Williamson's releases often outsold Muddy's, though in the long run they proved to be not nearly as influential. Actually older than the first Sonny Boy, *this* one was born to sharecroppers in Glendora, Mississippi, in 1910 or long before—his exact birthdate has never been ascertained, and Sonny Boy #2 (he would hate being called that) considered it nobody else's business. Suffice it to say he was already middle-aged when he cut his first sides, for the Trumpet label in 1951. A decade earlier, he had become something of a Delta radio star, hosting and performing on "The King Biscuit Hour," a show sponsored by the Interstate Grocery Company and broadcast daily over KFAA in Helena, Arkansas, for three years beginning in 1941. Sonny Boy wasn't paid much, but the job gave him an opportunity to plug his upcoming live appearances. The show was so popular that he toured groceries to tout the virtues of King Biscuit flour. The company briefly even manufactured a brand of cornmeal with Sonny Boy's picture on the sack.

From what people have had to say about him over the years, Sonny Boy #2 hardly resembled his namesake temperamentally. He has variously been described as "tough," "mean," "embittered," a hothead, a loner, and an opportunist (his taking the name he did and occasionally telling interviewers that Charley Patton had died in his arms is proof enough of the last). But no one ever disputed his droll wit or drive as a singer and harp player. A big, prematurely elderly, flatfooted-looking man, he moved surprisingly gracefully on stage, to judge from film clips. His sound on harmonica was piercing, and he had few rivals at cupping and fluttering his hands over the instrument to alter its tone and control the flow of its sound. In Alan and Susan Raymond's *Sweet Home Chicago* (one of the films in the PBS series, *The History of the Blues*) there's footage of Williamson jamming his harmonica in his mouth and practically swallowing it while continuing to play it—riffing on the beat simply by breathing in and out. His sidemen in this footage are white, and he himself is dressed in a derby and a modified

Howlin' Wolf, 1970
(DOUG FULTON)

Carnaby Street pinstripe—a reminder that Sonny Boy, who died back in Helena in 1965, spent the few years before that in England and on the Continent, playing for adoring fans who cared not one whit whether he was really the "original" Sonny Boy.

HOWLIN' Wolf was also a flamboyant performer, to say the least, given to simulating sexual ecstasy or epileptic seizure (difficult to know which it was supposed to be) by writhing on stage floors and treating his audiences to the spectacle of a three hundred–pound man skipping lightly while shaking his ass to the beat. It was only fitting that when the Rolling Stones made their American television debut on *Shindig* in 1964, they stipulated the Wolf also be featured on the broadcast. A claim could be made for him as the first rock 'n' roller, if only in terms of sensibility. He once confessed that he played both guitar and harmonica in public back home in Mississippi before he even *knew* how to play either; the music moved him, he wanted in on it, and he figured he could learn as he needed to know as he went along. *Desire* was what counted. As a young man in West Point, Mississippi (where he was born in 1910), he heard Charley Patton and tried his best to copy Patton's guitar licks, cement-mixer vocal style, and physical contortions (Wolf also named Tommy Johnson and the white yodeler Jimmie Rodgers as influences). Later on, he called on Rice Miller, who was then his brother-in-law, to teach him harmonica. As Miller had, Wolf took the nickname of another performer, in this case J. T. "Funny Papa" Smith, a Texas songster of the late 1920s who had recorded the two-part "Howlin' Wolf Blues."

But Wolf was a far more animalistic singer than the "original" Howlin' Wolf, and was ultimately to become much better known. Like his brother-in-law, Wolf was a late starter in terms of recording. Still a farmer when he decided to try his luck as a professional musician in Memphis after serving in the army during the war, he might have returned to his farm had fate not intervened in the shape of Sam Phillips and the brothers Chess. Phillips is, of course, famous as the man whose Memphis-based Sun label subverted Eisenhower-era America with Elvis Presley, Johnny Cash, Roy Orbison, Carl Perkins, and Jerry Lee Lewis. But Sun didn't yet exist in 1951, when Phillips recorded Wolf doing a song called "Moanin' at Midnight" ("Baying" would have been better) and leased it to Chess. The song was a hit, and though several other of Wolf's early recordings for Phillips or Ike Turner were leased to RPM—a subsidiary of Modern, a West Coast label whose big seller was B. B. King (on yet another subsidiary, Crown)—"Moanin' at Midnight" initiated what would be a quarter of a century association between Wolf and Chess, lasting until Wolf's death in 1976. Wolf moved to Chicago in 1953 in order to be closer to Chess, which by that time had him under exclusive contract. Muddy Waters helped him to land his first Chicago bookings, but Wolf soon realized that Muddy was the man he would have to topple if he was ever going to rule the South Side. Wolf found himself in direct competition with Muddy for the songs of Willie Dixon, a session bassist and prolific composer who, if anything, favored Wolf, giving him a "Spoonful," a "Little Red Rooster," and a "Back Door Man" for every "Hoochie Coochie Man" he gave Muddy. Dixon, who supervised some of Wolf's Chess sessions, used to say that in order to convince Wolf to have a go at a new song he had written for him, he would sometimes have to lie and tell Wolf that Muddy had expressed interest in it.

Wolf never amounted to much as an instrumentalist. Once settled in Chicago, he wisely assigned most of the guitar work to the fiery Hubert Sumlin, and then to a variety of guitarists after he and Sumlin had a falling out and Sumlin joined Muddy Waters's band in retaliation. Although only a functional harmonica player, the sight of such a big man squeezing not just his breath but seemingly his entire being into so small an outlet no doubt tickled live audiences, and something of the same wonderment comes across on his records.

It was with his voice that Wolf made his deepest mark. He was less a singer in the conventional sense than an indomitable force of nature. He didn't so much sing as cackle with malevolent glee, and as gargantuan as he was (he wore a size-sixteen shoe, to give you some idea), on listening to him on record you think of him as somehow even bigger—Godzilla about to stomp Tokyo, because it was in his nature and because it would be fun. He never unseated Muddy, but he was undisputed ruler of his own primitive swamp.

THE second Sonny Boy Williamson was Muddy Water's equal as an instrumentalist, and Howlin' Wolf was more than a match for him as a singer and showman. But neither could hold a candle to Muddy as a bandleader, perhaps because only Muddy had a sense of the blues band as a unified *ensemble*, not just a headliner and his backup. Part of this was temperament; unlike Wolf and Sonny Boy, he didn't mind sharing the spotlight (no less a luminary in the making than B. B. King was briefly in one of Sonny Boy's bands in Memphis, but so long as Sonny Boy was on the bandstand, there could be only one star), and he had a knack for getting a unified sound from a disparate crew of sidemen. Everyone has his or her own favorite Muddy Waters record of the 1950s; mine is a song called "I'm Ready" from September 1954, only a middling hit for him but (if you listen to his early releases chronologically) the number on which I think everything fell into place for him as a bandleader—even more so than "I Just Want to Make Love to You," recorded by the same personnel five months earlier. This was his first great unit, with Little Walter (Jacobs) on piano, Otis Spann on piano, Jimmy

Rogers on second guitar, and Fred Below on drums, with the song's composer, Willie Dixon, added on bass. Today, we're likely to think of this lineup as an all-star outfit. But except for Dixon, they were just members of Muddy's working group back then.

On his own, Rogers has proved to be one of the most durable of blues performers, still maintaining a hectic touring and recording schedule as this is written—the last surviving link to the greatest of all blues bands.

Spann, a former semipro boxer and football player who was then in his early twenties and on his way to becoming Chess's unofficial house pianist, stayed with Muddy the longest, until just a few years before his death from cancer in 1970. An ideal accompanist, with an attack as fierce or spare as a song called for, Spann was also a major performer in his own right—an intimate, smoky-voiced singer who could give *you* the blues in the process of explaining why *he* had them. Despite this, he was an extremely reluctant singer, content for the most part to face away from the audience on his piano bench. Sessions under his own name inevitably gave the impression of having occurred as if by accident, as though Spann had somehow been *talked* into singing.

Dixon started his career in the Big Three Trio, an overly slick Chicago lounge act modeled on Nat Cole's group. He, too, would go on to record under his own name, though he made his most valuable contributions out of public earshot, as a songwriter, record producer, and behind-the-scenes stringpuller. To some, Dixon was nothing more than a Lester Melrose of color. It used to be said that he could get you a date with Chess or one of the smaller labels he also worked for if you were willing to give him a "taste"—that is, willing to kick back some of your session fee. Rumor has long had it that he purchased or stole many of the songs he copyrighted. Yeah, yeah. But if he wrote only half of the numbers credited to him, that's more than enough great songs for any one man. In addition to those already

Otis Spann
(RAY AVERY'S JAZZ
ARCHIVES)

Willie Dixon, Ann
Arbor Blues and Jazz
Festival
(DOUG FULTON)

mentioned, his hits included Little Walter's "My Babe," Koko Taylor's "Wang Dang Doodle," and Sonny Boy Williamson's "Bring It on Home." He helped to reshape the blues into a style of pop, combining a Delta bluesman's flair for plain but expressive language with a pop songwriter's sense of what made for a great hook.

Little Walter was the first of Muddy's sidemen to emerge as a star, even outshining Muddy for a few years after the success of "Juke" in 1952—an instrumental with which Muddy's band ended its club sets. As a harmonica virtuoso, Walter represented the next step after the first Sonny Boy Williamson. He made the mouth organ a lead instrument, giving it the same cutting prominence in the blues that the saxophone enjoyed in jazz. He utilized amplification to unprecedented advantage, cupping both his harmonica and the microphone in his hands as though playing both—which in a sense he was. Despite also being a good-enough singer, he never rose to Muddy's stature as a bandleader. The exact opposite of his former boss in temperament, Walter was too distrustful and hotheaded to command the loyalty of his men. He died brutally and ignobly in 1968, suffering a heart attack after being beaten over the head with a lead pipe in a back-street brawl. The up-close, black-and-white photo of him on the cover of *Hate to See You Go*, a compilation of his early recordings released shortly after his death, suggests that he was no stranger to violence—there's what looks like a deep knife scar crisscrossed by stitches above his eyebrows and a don't-you-*fuck*-with-

195

me-*motherfucker* glint in his eye falsifying the smile on his lips. He was only thirty-seven when he died, but in this photo, he looks (as my grandmother used to say) as old as sin.

FROM Muddy's first real band, that leaves only Fred Below, a former jazz musician who went on to supply cross-rhythms on several of Chuck Berry's biggest hits, including "Roll Over Beethoven" and "Sweet Little Sixteen," but who never became a star because blues drummers simply don't become stars. Yet it's Below who makes the difference on "I'm Ready." From the down beat, the song is so rhythmically contagious that you can hear it hundreds of times before realizing that only Spann, Rogers, and Dixon are phrasing on the beat. Midway through "I'm Ready," Little Walter takes a solo that sounds like one long leer and provides the perfect instrumental complement to Muddy's croak of unshackled masculinity. Even so, what *rocks* the song—what links it to Berry and the British invasion—is Below's proto-backbeat: those jazzlike fills and bass drum syncopations which are somehow both heavy and light, and in marked contrast to the emphatic but metronomic timekeeping on Muddy's first few records with drummers.

Muddy once described himself as a "delay" singer, and in talking of his role in updating the Delta blues, never spoke of putting a beat *to* the music he grew up with, but of putting a beat *behind* it. Even the echo and reverb you hear on his early records was based on a principle of delay, the result of Leonard Chess running a sewer pipe between an amplifier and a recording mike, so that part of the sound arrived on the tape a fraction of a second late. The "tempo" on "I'm Ready" is stoptime from beginning to end, with Muddy's voice and Below's drums trailing the beat and emphasizing it in a way that would be impossible if they landed solidly atop it. Despite the rural echoes, this is unequivocally a city blues. Thanks to Muddy, it had that gravel that the Beatles and the Rolling Stones later wanted in their own music, and in their own lives. Thanks to Below, it also had that *thump*.

MUDDY'S band became a sort of blues graduate school in much the same way that Art Blakey's Jazz Messengers and the Miles Davis Quintet were in jazz during the same era. In addition to Below, Rogers, Spann, and Little Walter, Muddy numbered among his musical "children" the pianist Pinetop Perkins; the drummers Elgin Evans and Francis Clay; the guitarists Earl Hooker, Pat Hare, and Luther Tucker; and an illustrious succession of harmonica players, including Big Walter Horton, Carey Bell, James Cotton, and Junior Wells. Many of these former Waters sidemen are still making the rounds of festivals, point men in the current blues revival.

Just as the Chicago blues scene had revolved around Tampa Red in the

Buddy Guy, Ann
Arbor, Michigan,
1971
(DOUG FULTON)

1930s and Big Bill Broonzy in the 1940s, it revolved around Muddy in the 1950s. And his leadership extended to more than just music. Muddy was the sort of man those from another culture would call a mensch. At one point, he even served as the under-age and delinquent Junior Wells's Juvenile Court–appointed guardian. The following is from a 1992 interview with Wells in Lois Ulray's magazine *Magic Blues*:

> I started walkin' and Muddy said, "Where are you goin'?" I said, "I'm gettin' on the bus." He said, "No, I just put my name on that thing in there. It says I'm responsible for you. So you get in the car. I'm takin' you home." I said, "I don't want to ride." I went to walk away. And he pulled me. When he pulled me, I snatched away from him. When I snatched away[,] he say boom, and knocked me down. He always carried a little old [.]25 automatic, like I do. He said, "You know what? I'll kill you. You ain't no good to your own self, your Mama, me or nobody else the way you're actin'." He said, "Now, get in the car." And I did.

Buddy Guy, another of Muddy's progeny though he never actually played in his band, often tells the story of arriving in Chicago from his native

Louisiana in 1957, broke and hungry after having spent all of his savings on bus fare. He immediately made the rounds of the South Side clubs, finally persuading one clubowner to let him play. It didn't take long for Muddy's phone to ring with the news that there was a new guitar player in town he really ought to hear. That's the way it worked in Chicago in those days: no matter how good a newcomer was, nobody was quite willing to *say* he was good until Muddy handed down his verdict. Muddy jumped in his car and hightailed it to the club. Because he liked what he heard, Guy was soon doing session work for Chess. But this is the part of the story I like best: figuring that someone just in from the South might be hungry, Muddy brought salami and bread to the club.

Guy was one of a trio of Chicago guitarists and singers—the others were Otis Rush and Magic Sam (Maghett)—whose emergence toward the tail end of the 1950s can be seen in retrospect as a harbinger of change. Though Guy and Rush each recorded a few sides under his own name for Chess, they and Magic Sam eventually wound up under contract to Cobra or Artistic, a pair of influential if short-lived West Side labels owned by a record store proprietor and compulsive gambler named Eli Toscano, who was smart enough to lure Willie Dixon away from Chess and appoint him music director.

All three of Toscano's star acts were former small-town Southerners born within a few years of one another in the mid-thirties. This made them members of the next full generation after Muddy's; a generation not in position to reap the benefits of postwar affluence on their arrival in Chicago. Their music aside, they were typical of those Southern blacks who migrated to the Windy City in the 1950s and settled on the West Side, where living conditions were even bleaker than on the city's overcrowded southern edge.

Guy, of course, has subsequently become the most famous of these three performers, teaming up with Junior Wells on the Fillmore circuit in the sixties and seventies and helping to anchor the current blues revival with his albums *Damn Right, I've Got the Blues* and *Feels Like Rain* (both of which relied on guest shots by rock luminaries to ingratiate Guy to white audiences). But Rush—the most smoldering singer of the three, and arguably the most inventive guitarist—was the first to land a song on the R&B charts, with his driven version of Dixon's "I Can't Quit You, Baby" in 1956. And Magic Sam, the closest thing sixties blues had to Jimi Hendrix for sheer excitement, was poised to cross into rock when he suffered a fatal heart attack in 1969.

All three of these performers, but Guy especially, had in common a gospel influence that revealed itself in melismatic vocal flights of the sort that we today associate with soul. This in itself would have been enough to set them apart from the Chicago bluesmen of Muddy's generation; vocally, theirs was a younger sound. But the other thing that united them and marked them as different from their elders was the urgency and flamboyance of their

Magic Sam, 1969
(DOUG FULTON)

guitar playing—more urgent and flamboyant even than Elmore James's. Their solos also tended to be lengthier than any heard in Chicago before, with their guitars slipping in and out of the responsorial role traditionally assigned to the instrument in Charley Patton's music or Muddy's—testimony, along with the gospel inflections, to the growing popularity and influence of a Delta-born singer and guitarist who set foot in Chicago only once or twice a year, and then only long enough to perform sets at Robert's Show Lounge or the Trianon Ballroom.

HIS name was Riley B. King, though while playing guitar and spinning records and singing the virtues of a 12 percent alcohol elixir called Pepticon on an electronic medicine show of a radio program on Memphis's WDIA in 1949 ("Pepticon sure is good/You can get it in your neighborhood"), he had started calling himself the "Beale Street Blues Boy," or "B.B." for short, and the diminutive had stuck. His regal surname wasn't his own doing, though it's turned out to be pretty apt.

B. B. King was born in Mississippi, on a plantation between Itta Bena and Indianola, in 1925, and began to make his mark in music on Beale Street

B. B. King,
1983
(RAY AVERY'S JAZZ
ARCHIVES)

in Memphis in the late 1940s. Since becoming a full-fledged star in the late 1960s, he has lived in Las Vegas, of all places. But neither he nor his music has ever *belonged* to any of those towns or cities in the same way that Mississippi John Hurt and his music belonged to Avalon, or that Muddy Waters and his belonged to Chicago. King has essentially been on the road for close to fifty years, ever since hitchhiking to Memphis to try his luck there in 1946 ("Before I was a superstar in the blues, I was a superstar on the plantation, because after years of picking cotton and pulling a plow, I was driving a tractor," King explained only half-jokingly to Terry Gross of National Public Radio, during a 1993 television interview). Strictly in terms of his on-the-go nature, King's route in life has been similar to Blind Lemon Jefferson's, Robert Johnson's, or that of any boxcar-riding nomad of the 1930s. But there's one crucial difference: that aforementioned ride to Memphis was probably the last that B. B. King ever had to thumb. Playing as many as three hundred one-nighters a year since the early 1950s, he's always known exactly where he was headed, and any vehicle with him on board is automatically first class. "The things people used to say about those I thought of as the greats in the business, the blues singers, used to hurt me," King told Stanley Dance in 1966. "They spoke of them all as illiterate and dirty. The blues had made me a better living than any I had, so this was when I really put my fight on. A few whites gave me the blah-blah about blues singers, but mostly it was Negro people, and that's why it hurt."

A star in the black community for two decades before his string-decorated 1970 pop hit "The Thrill Is Gone" won him a mass following among whites,

King sees himself as an ambassador for the blues; and no one has ever been better qualified for the job, whether in terms of musicianship (if not the only blues guitarist to teach himself the Schillinger harmonic system, he must certainly have been the first) or professional deportment (despite fathering eight children out of wedlock by as many different mothers).

KING'S first record to chart R&B was his 1951 cover of Lowell Fulson's "Three O'Clock Blues," and that era's black record buyers probably were as enchanted by King's impassioned voice as by his prowess on guitar. In listening to King's Crown releases of the 1950s, it's a little startling to hear the punch of his falsetto and realize what an extraordinary vocal range he once had. As an older man, he still knows how to put across a song, even though his vocal compass is more narrow. The problem he faces is that everything we know about him (and everything we sense about him) suggests that he's far too sensible—far too big a man—to put much stock in the woman-baiting lyrics of most of the songs he chooses to sing (they're the musical equivalent of "One of these days, Alice . . . straight to the moon!). In recent years, his most satisfying albums have been those which encouraged him to stretch beyond a finite definition of the blues: an album mostly of tunes by the pop songwriter Doc Pomus (including the poignant "There Must Be a Better World Somewhere"), another mostly of standards with a jazz big band, even an album of duets with the ersatz jazz diva Diane Schuur. On all of these, his voice has sounded positively baronial, fully worthy of him as an individual.

But the condition of King's voice and his investment or lack of same in the lyrics he sings is almost beside the point, because in live performance his guitar has always received top billing, and this second "voice" has gained in eloquence over the years. In the interview with Gross, King told her that as a kid he used to listen to a country music station and was fascinated by the way that the guitarists would bend notes by seeming to bend their strings. It must have sounded to him as though the guitar was speaking. Hawaiian guitarists achieved the same effect, and so did King's older cousin, Bukka White, when he used a slide. B. B. either never mastered slide, or it never occurred to him to try. But where there's a will, there's a way has been the story of black American music from the days of washboards and animal bones to rap. "By trilling my hand, my ear would tell me it sounded similar to it."

In addition to Blind Lemon Jefferson and Lonnie Johnson, his early role models included Django Reinhardt and Charlie Christian, jazz guitarists who seemed to him to have "that certain something that Johnny Hodges had on the saxophone, or Bobby Hackett on trumpet. They seemed to sing."

The hornlike lilt of B. B. King's guitar lines is no coincidence, in other words. As an experiment, pop the Duke Ellington Orchestra's 1956 Newport Jazz Festival recording of "Jeep's Blues" into your CD player and listen to Johnny Hodges's alto gliss with emphatic vibrato. Now imagine an electric guitar playing the same thing, and you've got B. B. King. He showed that in order for a guitar to sing like a horn, it had to breathe like one (though the lesson has been lost on most of the note crowders who have followed him). Borrowing from jazz to an even greater extent than T-Bone Walker, and setting a standard only the most gifted and hardworking of blues guitarists could ever hope to match, King would be a downhome sophisticate even without the black tie and tux he wears to collect his Grammys.

KING'S is now the name most synonymous with the blues, much as Louis Armstrong's once was with jazz. You don't have to be a blues fan to have heard of King, and you certainly don't have to be black. Yet there was a time, now almost thirty years ago, when (as Charles Keil pointed out in his groundbreaking *Urban Blues*) the number of white Americans who had heard King's music or were likely to recognize his name probably numbered in the low thousands. Despite taking up permanent residence on *Billboard's* R&B charts in the 1950s, King didn't cross over then. Nor did Junior Parker and Big Mama Thornton, the first to record "Mystery Train" and "Hound Dog," respectively, and both then under contract to Duke, a Houston-based blues and gospel label run like a plantation by a cigar-smoking, half-black, half-Jewish, one hundred percent sleezeball named Don Robey (as if claiming co-composer credit for most of his performers' songs wasn't bad enough, he also threatened them with bodily harm or death when they objected).

Bobby "Blue" Bland, another of Robey's field hands and briefly B. B. King's chauffeur, rode a song called "Turn on Your Love Light" to number 28 on the pop charts in 1962, and followed this with "Call on Me" and "That's the Way Love Is" in 1963, and "Ain't Nothing You Can Do" in 1964. But Bland had been recording for over a decade by then, and though that era's white teenagers were likely to confuse him with Billy Bland, a Brill Building one-hit wonder from 1960 (remember "Let the Little Girl Dance"?), Bobby's was practically a household name among black adults. As shamelessly emotive and wondrously expressive as any gospel singer (he did, in fact, emerge from a church background), Bland was especially popular with women. No wonder. His songs were addressed directly to them, and their message usually boiled down to a tortured plea not to two-time him. Striking the pose of the lover as disrobed supplicant long before soul men like Sam Cooke and Teddy Pendergrass, Bland wasn't above paraphrasing the Good Book in order to make his woman think twice about screwing around. One of his R&B charters that didn't go pop was called "Yield Not to Temptation"; in another he warned a straying lover that she was "gonna reap just what you sow";

and in yet another, he asked accusingly "How Does a Cheating Woman Feel?" If Bland's greatest natural gift was his ability to make even his shouts sound intimate, his genius (or Robey's) was in realizing that women bought blues records, too. He presented himself to them as putty in their hands. Despite his pudginess and grotesque, lopsided conk, he was a major black heartthrob. Yet few whites heard his best records when they were first released, and sixties blues revivalists looked with disdain on a nonself-accompanied black singer so recently on the hit parade.

Bobby "Blue" Bland
(RAY AVERY'S JAZZ ARCHIVES)

LIKE Bland, Jimmy Reed also had a handful of early sixties pop hits, including "Baby, What You Want Me to Do" on Vee-Jay, a black-owned Chicago label whose catalogue also included the Four Seasons and the first U.S. album released by the Beatles. Reed, who accompanied himself on both guitar and harmonica, was an epileptic whose lazy, stuttering vocal style

203

was the starting point for a group of singers and instrumentalists who recorded under colorful pseudonyms (Slim Harpo, Lazy Lester, Lightnin' Slim, Lonesome Sundown) for Excello, a Louisiana label distributed almost exclusively in the South.[1] More typical than Reed of the era's ghettoized blues performers was Clarence "Gatemouth" Brown, another member of Robey's stable, a Texan who shouted the blues in a hair-raising manner and generated heat on fiddle as well as guitar. One of the best-selling blues records of 1954—and one of the most exciting of any year—was "The Things That I Used to Do" by a New Orleans performer who called himself Guitar Slim, with an arrangement by the then unknown Ray Charles. But it never charted pop. Nor did "Grits Ain't Groceries" and "If Walls Could Talk," ghetto anthems by Little Milton (Campbell), a singer on the Chess subsidiary Checker, whose only pop hit was "We're Gonna Make It," in 1965.

What's curious about the failure of blues performers to appeal to white record buyers in the fifties and early sixties is that this was an era in which Chuck Berry, Sam Cooke, Fats Domino, Jackie Wilson, and black doo-wop groups regularly climbed the pop charts. But this actually isn't such a mystery. Their music was pop, not blues. There's another, less obvious, explanation. No one was trying especially hard to expose B. B. King or Bobby "Blue" Bland to white listeners. For that matter, the entrepreneurs behind such labels as Duke and Crown made only the slightest effort to sell their records to Northern blacks. The same was true even of Chess, if only in terms of its blues releases. Not even Muddy Waters sold very well in Harlem or North Philadelphia.

Schwab's, the venerable Memphis dry goods store, sells something called John the Conqueror roots, dank-looking things in bottles bought by superstitious black men from the surrounding countryside in the belief that the amulet will put women under their spell. Tourists buy John the Conqueror roots, too, thinking that they're bringing home a Southern hoodoo artifact. Maybe, maybe not—according to Studs Terkel, John the Conqueror roots are manufactured in Chicago, just like Muddy Waters's singles used to be. In a sense, Chess and its competitors were the last race labels, run by men who, as visionary as they might have been in other ways, were late

1. Another footnote of the "and-here's-another-thing" variety, this one encapsulating a few quick asides. Excello's artists and their producer, Jay Miller, apparently liked Lightnin' Hopkins as much as they did Reed. Excello's swampy, schmutz-on-the-needle mix is supposed to be what the Rolling Stones were striving for on *Exile on Main Street*, almost every writer I respect's choice as the group's most enduring record, though not necessarily mine. On the subject of Louisiana in general and New Orleans in particular, some enterprising graduate student ought to write a thesis on how a region so identified with zydeco and so crucial to the births of both jazz and rock 'n' roll could be so minor a port for blues (the contributions of such pianists as Professor Longhair, Champion Jack Dupree, and James Booker notwithstanding). I don't know the answer—only that the very question should caution us against regarding all of black music as (in Amiri Baraka's term) an ever-changing same.

in spotting the evidence right in front of their faces that black America was no longer predominately Southern and rural, even if the audience for the blues still was.

Duke did have its share of pop smashes, most notably Johnny Ace's haunting "Pledging My Love" in 1955. (Ace was dead by the time the song made the charts, the loser in a game of Russian roulette—though some still believe that Robey shot him). So did Chess, though mostly with vocal groups like the Moonglows and Johnny and Joe, rather than with blues performers. The label's biggest hits of all were by a young singer and guitarist named Chuck Berry, from St. Louis, who was brought to the label's attention by Muddy Waters (naturally) and who recorded his first session for Chess in the late summer of 1955. Muddy and other Chicago musicians especially liked Berry's "Wee, Wee Hours," a slow but hardly mournful blues. But it was the intended B-side that clicked with the public: a song that Berry originally called "Ida Red" but later changed to "Maybellene," and that sounded for all the world like a hillbilly tune to Berry's indulgent sidemen (including Willie Dixon).

Except that back in Memphis, there was an honest-to-God hillbilly named Elvis Presley singing what sure as hell sounded like the blues. With Elvis's debut for Sun Records in 1954 and Berry's for Chess a year later, the earth completed another of its baffling revolutions.

. . . .

CHAPTER 8

CHUCK AND ELVIS, HANDS-ON PRESERVATIONISTS, AND SOUL IN THE BIBLICAL SENSE

a blues performer is like a doctor who prescribes the blues as a cure for the blues, Roosevelt Sykes told Margaret McKee and Fred Chisenhall, the authors of *Beale Black and Blue.* "Doctor studies medicine—'course he ain't sick, but he studies medicine to help them people," Sykes explained. "A blues player ain't got no blues, but he plays for the worried people. . . . Like the doctor works from outside of the body to the inside of the body. But the blues works on the insides of the inside. See?" Sykes went on to say that practically everyone he'd ever met had the blues, including "thousands a people worried to death, house done burned down, lost their family," who couldn't play or sing a lick. That was Sykes's job.

In other words, the blues at the professional level is never just self-expression. It isn't necessarily just the blues performer who's down with the blues: it's his or her listeners too. He or she is singing from their point of view. As Sam Charters put it, referring to Lonnie Johnson's brooding, borderline misogynist recordings of the 1930's, "Despite all that has been written about blues singers and their 'honesty,' most of the blues is metaphoric." According to Charters, this often means that "the singer is only reflecting the mood of the audience." A folklorist might amend this last statement to read "the mood of his community," the singer being a member of said community. That the point of view expressed by a song's lyrics might not be the singer's is probably true of all forms of popular song, including rock 'n' roll. But a difference between the blues and fifties rock was that the latter first reached most of those who became its audience via radio or phonograph records—two forms of mass media that stretched the notion of "community" beyond meaningful definition.

Consider the point of view, or seeming absence of one, in Chuck Berry's "School Day," which debuted on radio at exactly the right moment in April

1957, as the weather got warm and the school year entered its excruciating final six or seven weeks (as I well remember). Thanks to oldies radio, the song has never gone off the air. Regardless of your age, you probably know its lyrics by heart: all that great stuff about American history and practical math, the teacher who doesn't know how mean she looks, the joker behind you who won't leave you alone, and (soon as three o'clock rolls around) dropping the coin right into the slot because you gotta hear something that's really hot. Et cetera, et cetera. It was the first teen anthem; also the anthem of elementary school punks like me whose only ambition in life back then was to *be* a teen someday.

But the question that usually occurs to me on hearing "School Day" now is, who the hell is "you," a question you (or "one," or "I") never have to ask when reading Hemingway. Though both the singer and the guitar shuffle that underpins the vocal are black, race is never mentioned in "School Day," or even implied. The lyrics are so racially neutral that their point of view becomes that of the record's intended buyer, the typical, mildly rebellious American teenage male of the mid-1950s. "Typical," in this case, as in most others, meant "white." Me, in other words, rather than the twenty-eight-year-old Chuck Berry, who had virtually nothing in common with most of his buyers, and who seems oddly absent from "School Day" save for his

Chuck Berry
(RAY AVERY'S JAZZ ARCHIVES)

crackling voice and guitar (though in his 1988 *The Autobiography*, Berry tells us that "School Day" was inspired by his own memories of high school). "School Day" was metaphoric in Charters's terms; but the people Berry was singing for weren't afflicted with the blues, just an itch to be done with books and number-two pencils for another year.

"School Day" was followed later that year by "Rock & Roll Music" (another anthem), and then by "Sweet Little Sixteen" early the following year. Pretend for a minute that there's someone in the world who's never heard "Sweet Little Sixteen," but who's well versed in the blues repertoire. On being told Berry's title, such a person might think that "Sweet Little Sixteen" was in the tradition of Sonny Boy Williamson's "Good Morning, Little Schoolgirl" and Muddy Waters's "She's Nineteen Years Old"— one more song about the appeal to older men of younger female flesh (or under-age female flesh in the case of Sonny Boy, who in his own innocence makes it plain that the cutie he's sniffing after is several years shy of legal). Even those of us so fond of Berry's song that we've become a little sick of it might be inclined to read things into those lyrics about "tight dresses and lipstick," given our vague recollections of Chuck's bust for violating the Mann Act with a fourteen-year-old Apache girl in 1960.

But unless you insist on hearing something between the lines, Berry's interest in the girl in the song is strictly avuncular, his point of view shifting between hers and that of an indulgent uncle or father. The song went to number two; number one R&B. But who bought it? People who liked rock 'n' roll, of course, which Berry's guitar licks virtually defined. But who else? Whose very favorite record was it? Girls who *were* sixteen that year and boys with crushes on them? Pre-teen girls who fantasized about being sixteen and dancing on *Bandstand*, like the girl in the song? In *The Autobiography*, Berry says his inspiration was a "small German doll" of around seven or eight who had been pursuing Paul Anka for his autograph!

Berry's other big 1958 hit was "Johnny B. Goode," about a little country boy who plays guitar "just like ringing a bell" and becomes the leader of a rock-'n'-roll band. Himself? Or every teenage American boy then playing air guitar in front of his bedroom mirror while duckwalking like Chuck or wiggling his hips like Elvis?

IN 1992, Jim Dawson and Steve Propes published a nifty little book called *What Was the First Rock 'n' Roll Record?* The usual answer to this question is "Rocket 88," a 1951 boogie by Jackie Brenston (fronting Ike Turner's Kings of Rhythm, of which he was then a member); this was the song that introduced fuzztone and distortion to pop by virtue of a busted amplifier cone nobody bothered to replace; the link between Robert Johnson's "Terraplane Blues" and the Beach Boys' "Little Deuce Coup" in terms of extolling the freedom that comes with driving a car. But Dawson and Propes offer forty-nine reasonable alternatives, ranging chronologically from a 1944 jam by a jazz group featuring Illinois Jacquet's tenor saxophone squalls to Elvis Presley's "Heartbreak Hotel" in 1956. Their list also includes a number of hardcore blues recordings by such performers as Big Boy Crudup, Lonnie Johnson, John Lee Hooker, Muddy Waters, and Big Mama Thornton.

So, any old way you choose it, rock 'n' roll was a fait accompli by the time "School Day" and then "Sweet Little Sixteen" hit the airwaves. Yet these two Berry hits seem to me to have been the first rock-'n'-roll records in quite another, more self-conscious sense. Their success was as sure a sign of a cultural shift in favor of youth as the network debut of *American Bandstand* in 1957 and Procter & Gamble's introduction of Clearasil around the same time (a *dedicated* pimple cream, unlike the multi-use Noxema).

In the late 1950s and early 1960s, as the great number of children born after the war began to exercise their own consumer options, American popular culture reconfigured itself into youth culture. These baby boomers may have been the first Americans to think of themselves not just as a generation, but as an age group. Just as important, they may also have been the first to be identified as a demographic. Rock 'n' roll had been the first sign of all of this, and given that American popular culture had traditionally drawn style and substance from black subcultures, rock's emergence should have brought an avid white following to those veteran blues performers who felt—with some justification—that rock 'n' roll wasn't anything but the blues mixed up with country and given a slightly more pronounced beat. Yet it didn't work out that way, or at least not at first. Muddy Waters may once have been a mannish boy, but he was never a teenager in the same way that the kids on *Bandstand* were, and he had absolutely nothing in common with them. The blues was understood to be adult music, which made it of virtually no interest to the largest segment of the record-buying public at a time when the Top 40 was breaking down racial barriers on a weekly basis.

"The blues had a baby," Muddy Waters sang, "and they called it rock and roll." Yeah, and once the brat began bringing home a paycheck, it looked as though he'd boot the old man out of the house.

A S long as I'm joining the cliché squad by bringing up that business about the blues having a baby, let me point out that what we're talking about was an interracial relationship with country music that actually produced twins, a black boy named Chuck and a white boy named Elvis. I know that some readers are going to feel that Elvis Presley keeps turning up like a bad penny in these pages, but there are a few quick points I feel need to be made about him in this context. It isn't enough to say that Elvis treated thousands of white teenagers to their first sugared taste of black music and perhaps gave them an appetite for the real thing. That's not giving him his proper due. He was one of the finest white blues singers. To put it in a way that acknowledges both the murky and possibly biracial roots of the blues and Presley's own double consciousness as a white boy from Tupelo, Mississippi, he was one of the finest singers ever spawned by the Southern United States.

Elvis Presley
(RAY AVERY'S JAZZ
ARCHIVES)

The proof of Elvis's mastery of blues idioms is on *Reconsider Baby*, an RCA compilation of his cover versions of songs written by and/or originally sung by Arthur Crudup, Lonnie Johnson, Lowell Fulson, and Percy Mayfield, among others. On many of these, Presley gives the original performers a real run for their money. The version included of "One Night" isn't the 1957 chart topper, but an unbowdlerized alternate on which Elvis sings "One night of sin/Is what I'm now paying for," just as Smiley Lewis did on the original recording of the song. On the version you're probably familiar with, he changed it to "One night with you/Is what I'm now praying for." Even so, he managed to convey more memory of sexual heat and fear of eternal hellfire than Lewis had by coming right out and saying what he meant. Should you remain skeptical after listening to *Reconsider Baby* from start to finish, I urge you to try *The Sun Sessions*, which has a version of "Blue Moon" in which Elvis's falsetto conjures up an abandoned lover's plea traveling across the Mississippi, the river serving as a natural echo chamber.

Better still, hear RCA's four-disc box of his complete fifties masters. Despite his admitted (and implausible) affection for Dean Martin, the singer Elvis seemed most taken with as a young man was Lonnie Johnson, whose influence is apparent not just on the cover of his "Tomorrow Night," but on those ballads Elvis half-speaks, those on which he actually recites, and especially those he phrases ever-so-carefully in that high, keening voice he mysteriously no longer had when he returned from the army.

If your image of Elvis Presley is that of pop's white elephant scuba-diving and rock-a-hula-ing, baby, in those dreadful movies he made one right after the other in baffled response to the British invasion, nothing I can say about him is going to change your mind. But it's a sign of his greatness, or at least of his historical importance, that it's virtually impossible to talk about him without starting a fight. To some people, Elvis is always going to be a thief. In the late 1950s, there were those who believed that not only could 50 million Elvis fans be wrong, but racist to boot. Forget the often-told story of Sam Phillips of Sun Records saying that if he could find a white man who sang like a black man, he could make a million dollars. And forget that, in Albert Goldman's telling, Phillips put it that he wanted a white man who sang like a "nigger." I know black people who believe Elvis once said that a black man was fit only to shine his shoes. But none of them has ever been able to play me the tape or show me the clip. Quite the opposite was true. In Elvis's early interviews, when the subject of his influences came up, he inevitably praised black performers, admitting that he wasn't doing anything they hadn't been doing for years.

Some people just have trouble believing that a piece of white trash from the depths of the segregated South could have been musically color blind. If Elvis hadn't been a Southerner—if, say, he had been a Yalie who went south to hunt for ancient blues singers and wound up singing the blues himself, or a Jew from Chicago who horrified his parents by risking life and limb to sit in with his black idols in the South Side clubs—well, then, maybe those who despise or ridicule him would be willing to give him a break. Or maybe if he hadn't sold zillions of records, amassing a wealth that many feel should have been spread among the black singers he allegedly pilfered from. But if he hadn't been a Southerner, he wouldn't have been Elvis and probably wouldn't have sung the blues with such natural feeling (in his case some of it really did rub off). And if he hadn't sold all those records, American popular music might be quite different now. So might the patterns of contemporary American life.

THOUGH it was surely no coincidence that the first phase of the blues revival of the 1960s unfolded almost simultaneously with the civil rights movement's appeals to white conscience, guilt wasn't the revival's primary motivation. Nor was it simply a growing disenchantment with rock 'n' roll on the part of its original audience as they left adolescence, though that's the way it probably seemed to record companies suddenly faced with a demand by college-age whites for acoustic blues LPs. As Peter Guralnick points out in *Feel Like Going Home*, a 1971 collection of his profiles of blues and early rock performers, "To the record producers [of the late 1950s] teenagers had just about the same status as blacks thirty years earlier and just about the same appeal, too. They represented a huge but totally unpredictable market subject to whims of taste and fancy no sane person could sensibly predict."

Later in his chapter on rock 'n' roll, though, Guralnick puts his finger on something else, something perhaps more to the point in explaining why so many white rock-'n'-roll fans of his generation embraced the blues with such fervor in the early 1960s. For its more thoughtful adherents, rock 'n' roll had served as an introduction to "a black subculture which had never previously risen to the surface, so that we were set up—I was, anyway, along with my friends—for the adoption of a purely black music and a purely black culture." Thus, to paraphrase Guralnick, the music and the adolescent culture that had helped to kill the blues as a form of popular music decided to resurrect it out of guilt "and out of necessity."

LOGICALLY, all of this should have led bookish rock 'n' rollers straight to Muddy Waters and B. B. King. This was ultimately what happened, but given the folkloric bias of most of the blues literature that existed at that time, plus the nightly TV battle footage from Mississippi and Alabama, it's not surprising that the revival initially focused on Southern rural blues.

The man who turned countless white adolescents on to the blues was Sam Charters, who was himself no former rock 'n' roller just out of his teens. Charters's *The Country Blues*, published in 1959, struck a new tone for such books. Though qualified as a folklorist, Charters wrote with the grace of a novelist and the flushed excitement of a fan. Unlike those who had covered similar ground, including John A. Lomax and his son, Alan, Charters focused on singers, not just their songs. For him and those who caught his fever, collecting examples of local song styles wasn't the rationale for combing the sleepy little plantation towns presumed to have given birth to the blues. The best country blues singers of the twenties and thirties weren't just agents of tradition (though they were that, too); they were genuine artists whose recordings inevitably told something about their personal lives and left anyone who listened to those records thirty years later hungry to know more. The goal of those who heeded Charters's call in the early 1960s was to come back from the South with as many singers from bygone decades as were still alive (or, in the case of those who weren't, death certificates and the personal recollections of family and friends).

Part and parcel of the Camelot-era folk craze—the era of hootenannies and topical singer/songwriters, although its only *genuine* folk music may have been the Beach Boys' studio celebrations of surfing, cars, girls, and teen solidarity—the blues revival also gained synergy from related developments in jazz, an art music then still subject to the same cultural forces as pop. The most popular style of jazz in 1960 was the funky, "sanctified" sort purveyed by Horace Silver, Bobby Timmons, Cannonball Adderley, and a host of organ combos who were following the trail blazed by Jimmy Smith. (These organ combos, usually featuring guitar, drums, and an optional honking tenor saxophone, would remain popular in Northern inner-city lounges for the next two decades.) Younger black jazz musicians were endeavoring to get back in touch with their "roots," by which they didn't mean Louis Armstrong and Jelly Roll Morton. They meant the blues and the music of the Baptist and Pentecostal churches. Their favorite singers were Ray Charles and Mahalia Jackson. Meanwhile, musicians associated with jazz's intellectual wing—Charles Mingus, Jimmy Giuffre, and George Russell, among others—

were writing compositions that incorporated elements of Southern Negro folk song. In 1955, Count Basie had reasserted his big band's supremacy with a hit recording of Memphis Slim's "Everyday I Have the Blues," featuring Joe Williams, the latest and most polished of Basie's shouters (not to be confused with "Big" Joe Williams, of Mississippi and Chicago). Then, in 1959, the Texas-born alto saxophonist Ornette Coleman exploded on the New York scene, startling as many listeners with his untempered, blues-inflected pitch as with his band's avoidance of chord changes and measured time.

For what it's worth, the label that released the most "folk" or "country" blues albums in the early sixties was Bluesville, a subsidiary of Prestige Records, one of the leading jazz independents. And at that time, jazz magazines such as *Down Beat, Metronome,* and *Jazz Review* were the only wide-circulation periodicals regularly offering in-depth analysis of regional blues styles and articles on individual blues performers.

So the blues revival drew its numbers from fans of jazz and folk as well as from postadolescents fleeing Fabian, Frankie Avalon, and Bobby Rydell. As already noted, Son House and Skip James were located on the same day in 1964. And the hunt for forgotten country bluesmen who had recorded for Paramount or Okeh yielded such unanticipated finds as the Texas farmer Mance Lipscomb and Mississippi Fred McDowell, missing-link songsters

Mance Lipscomb
(DOUG FULTON)

Fred McDowell
(DOUG FULTON)

Robert Pete Williams, Ann
Arbor, Michigan 1972
(DOUG FULTON)

who had never previously recorded or earned their livings as professional musicians. (Make of it what you will that Lipscomb's favorite tune was "Shine On, Harvest Moon," and that he would confound interviewers by telling them that the blues as such began to take shape not around the turn of the century, but in the years just after World War I—around the time all manner of performers began to be recorded as "blues" singers, in other words.) A trip to the Angola prison by the folklorists Henry Osser and Richard Allen turned up a mesmerizing singer and guitarist in Robert Pete Williams, a convicted murderer whose life sentence was eventually commuted largely as a result of the recordings he made for them.

Not all of the singers recorded as part of this boom were lifelong Southerners; not all of them were well along in years; and not all of them had long before drifted into obscurity. The Reverend Gary Davis, said to have been an influence on Blind Boy Fuller in North Carolina in the 1930s, a decade when he himself recorded widely, was living in New York and earning his living as a street singer and guitar instructor when he became the focus of renewed attention (his students included Dion DiMucci, of Dion and the Belmonts). Though Davis consented to perform only religious material, his rousing vocals and intricate fingerpicking made him a coffee-house favorite until his death in 1972.

Another performer who found great favor during this period was Jesse Fuller. Best remembered as the man who wrote "San Francisco Bay Blues," he was a one-man jug band who sang and winningly played harmonica, washboard, kazoo, Piedmont-inspired twelve-string guitar, and what he called "fotdella," a homemade, piano-wire bass operated by a foot pedal. Originally from Georgia, Fuller was living in Oakland, playing on the street and recording for a Dixieland label when the blues craze created a new audience for him.

Juke Boy Bonner and Snooks Eaglin—born in 1932 and 1936, respectively—were among the very few younger black performers deemed "authentic" by that day's white blues audiences. Bonner, a Texan who had migrated to Southern California, was another one-man street band, though he limited himself to such conventional instruments as guitar, harmonica, and drums. He wasn't exactly a dynamic singer, but he did write well-crafted and fully original songs, many of which were topical in nature and deviated from that day's liberal party line; his response to the 1965 Watts Riots, for example, was a song called "I'm Going Back Home Where They Don't Burn the Buildings to the Ground."

Eaglin, from New Orleans and blind since birth, was barely out of his teens when he recorded his first album for Folkways in 1958; those labels for which he recorded in the years just after desired traditional-sounding songs from him, and his ability to give these producers what they wanted made him almost everybody's first choice as bright-young-hope-for-the-country-blues. It turns out, however, that these early records misrepresented Eaglin, in allowing only a partial look at his repertoire. Still active today, he's likely to follow a blues song with a Mardi Gras Indian tune, his rendition of a fifties R&B hit, or maybe some funked-up flamenco. In this sense, he's a typical product of New Orleans, a city whose music has always been a gumbo. The same is true of the entire state of Louisiana, and a good example of this is zydeco, the homespun but exotic result of centuries of intermarriage between French Acadians (or "Cajuns") and the bayou's black and Native American inhabitants. Sung with gusto in a nearly unintelligible patois and typically played on guitar, fiddle, button accordion, and chest washboard, zydeco dates from the 1930s as a form of recorded music, and (in its postwar form) sounds more like R&B than it does like the blues. That should have put it off-limits to sixties purists, but perhaps because it was clearly still folk-based, many found room in their hearts for Clifton Chenier, a euphoric singer and accordion player who still ranks as zydeco's greatest ever performer nearly a decade after his death in 1987.

YOU won't get many of them to admit it, but some of the idealistic young white men who were going south to hunt for elderly blues singers must have been bitterly disappointed by many of the men they found. There were performers who were unable to blow off the cobwebs, and one of the reasons for Charley Patton and Robert Johnson's continuing allure might be that they didn't live to be palsied old men. In our minds, they're always going to be as vital as they sound on their records.

As defiant, too—which raises another point. On records as young men, the singers of the twenties and thirties sounded like black men risking their necks (literally, as it were) to assert their right to be *treated* as men. Against a backdrop of Freedom Rides, lunch-counter sit-ins, and voter registration drives, it was easy to imagine heroic qualities in these men, to see them as unofficial spokesmen for their race. What a shock it must have been for some Northern whites to realize that these were men who had survived as long as they had by saying as little as possible around white folks.

Finally, there was something amusing and, maybe a little bit tragic about the tortured reasoning of so many of that day's white blues enthusiasts. They boxed themselves into an ideological position in which the music of a Muddy Waters or a B. B. King was deemed commercially debased not just on account of being amplified, but because it still appealed to sizable numbers of blacks. In *Urban Blues*, which must have read like a polemic on behalf of the likes of King, Waters, and Bobby "Blue" Bland on its original publication in 1965, Charles Keil bitterly joked that the ideal bluesman as envisioned by Charters, Alan Lomax, Harry Oster, Paul Oliver, and others was "more than sixty years old, blind, arthritic, and toothless," "should not have performed in public nor have made a recording in at least twenty years," and "should have lived the bulk of his life as a sharecropper, coaxing mules and picking cotton, uncontaminated by city influences."

This eliminated Waters, King, Bland, and Howlin' Wolf, among others. It should also have eliminated John Lee Hooker and Sam "Lightnin'" Hopkins. Fortunately, it didn't. Two of the sixties blues revival's biggest draws, Hooker and Hopkins had much in common. Both recorded for any company, big or small, black-oriented or white-oriented, willing to pay up front. In other words, both were overrecorded, and were as capable of giving lackluster performances as they were inspired ones. Each was rhythmically and metrically unpredictable, not given to worrying how many bars of music a tune was supposed to have, where the bar line was, or how many beats there were supposed to be per measure. Needless to say, each was a bitch to accompany. Hopkins, a younger cousin of Texas Alexander's and another of Blind Lemon Jefferson's apprentices and guides, was living in relative obscurity in Houston, singing for coins on street corners when Charters took him to a hotel room and recorded him on a portable tape player for Folkways in 1959. But he had been a big favorite on Southwestern juke boxes only five or six years earlier, recording singles for a variety of latterday Texas and West Coast race labels, including Aladdin and Gold Star. Hooker, when he signed up for work on acoustic guitar at colleges and in coffee-houses, was still recording with jumping little bands for Vee Jay, sometimes even making the R&B charts. Remember Big Bill Broonzy's "two-way" picnics, blacks on one side and whites on the other? Hopkins and Hooker were crafty pros who realized that the time had come to unplug and turn the other way.

LIGHTNIN' Hopkins was born in Centerville, Texas, in 1912, and died of cancer in Houston in 1982. Practically anything else you'd ever want to know about him, no matter how trivial, is in a song somewhere. One of his most stinging numbers was "Tom Moore's Farm," which he recorded for Gold Star in 1948; it told the story of how Hopkins and his wife once hired themselves out to a white landowner who cheated them out of money and generally treated them like livestock. It's an angry song, and though Lightnin' is the one singing, he could be any black Southerner railing against a legally sanctioned dirty deal.

In general, however, Hopkins was the least bardic of the great blues singers: less interested in telling a story than setting a mood and speaking whatever happened to be on his mind the second the tapes started to roll.

Lightnin' Hopkins, 1969 (DOUG FULTON)

John Lee Hooker
(RAY AVERY JAZZ ARCHIVES)

On his singles from the late fifties and early sixties, he played pricking electric guitar; the albums he made for a mostly white listenership after 1959 might feature him on acoustic or electric, by himself or with bass and drums, depending on the producer's whim. But Hopkins could start you furiously tapping your foot even when he was playing solo and unplugged, and stating his observations in a slow drawl much too lazy to be accurately described as "conversational." In the middle of lyrics about nothing in partic- ular, he could startle you with a telling, almost surreal aside: "Did you ever see a one-woman cry?" he asked in one song. No, Lightnin', but it sure is something to think about.

J O H N Lee Hooker is still with us, of course, drawing larger audiences than ever and selling more albums, too, in the aftermath of his 1989 Grammy winner *The Healer* (produced by his former sideman Roy Rogers and featuring cameos by Bonnie Raitt, Carlos Santana, and Robert Cray) than he did even in the early 1970s, when he hooked up with the band Canned Heat. Since Muddy Waters's death, Hooker has become the grand old man of the blues, and even those of us aware that he was born in Clarksdale in 1920 and that he was working as a janitor in a Detroit automobile factory when he began his recording career with "Boogie Chillen" in 1948 sometimes fantasize that he must have been in the Delta and already an old man before the turn of the century, when the first blues was sung. Part of it is his thick guitar sound and riverbottom baritone, which combine to make his music sound indigenous to the Delta. But part of it is his physical appearance, especially now that he's in his seventies. With his sunken cheeks and dark shades, he looks like a lifesize version of a voodoo icon you'd expect to find on sale at Schwab's. Even on an off night, his patented one-chord boogies can rattle your bones, and his slow incantations can be as thick with atmosphere as the Mississippi is deep. No one back in the 1960s was going to dare to question John Lee Hooker's authenticity, even if his blues sometimes echoed the roar of black urban life rather than the tense moonlit quiet of the rural South.

DICK Waterman, one of the men who tracked down Son House in Buffalo (and in Waterman's case, went on to manage him), told researchers for the PBS series the following story:

> A month or so later, we brought Son to Cambridge, Massachusetts, to get him ready for the Newport Folk Festival [and introduced him to] Al Wilson, who later moved to Los Angeles and was a founding member of the group Canned Heat. Al played open-tuning bottleneck and could play all the styles. He could play Bukka White, Son House, Charley Patton, and Blind Lemon Jefferson— he could really play. And he sat down with Son, knee to knee, guitar to guitar, and said, "Okay, this is the figure that in 1930, you called 'My Black Mama,' " and played it for him. And Son said, "Yeah, *yeah*, that's me, that's me. I played that." And then Al said, "Now about a dozen years later, when Mr. Lomax came around, you changed the name to 'My Black Woman,' and you did it this way." He showed him. And Son would say, "Yeah, yeah. I got my recollection now, I got my recollection now." And he would start to play, and the two of them played together. Then, Al reminded him of how he changed tunings, and played his own "Pony Blues" for him.
>
> There would not have been a rediscovery of Son House in the 1960s without Al Wilson. Really. Al Wilson taught Son House how to play Son House.

Alan Lomax's friends and associates say that Lomax is a fine singer. The rest of us have little way of knowing. Folklorists of Lomax and his father's generations were passionate about the songs they collected and the singers they documented. But they saw themselves strictly as preservationists. It wouldn't have occurred to them to sing those songs themselves in public.

In the 1960s, blues preservation became a hands-on proposition, as young whites like Al Wilson endeavored to keep the blues alive by performing it (maybe after realizing that blacks their own age were, for the most part, not about to—though by so guessing, I'm making this sound like a conscious decision, which it almost certainly wasn't). Rock 'n' roll exerted an influence here, even on those hands-on preservationists who denounced it. One of the most liberating things about rock 'n' roll is that a lack of musical training has never prevented anyone from trying his hand at it. All that's required is passion; there are only three chords to learn, and by 1964, there was already an honorable tradition of learning them on the job. Plus, early rock was a music in which expressiveness was equated with blackness, though

219

John Hammond, Sr.,
1939
(FRANK DRIGGS COLLECTION)

often only subliminally. It sanctioned an invisible, but audible, blackface.

Many of the white blues performers of the 1960s whom I refer to as hands-on preservationists differed from older men like the Lomaxes and Sam Charters in yet another respect. As knowledgeable of black folk culture as Lomax is, I doubt he's ever thought of himself as a White Negro, black all but for the skin. But who knows about the young John Paul Hammond, nicknamed "Jeep" by his father, the famous record producer and liberal activist? "Jeep left [Antioch College] to work as a handyman in Boca Grande, Florida," the elder Hammond recalled in his 1977 memoir *John Hammond on Record*. "He bought a pair of blindman's glasses and a tin cup, and took to the streets to play and sing the blues. He felt that only by disguising himself would he be allowed to enter black taverns where he could learn more about singing the blues." If he couldn't pass for black, as the Los Angeles–based singer and bandleader Johnny Otis had for so many years, to pass for blind was the next best thing.

Not every sixties hands-on preservationist fancied himself darker than he looked, and for all I know, the younger John Hammond didn't, either (though even today, there's something vaguely offensive about those note-perfect

Charlie Musselwhite
(RAY AVERY)

recreations of Son House's voice and slide guitar emanating from a high-born white man handsome enough to be a movie star). Still, in order to sound "authentic," it was necessary to sing and play with a black inflection, which gave Southern-born whites like the harmonica player and singer Charlie Musselwhite an edge over those Northern Whites who sounded like they first heard the blues in college.

Al Wilson, the young white man who taught Son House how to play Son House, was a hands-on preservationist, and so was Bob "The Bear" Hite, another charter member of Canned Heat who was rumored to own the world's largest collection of vintage blues 78s. Other hands-on types included the harmonica player and singer Paul Butterfield and the two guitarists he enlisted for the electric (and racially mixed) blues band he put together in Chicago in 1963, Elvin Bishop and Michael Bloomfield. Though she happened on the scene a few years later and probably didn't think of herself as one, Janis Joplin was a preservationist by virtue of her conscious debt to Bessie Smith. Taj Mahal was one of the few black hands-on preservationists, a likable eclectic whose interpretations of older blues songs and originals in the same vein were ingratiatingly eccentric, if sometimes a trifle bookish.

WE need a guitar chord to announce the entry of phase two of the sixties blues revival, and it might as well be the one struck by Bloomfield and Bishop to begin the Paul Butterfield Blues Band's set at the 1965 Newport Folk Festival. This is the festival remembered as the one at which Bob Dylan first "went electric," as they used to say then; his set with a band that included his and Bloomfield's electric guitars drew catcalls from an audience that equated plugging in with selling out. Less well publicized at the time, and less remembered today, was an earlier incident at the same festival, during Butterfield's set.

As Charles Sawyer tells the story in *The Arrival of B. B. King*, Alan Lomax was the emcee for an afternoon blues workshop that, in addition to Butterfield, included performances by Son House and Mississippi John Hurt. It took some time for the stagehands to assemble what Sawyer describes as the Butterfield Band's "formidable tiers of amplifiers and speakers," and Lomax filled the lengthy delay by reminding the audience that

> they had already heard the best bluesmen in the world during the first half of the workshop. Then, he reflected that in a bygone age people fashioned their own instruments and made their blues music in the shade of a tree, where [as] nowadays people seem[ed] to need mountains of fancy hardware to make even a toot or a squeak. Finally, he introduced the Butterfield Band, saying, in effect, that now the truth would be out: the world would see if these smart alecks [could] really play blues.

221

Mississippi John Hurt, Newport Folk Festival, 1964
(DICK WATERMAN)

These were fighting words to Albert Grossman, who managed both But-terfield and Dylan. He and Lomax exchanged unpleasantries, and a few minutes later, "they were on each other, rolling in the dirt."

The audience remained oblivious to this comic tussle, more accepting of amplified music from a newcomer like Butterfield than they were from an established paragon of folk virtue like Dylan. And a year or two later, nobody (except perhaps for Lomax) would have raised an eyebrow at the sight of an electric guitar at a folk festival or a blues workshop.

Other factors that turned the tide in favor of "urban" blues were (on the academic level) the publication of Keil's *Urban Blues* and (in the popular arena) the enormous influence of the Rolling Stones, whose early Chess covers amounted to love letters to that label's performers. (The Beatles drew no distinction between Carl Perkins and Little Richard, and the Stones admitted none between Chuck Berry and Muddy Waters. Anything that was American and made a lot of noise was all right to the first great British postmods and rockers, and maybe they had the right idea.) Another turning point was the sudden emphasis on instrumental prowess in rock 'n' roll, with the greatest emphasis of all on guitar. In the fifties, teenage boys had dreamed of singing like Elvis. By the late sixties, just as their fathers had dreamed of playing clarinet like Artie Shaw or Benny Goodman, teenage boys were itching to spew licks like Jeff Beck or Jimmy Page or Eric Clapton and form their own bands.

This opened the doors of the Fillmores East and West to urban blues performers such as Buddy Guy and B. B. King, acknowledged masters of a music in which guitar was undisputed boss. The last years of the 1960s were a time of guitar heroes American and British, black, white, and even albino (the biggest hype of 1969 was the paler-than-pale Texas blues guitarist Johnny Winter, who didn't begin to live up to the fanfare until it subsided). The most idolized of these guitar heroes was Eric Clapton, who even before becoming a superstar in America (with Cream, after stints with the Yardbirds and John Mayall's Blues Breakers), had inspired British graffiti to the effect that he was God (from which, as I recall, some of us concluded that God took interminable guitar solos and sounded extremely uncomfortable when He was called upon to sing—though, in all fairness, Clapton has long since

Johnny
Winter, 1970
(DOUG FULTON)

223

Jimi Hendrix

found his voice as a low-key pop performer who carries a torch for the blues). Jimi Hendrix, until his death in 1970, rivaled Clapton in popularity. Just as there's a revisionist school of thought that sees Hendrix as the most innovative jazz guitarist of his era (notwithstanding the fact that he never played jazz), there's another that sees his music as sure-'nuff blues marketed as a psychedelic. Exhibit A has become *Blues*, a 1993 compilation of Hendrix's more conventional blues jams, most of which were unreleased during his lifetime. I was one of those who preferred his paisleys (as it were) to his blues. And I still do, which might be another way of saying I think that he was at his most innovative when his music was most difficult to put a label on. Early in the next decade, Duane Allman emerged to challenge Clapton for his throne, even meeting him head on in the studio one-off band Derek and the Dominoes. Like Hendrix, Allman died young.

In addition to B. B., two other veteran black guitarists named King gained white followings during this period. One was Freddie King, a Texan by way of Chicago who had reached the pop charts with a blazing instrumental called "Hideaway" in 1961, and whose R&B hits had been memorized by such British rockers as Beck, Clapton, and Peter Green of Fleetwood Mac. The other was Albert King: like B. B. a native of Indianola, Mississippi, who had migrated to Memphis as a young man. Unlike Freddie King, Albert was a confident (if rather phlegmy) singer and a dynamic stage performer, which increased his standing among rock audiences. Playing his guitar left-handed and "upside down" (that is, with the strings tuned for a right-handed reach),

Albert King was also one of very few blues performers to win a following among blacks during this period. He accomplished this largely as a result of recording for Stax, a Memphis-based label whose name was then practically synonymous with a new form of black popular music called soul.

MENTION of which necessitates another abrupt transition, but not before making three final observations about this second phase of the sixties blues revival.

First, though it would have a wide-ranging and long-term influence on American popular music, the country blues revival of the early sixties (what I've been referring to as the first phase) hardly caused immediate commercial tremors. The first LP reissue of Robert Johnson's recordings in 1961 was one of the revival's touchstones; it sold just over 20,000 copies, in contrast to the 500,000 units sold of the 1990 CD package. The early sixties revivalists were a cult, not a mass audience.

Freddie King, 1969 (playing the guitar
behind his back)
(DOUG FULTON)

Albert King, 1971
(DOUG FULTON)

225

Second, it's always been easier for whites to play an instrument in a "black" manner than it's been for them to sing black. A consequence of this, in the late sixties, was an even greater emphasis on guitar in white blues than in rock in general. This hardly would have mattered except that as black audiences drifted away from the blues and young whites gradually became the primary consumers of both blues-rock and unhyphenated blues, black blues guitarists began to emulate the most dubious traits of their white imitators, playing solos that droned on and on and thereby upset the balanced interplay between voice and instrument that had been a hallmark of the blues from Charley Patton's time to Muddy Waters's. This remains a problem in much contemporary blues.

Third, it was inevitable that white acolytes of the sixties would eventually share both stages and vinyl with their high priests. This had the immediate effect of exposing bluesmen such as Muddy Waters and Howlin' Wolf to audiences who might otherwise never have known of their existence. Record companies still use this strategy, and the huge sales of recent albums by John Lee Hooker and Buddy Guy, among others, surely owes something to guest shots by veteran rockers. Yet this can create a tension that makes such albums practically unlistenable. A twofold drama is being played out. Recording with Muddy Waters or John Lee Hooker amounts to a form of validation for white rockers. But from the point of view of the typical record buyer, whose point of view is the only one that finally counts in the market-place, the participation of an Eric Clapton or a member of the Rolling Stones validates the older black performer whose name was on the cover. These are usually records at cross purposes with themselves. Last and most important, it needs to be stressed that when we speak of "blues revivals," we're not necessarily talking about a stylistic revitalization of the blues, nor about black audiences returning to the fold. All we're really talking about are spurts of interest in the blues on the part of record-buying and concert-going whites. Black audiences for the blues were dwindling even as Alan Lomax and Albert Grossman wrestled over scripture in the dirt at Newport in 1965, the year of James Brown's "Papa's Got a Brand New Bag" and Otis Redding's "Respect" (with only two years to go until Aretha's version and only three until Brown's "Say It Loud—I'm Black and I'm Proud"). While their kids danced to Motown, many black adults continued to listen to some variety of blues; and for those originally from the South, the blues continued to be a reminder of both good times and bad. But soul music gave both them and their Northern-born offspring a different fish to fry.

SOUL overshadowed blues in the late 1960s, then merged with it into something called "deep" soul some twenty years later. (Deep soul is a South-ern-fried style of black pop understood by its fans to be for adults, just as

Otis Redding
(RAY AVERY)

the blues has always been, but also taken by many to be a last stand against teenage, ghettocentric rap.) The best history of soul, though it pretends to be only the story of Stax/Volt's rise and fall, is Peter Guralnick's *Sweet Soul Music*. For our purposes, however, it might be best to treat soul as tangential to the subject at hand and let a pair of vignettes suffice.

Big Bill Broonzy was upset on first hearing Ray Charles play the role of a sanctified preacher, with horns and the Raelets serving as his amen-choir. "He's got the blues, [but] he's cryin' sanctified," a reproachful Big Bill— briefly a preacher as a young man—lectured a reporter, presumably in the late 1950s (I'm quoting from Kenneth Lee Karpe's liner notes to the 1959 album *Ray Charles at Newport*, which fail to acknowledge his source). "He's mixin' the blues with spirituals. I know that's wrong.

"He's got a good voice," Broonzy admitted. "But it's a church voice. He should be singin' in a church."

Now, jump ahead to the Academy of Music in Philadelphia in 1991, where Al Green is headlining a show that also features Little Milton and Bobby "Blue" Bland.

227

Ray Charles
(RAY AVERY)

Al Green
(RAY AVERY'S JAZZ ARCHIVES)

"*Whoa*," Green exclaims midway through a song called "In the Holy Name of Jesus," then turns his back to the audience in order to rezip his fly, the first of many times he will have to do so tonight.

"We got somethin' *goin' on* up here," he explains in a stage whisper, making it plain that he isn't talking about the *resurrection*.

The show is crammed with many such incongruities, not the least of which is that this is an old-fashioned Apollo Theatre–style revue being presented as part of a jazz festival at a decidedly unfunky venue where Eugene Ormandy and then Ricardo Muti used to lead the house band. But the strangest touch of all might be that although both Bland and Little Milton sang what might be described as songs of vaginal enslavement during *their* sets, it's Green, singing mostly about his love for Jesus (as he has for the last decade or so, since becoming ordained) who's sending erotic chills through the well-dressed, predominantly black, female, middle-aged crowd.

Soul has always sounded like church to white people, but to blacks it signifies sin as well as salvation, both the acceptance of faith and the shattering of religious taboos. The official attitude of the Baptist Church has always been that blues are one thing and spirituals another; you really shouldn't mix the two, but if you do it outside of church, it's your own business. Pentecostal churches forbid secular song altogether, in church or out. Yet soul is clearly Pentecostal-derived, the music of men and women singing to one another in a tongue understood to be for God's ears only. Green—not just the last of the great soul singers, as he is sometimes hailed, but arguably the greatest ever—confuses the issue even further by begging Jesus for deliverance as he would a woman for climax of another kind, with falsetto love wails and preening sexual semiotics.

In addition to newer gospel numbers, Green—dressed tonight completely in white, and with enough red roses behind him to make you think simultaneously of Jesus and drops of blood from deflowered virgins—also sings a few of his earlier secular hits, including "Let's Stay Together." Or to be more accurate, *his three backup singers and the audience* sing Green's old hits while he leaves the stage and bounds through the aisles shrieking counterpoint into a handmike, moving among his flock and encouraging the laying on of hands.

I N some ways, soul simply replaced the blues. Motown was black pop whose success could be attributed to a slickness blues listeners prided themselves on not needing. But soul as exemplified by Ray Charles, Otis Redding, Aretha Franklin, Al Green, and early James Brown was another story: pop more urgently contemporary than Motown, but as downhome as the blues in dialect and frame of reference. Maybe more downhome, in a way, because it caught the echoes of Sunday morning as well as those of Saturday night. But soul was itself eventually usurped by its offshoot, funk, which by pinning its rhythms to the first beat of the measure instead of the second, turned the familiar beat of black music completely around. Or maybe on-the-one funk, and then rap, which replaced soul's implicit "hallelujah" with explicit "fuck you's," were nothing more than black music catching up with the enormous changes in black life since the beginning of this century. With that simple displacement—one-*two* giving way to *one-two*—black pop finally shook its Southern accent, so much so that it was a shock to hear it again on the Atlanta-based rap group Arrested Development's 1992 hit "Tennessee." And if you're looking for irony, you can find it in the fact that James Brown, a native of Georgia but a citizen of the world, became the first black man on the one, around the same time white men walked on the moon.

three

BLUES CONNOTATION/ FROM SONGSTERS TO SOULSTERS

he best feature-length movie ever made about what I'm tempted to call the blues experience is Charles Burnett's *To Sleep with Anger*, which opened in theaters in the fall of 1990, around the same time that Columbia Records released Robert Johnson on CD and the weekly newsmagazines decreed a blues revival. No review I read of Burnett's movie noticed the parallel, probably because despite a cameo appearance by Jimmy Witherspoon and records by Little Milton, Bobby Bland, and Z. Z. Hill on the soundtrack, *To Sleep with Anger* wasn't about the blues—merely imbued with its moods and essences in a way that eluded film critics, much less paying moviegoers.

As *To Sleep with Anger's* opening credits roll and Sister Rosetta Tharpe's worried voice wells up on the soundtrack (singing the spiritual "Precious Memories"), we see what looks at first like a still photograph of uncertain vintage of a black man—not quite elderly, but not quite middle-aged, either—wearing a white summerweight suit and sitting next to a table with a basket of fruit on it. The man is completely still, his eyes and presumably his thoughts as motionless as the rest of him. But a close-up that comes and goes so quickly it's easy to miss reveals that he's twiddling his thumbs, as though to recall the aphorism about the Devil finding work for idle hands (practically the movie's theme, though never directly stated). What happens next is difficult to describe: a sequence of events as might occur in a dream, in defiance of physical laws. The fruit catches on fire, or not exactly; smokeless flames like those in religious paintings suddenly appear in the bowl. The fire doesn't exactly spread; it flares in isolated places, including the legs of the table and in a framed painting or photograph whose details we can't quite make out. Finally, it licks the tops of the man's patent-leather shoes; but his expression never changes.

A close-up of the shoes dissolves into one of the bare feet of a man wearing jeans and feeding chickens as a sour trumpet sounds in the near distance.

The setting appears to be rural, until the camera draws back to establish that what we're looking at is the small backyard of a city or suburban row house, possibly in or just outside of Los Angeles (generally the locale when a movie appears to be happening no place in particular). The trumpet is coming from the second floor of the house across the fence; it's the neighbor's kid practicing, which we're given to understand he does day and night, driving even the chickens crazy. The man feeding them and complaining about the kid's trumpet is named Gideon (an irony Burnett wisely never underlines), and he's the same man whose shoes were on fire in the opening scene.

Gideon's wife, Susie, is in their living room, teaching a Lamaze class. She's a former country midwife, and this is her way of putting what she knows to use in the city, which is more than Gideon can say for himself. We learn that once he was a Southern farmer. One of his and Susie's two daughters-

Z. Z. Hill
(RAY AVERY'S JAZZ ARCHIVES)

in-law, who usually waits in the car when her husband goes in the house to drop off or pick up their son, complains that she's sick of Gideon's incessant talk of "how the corn was this fall and how to get rid of gophers." What sort of job drew Gideon to the city is never specified, but he's obviously a man who's worked hard all of his life and is now retired, with nothing but time on his hands. Even fattening up the chickens is a pointless exercise, because he wouldn't dream of slaughtering them and giving them to Susie to cook; they buy their poultry from a butcher, like everyone else. The elder of Gideon and Susie's sons takes after them in the value he places on family and honest labor. Their younger son—the one whose wife dreads entering Gideon and Susie's house—is more inclined to drift from job to job, and to use his parents as full-time baby-sitters. Tension is building between him and Gideon, but a more immediate source of vexation for Gideon is that he's misplaced his lucky toby stone.

Right after he realizes it's missing, a fruit basket containing his grandson's marbles breaks unnoticed, seemingly of its own accord, the marbles spilling on the floor with Gideon's amulet perhaps among them. That's when Harry shows up, a friend of Gideon and Susie's from back home whom they haven't seen for thirty years or more, his arrival at their door marked by the sound of an ominous slide guitar.

It's Harry who explains to the puzzled grandson that a toby is a good-luck charm you want to have safely tucked in your pocket should you come to a crossroads. Harry ought to know, because he's a crossroads trickster whose charm lies in a manner reminiscent of an earlier place and time (one of his first suggestions is an old-fashioned fish fry) and in superstitions even quainter than Gideon's—but only on face value.

"You're not like the rest of Gideon's friends," the daughter-in-law that Gideon and Susie don't get along with compliments Harry. "Most of them believe that if you're not hard at work, you're hard at sin."

"Sin *is* something you work at," he replies with a little curtsy and a sinister gleam.

The daughter-in-law is unaware that Harry boasts of once having "carved" a man on Beale Street with his "crabapple" knife. According to rumor, he also once precipitated a small-town race riot by stringing another of his victims to a tree and setting him on fire in order to make his foul deed look like the work of an angry white mob. But maybe not. "I don't know if I actually did what I did or I got my life story mixed up with other folks," he says about himself at one point. He's as much a creature of myth as Charley Patton or Stagolee, and in the days and weeks that follow, he brings poker, moonshine, and a nefarious group of cronies into Gideon and Susie's home, and then into their younger son's house.

Planting suspicion in everyone's mind, Harry pits husband against wife and brother against brother. He takes Gideon, who's badly out of shape, for a long walk by a railroad crossing, and stands slicing an apple with his penknife as Gideon hallucinates about a railroad labor gang and collapses to the ground. Neither dead nor fully alive, Gideon lies in his marital bed paralyzed with fever, stirring warily only when Harry draws near. Harry gradually replaces him as husband and head of the family. Under his spell, even the rational and assimilated Susie reverts to country superstition, trying to cure Gideon with home remedies that may have the opposite effect of strengthening Harry's hex on him.

HARRY'S demon grip on the family is finally broken by that missing toby (or maybe just a marble), but not before he leads them to within inches of hell—and not before Susie spills blood on behalf of her warring sons. The past may be another country where they do things differently, but in Burnett's Joycean scheme of things, its boundaries are uncertain. It's contiguous with the present in the same way that superstition is with certifiable knowledge, cultural identity with individual experience, dreams with waking life.

In Philadelphia where I live, *To Sleep with Anger* played first run at a Society Hill art house, which meant that despite the presence in the cast of Danny Glover as Harry, the movie went virtually unnoticed by the black audiences who flock to his *Lethal Weapon* movies, in Philly's equivalent of Times Square. Moviegoers are racially polarized in my hometown, as they now tend to be in most large U.S. cities. But it probably wouldn't have made any difference where *To Sleep with Anger* opened. Recent black movies as otherwise different from one another as Lee's *Do the Right Thing*, John Single-ton's *Boyz N the Hood*, and the Hughes brothers' *Menace II Society* engage their audiences in games of call-and-response. The crowd's ongoing dialogue with the characters on screen is part of the narrative for Lee, Singleton, and the Hughes brothers; an element of their self-consciously streetwise mise en scène. Moody and resolutely unmanipulative, *To Sleep with Anger* was more like an inducement to its small audiences to dream in public, as Burnett had in writing and shooting it.

I know people in their thirties or forties who have stopped going to the movies altogether, except for the occasional foreign film. Such adults put themselves in a no-win situation. By waiting for the video, they allow their adolescent children to call the shots at the box office. This is one of the ways in which black audiences are no different from movie audiences in general. I suspect that *To Sleep with Anger* failed to excite distributors because they knew that those black urban adolescents who recognized something of their own lives in Lee's boom boxes, pizza slices, fade haircuts, Air Jordans, Tawana Brawley graffiti, and Public Enemy would be thrown for a loss by Burnett's toby stones, swamp roots, salted meats, railroad crossroads, and Bobby "Blue" Bland. And because an ominously quiet movie about the vexations of middle-aged black city dwellers originally from the rural South wasn't what white moviegoers were looking for, either. At least not in 1990, by which point audiences of both races had concluded that the only "authentic" contemporary black experience was that of the urban ghetto.

THE analogy between Burnett's movie and the blues records he chose for his soundtrack should be obvious. Generalizations are inaccurate by definition, and to say that black people no longer listen to the blues simply isn't true. For one thing, it depends—as it always has and probably always will—on what you mean by the blues. And even if you insist on a strict definition that eliminates music merely tinted with the blues, you find yourself having to rationalize the success of Malaco Records, a small, Delta-based company that's carved a comfortable niche for itself by selling albums and CDs by the likes of Little Milton and Bobby Bland to a largely middle-aged (and otherwise ignored) black Southern consumership.

For the most part, though, guardianship of the blues has passed from the black community to white bohemia. This is what many observers warned in the 1960s; a quick look around at a blues festival or even in a South Side club should be enough to tell you they were right. Instead of "guardianship," I almost wrote "ownership," a word to which some might object but one which perhaps reveals why so many white blues fans view this turn of events with such dismay. In one sense, it hardly matters who listens to the blues. Everyone's entitled to listen to whatever he or she chooses, and more power to those white audiences who are helping to keep the blues commercially aloft. In another sense, who's listening matters a great deal. If four decades of rock 'n' roll and close to three of rock criticism have taught us anything, it's that audiences play at least as great a role as performers in determining music's *meaning*. The notes I hear when I pop Charley Patton in my CD player are the same notes black Victrola owners heard in Mississippi in the late 1920s, aren't they? When John Lee Hooker performs at a blues festival, am I not hearing the same music that a black man of Hooker's own generation who might happen to be in the same audience is hearing? I think so, but I honestly don't know.

What I do know is that someone like Hooker once performed almost exclusively for black audiences approximately his own age; now his audience consists mostly of whites young enough to be his grandchildren. Who now has more in common with his audiences, a younger black blues performer like Lonnie Pitchford or a grown-up white sixties revivalist like John Hammond? Thankfully, the question of whether whites are capable of performing the blues credibly no longer triggers much debate. By this point, almost everybody is willing to concede that some whites sing and play the blues very well indeed (and that some always have, beginning with Frank Hutchinson and Jimmie Rodgers). Whatever you think of the music of a Charlie Musselwhite or a John Hammond (I'd vote "yea" on the former, a reluctant "nay" on the latter), you can't question either's dedication. They and Johnny Winter and John Mayall have stuck with the blues through thick and thin. If someone happens to announce a blues revival and that brings people through the doors, so much the better. But these performers are in for the long haul, blues revival or no. They've long since paid all dues required of them.

Besides, the (relative) lack of black faces in the crowd has become a greater cause for concern, because without them the blues no longer represents an oppositional black subculture, merely an upmarket consumer option. This seems to disturb whites more than it does blacks, and it's easy to understand why. In general, whites who embrace black music—be it blues, jazz, rap, whatever—are opening themselves up to aspects of black experience they worry will finally elude them. To be part of a sea of black faces offers both a thrill and a validation: one is being granted a privilege denied to other whites. On the other hand, most whites who listen exclusively to black music inevitably feel unworthy of it on some vague, existential level. For some whites, this is part of the attraction; far from the least curious aspect of a love whose fulfillment depends on remaining unrequited.

N O T I C E that I was careful to say "in general" and "for such whites." Some of us people of pallor just fall in love with the music, and I have no inkling of what, if anything, is going on in the souls of those white folks who show up at summer blues festivals shirtless, spill beer on themselves, trade high-fives with their girlfriends after every number, and shake their asses like poster children for rhythmic deficiency anemia. (Let's face it: if they *could* dance, they'd be someplace else.) Also, in saying that hardly anybody now contests the right of whites to sing the blues, I'm not saying that a performer's race goes virtually unnoticed. This controversy was given a brand new twist in the June 1993 issue of *Living Blues*. Paul Garon, one of the magazine's founding editors, wrote a piece in which he defended its policy of not publishing articles on white performers, no matter how dedicated or skillful:

> Only the very specific sociological, cultural, economic, psychological, and political forces faced by working class African Americans—forces permeated with racism—produced the blues. *Nothing else did. . . .*
>
> No matter who plays and sings the blues, no matter how wonderful they may be, no matter how much they have suffered or "lived the blues," for *Living Blues* and for many of its founders, *black culture is an inseparable part of the blues* to which the magazine has dedicated its existence.
>
> That is to say, for us the blues is defined *culturally* and not *acoustically*. This

explains why . . . the magazine has devoted space to "soul artists" like Tyrone Davis and Denise LaSalle but not "blues artists" like Stevie Ray Vaughan. From a *cultural* point of view, Davis and LaSalle are of far greater concern. [All italicized passages in the original.]

Garon concluded by hoping that *Living Blues* would continue "to perform the function for which it was created: To document a vital and important aspect of African American culture." As you can well imagine, his piece prompted a deluge of letters pro and con, but mostly the latter. In reference to his first point—about the blues owing its existence to white racism and *nothing else*—my own feeling (and probably that of most black Afrocentrics) is that this gives the white race entirely too much credit. His overriding point—about the blues being "*an inseparable part*" of black culture—strikes me as myopic. Important, definitely. But vital? Let's face it: if your reason for listening to black music is "cultural" rather than "acoustic," the music you ought to be listening to at this point is hip-hop.

Say what you will about rap—revile it as the crack baby of soul and funk—but admit that it might be the only remaining form of African-American music to meet every test of "folk" music, including the crucial one of its performers addressing the direct concerns of their audiences in their own language. The blues was a form of escape for its first performers and their audiences, whoever they were. The problem with hearing the early blues as a coded form of social protest has always been that it's just as easy to hear it as an imagined world without whites (which, granted, can itself be regarded as a form of protest). Whites are anything but absent in hardcore rap, where white cops in particular vie with "ho's," "bitches," and Asian grocers as targets of abuse. The people conspicuously missing from most hip-hop are black adults, especially those old enough to have firsthand or even inherited memories of the rural South (or memories of what it was like to swoon to Bobby Bland or Al Green, or to hear "I Can't Be Satisfied" blaring from a Chicago barber shop that day in 1948). Arrested Development aside, rap is the first black pop style entirely free of Southern inflections. And when its leading performers give props to their ancestors, they're more likely to be thinking of mythical African royalty than Delta sharecroppers.

At its most Afrocentric, rap is as much a memory song as the blues once was. But the South is now remembered as a place of shame and subjugation when "remembered" at all. Rap's bohemian-intellectual fringe (pushovers for onomatopoeia and a good end-rhyme) draw parallels between hip-hop and bebop—not between hip-hop and the blues, where parallels clearly do exist (including, as Giles Oakley put it about Original Gangster Peetie Wheatstraw, "the presentation of the singer himself as an almost mythical figure"). It used to be fashionable to blame the black bourgeoisie for "forgetting" the blues, and for wishing that everyone else would forget them, too.

239

B. B. King
(DOUG FULTON)

But the problem is now generational rather than one of class. To young men in South Central L. A. these days, "blues" refers to the prison uniforms large numbers of them will wind up wearing, not to a kind of song still sung and played by men of such genuine stature as John Lee Hooker and B. B. King.

T H E blues is dead; the blues will never die. I don't know which it is, though I suspect it's both. I seem to have developed the habit of misreading Big Bill Broonzy. In *Big Bill Blues*, he tells of how he once went fishing with his uncle as a young boy. They didn't catch any fish, but they did hook a very large turtle. They dragged the turtle home (I guess to make soup), and proceeded to chop off its head at the shell.

> [Then] we went in the house and stayed there a while. When we came back, no turtle. So we looked for him and the turtle was nearly back to the lake where we caught him. We picked him up, brought him back to the house and my Uncle said:
>
> "There's a turtle who's dead and don't know it."
>
> And that's the way a lot of people is today: they got the blues and don't know it.

When I first read this, I thought Big Bill's punch line was going to be something like, "And that's the way the blues is, too. If it's dead, it sure don't know it."

Though everyone more or less agrees that the last blues innovation was the discovery of electricity almost fifty years ago and that no more innovation is in store, the blues has never been more popular than it is now—not even during the 1960s. The April 1994 issue of *Living Blues* carried announcements for well over a hundred summer blues festivals in North America alone, and for another three dozen in Europe. But the biggest overseas market for the blues might be in Japan, where the Robert Johnson reissue has sold more than 100,000 copies (in the United States, it went platinum, with sales in excess of 500,000). MCA, Columbia, and Rhino report sales of as much as 100,000 for some of their blues reissues. As I hope I have at least suggested, technology has altered the course of popular music throughout this century, up to the present day. The introduction of compact discs in 1983 created a demand for instant product, and record companies began to exploit the bounty tucked in their vaults. But it isn't only vintage material that's flying out of the stores, and it isn't just the majors who are cleaning up. Alligator Records, an independent operated by Bruce Iglauer out of his Chicago apartment since 1971, probably releases more new blues recordings annually than any other label. With a roster including Lonnie Brooks, Son Seals, the reborn Johnny Winter, and Saffire—The Uppity Blues Women, Alligator grossed $4 million in sales in 1993. Robert Cray's new releases routinely crack the pop charts, as do John Lee Hooker's and Buddy Guy's. You have your choice of blues clubs in most large U.S. cities, and Isaac Tigrett, one of the founding partners in the Hard Rock Cafe chain of rock-themed restaurants, has started a chain of modern-day "juke joints" called House of Blues.

About the only place where blues is still ghettoized and severely underrepresented is on radio, a medium that once set trends but now generally lags several years behind. The newest format on public radio is something called "Triple A," for "adult acoustic alternative," though what it really seems to mean is white singer/songwriters and plenty of them. It's surprising that some bright public radio program director looking to increase his over-twenty-five share hasn't initiated something called "roots" radio. In addition to the blues, the "roots" format could include lots of New Orleans, vintage rock 'n' roll, modern country, reggae, R&B, zydeco, and smatterings of gospel and Afro pop. I have to think that there's an adult audience out there who wouldn't mind hearing B. B. King after Johnny Cash, or hearing either one of them after Richard Thompson or King Sunny Ade. I also have to think that such an audience would banner its eclecticism by making those phones light up during fund-raisers. So "roots" radio may be just a matter of time.

Meanwhile, that the current blues boom isn't the latest teenage eruption qualifies as good news insofar as people's taste in music tends to stabilize once they reach their late twenties. The people who are blues fans now are going to be blues fans for life, which means that this latest revival figures to be permanent.

I T ought to be, because it was a long time in coming. In one way, the sixties blues revival never ended, and what we're experiencing now is just an aftershock. It was in the sixties, after all, that whites became the primary audience for the blues, and this remains true. Stevie Ray Vaughan's *Texas Flood* in 1984, Robert Cray's *Strong Persuader* in 1986, John Lee Hooker's *The Healer* in 1989, and Robert Johnson's *The Complete Recordings* in 1990 are usually pointed to as the albums that launched this current blues revival. Around the same time, the huge sales racked up by such middle-aged pop performers as Bonnie Raitt and Eric Clapton pinpointed the existence of a similarly middle-aged audience bewildered by what they heard their kids listening to and ready to spend money on what I've described elsewhere as handmade music.

But the stage for this particular revival was set long before any of this. The first issue of *Living Blues* in 1970 and Alligator's debut release by the Chicago journeyman Hound Dog Taylor a year later are this revival's links to the sixties. *Living Blues* was the first magazine of its kind to be published in the United States. It created a forum for serious discussion of the blues. Taylor's album, which became a campus bestseller and put Iglauer's label on the map, was a different story: a happy, hard-rocking effort with no pretensions to depth. For better or worse, this also describes much of the blues heard since.

I like to shock people by telling them I think a real turning point in white America's perception of the blues was the release of John Landis's *The Blues Brothers* in 1980. I'm usually only half kidding. The whole thing was a gag that got out of hand. One night in 1977, on *Saturday Night Live*, Dan Aykroyd and the late John Belushi sang the blues dressed in dark suits and blindman's glasses like those John Hammond wore in those Florida bars. They called themselves Elwood and Jake Blues, and what was funny about the routine was that they weren't imitating black blues performers so much as spoofing a breed of white enthusiast who comes to *think* of himself as black. As with Spinal Tap a few years later, America failed to get the joke but laughed anyway. And Aykroyd and Belushi wound up laughing all the way to the bank, as the saying goes. They toured as Elwood and Jake, and even recorded a series of best-selling albums for Atlantic. To their credit, they seemed completely baffled by their success. "What can I tell you?" a winded Belushi asks the cheering throng on one of the Blues Brothers' live albums. "Buy as many blues records as you can." He sounds as though he'd like to add, "Just don't make the same mistake Aykroyd and I did and start your own band."

But it was the Blues Brothers' movie rather than the records that marked a turning point in the way white audiences interpreted urban blues and deep-fried R&B. Let's not be ideological or naive. White Americans have long assigned their own connotations to the music of their black countrymen, and these connotations have usually gone unquestioned. At any given point in blues evolution whites have been the ones who have determined what the blues was supposed to mean. This has been true since the very beginning. It's possible that whites named the blues. Among the meanings given by the *OED* for "blue" in the sense we're talking about are "affected with fear, discomfort, anxiety," "dismayed, perturbed, discomforted," and "depressed, miserable, low-spirited." British authors of the sixteenth and seventeenth centuries used to write of being in a "blue funk." The phrase "the blues" is derived from "the blue devils," a mental affliction of the early nineteenth century defined by the *OED* as despondency or spiritual depression. Think it over: If you enslaved a race of people and put them to work like mules, might not the music you heard them making for one another in their few unguarded moments sound to you like an expression of fear, discomfort, or anxiety?

The blues often was this, but it was just as often an attempt to forget all of this, dance music even at its most downhearted. This is increasingly the way today's white blues fans hear it; as endless boogie, a black party favor, the music of real-life Elwoods and Jakes. And maybe that's not such a bad thing, though I wish that those who do so had read Albert Murray's case for the blues as celebratory music in *Stomping the Blues* instead of drawing their conclusions (if only indirectly) from an awful movie that amounted to a minstrel's misinterpretation of the same message.

MAYBE what I'm blaming on the Blues Brothers should really be blamed on ZZ Top, or on one of those cultural mood swings that nobody ever sees coming (in this case, nostalgia for a time before rap, when black music was still a bridge between the races?). Myself, I've always liked Ralph Ellison's casual definition of the blues as "an autobiographical chronicle of catastrophe, expressed lyrically." I guess I want both, the celebration *and* the foreboding. I guess I want contemporary blues to be about what the best blues have always been about: not just good times but the transcendence of pain that makes good times possible.

Whatever it is I'm listening for, I don't find it in much of today's blues. I don't hear it in the preening slide work of Tinsley Ellis and Roy Rogers, in the self-conscious moans of the late John Campbell, or in the good-time shuffle of Little Charlie and the Nightcats, Anson Funderburgh and the

Rockets, and the legion of interchangeable Austin barroom bands. I don't even hear it in the music of such veteran black performers as A. C. Reed, Hubert Sumlin, Pinetop Perkins, and Katie Webster, crackerjack instrumentalists with no special aptitude as singers who did scintillating work behind the likes of Muddy Waters or Howlin' Wolf in decades past, but now release humdrum albums under their own names. They and others of their generation are frequently hailed as survivors. A cruel way of putting it would be to call them Muddy and the Wolf's remains—living reminders of seismic voices long stilled.

THE contemporary picture isn't nearly as grim as I'm making it sound. If you listen to enough contemporary blues, you're bound to hear plenty of music that moves more than your feet. The field includes performers roughly classifiable as Soulsters, Gloomy White Guys, Great Black Hopes, and Women with Guitars.

By Soulsters, I mean those who've recorded for the aforementioned Malaco Records and a good number of singers who haven't but just as well might—Johnny Adams, Otis Clay, Travis "Moonchild" Haddix, Denise LaSalle, Little Milton, Mighty Sam McClain, Johnnie Taylor, Maurice John Vaughn, Robert Ward, the late Z. Z. Hill, the late Arthur Alexander, and the getting-up-in-years and becoming-increasingly-more-bronchial Bobby "Blue" Bland. In other words, singers once dismissed by purists as mid-level soulmen, though to older black audiences it's always amounted to the blues (plenty of younger audiences are beginning to feel this way, too). The greatest of the Soulsters might be Ted Hawkins, a singer and guitarist who has virtually no black following at all. But I want to save him for the end.

THE Gloomy White Guys serve their purpose by refusing to circulate at the party. For Dave Alvin, a former member of the Blasters whose current songs draw from both blues and country, and whose *Museum of the Heart* was one of the most enjoyable wallows of 1993, "barroom" signifies a man pushing them back in an otherwise empty tavern and sometimes not wanting even a bartender and a juke box for company—a trip from the roadside motel to the nearest package store will do the trick just as well. The gloomiest of all white blues performers was probably John Campbell, a former substance abuser from Shreveport who died of a fatal heart attack in 1993, at the age of forty-one. Campbell was a man stranded at a personal crossroads, never sounding remotely black but never sounding remotely like himself, either.

By far the most talented of the Gloomy White Guys is Chris Whitley, a debauched Jesus-man whose only album so far is one of very few that wouldn't sound hopelessly anticlimatic after an hour or so of Robert Johnson.

As in Johnson's music (but in so little of today's blues), something more than groove sounds at stake in Whitley's best songs—possibly the singer's immortal soul. And as in Johnson's, the guitar combines with the voice in such a way as to make it seem as though both are shivering with an emotion somewhere between joy at being alive and dread at what life might hold in store. Whitley's career will be worth following closely.

A group of Gloomy White Guys I especially liked were the members of a Boston-based echobilly band called Treat Her Right, which has since splintered into the alternative radio favorites Morphine. Treat Her Right frequently sounded like Muddy Water's band with Maureen Tucker of the Velvet Underground on drums; or maybe I mean the Velvets with Hubert Sumlin on lead guitar. I'm tempted to describe their three murky albums as punk blues, though that may be a contradiction in terms insofar as punk was about tightening the same sets of muscles the blues loosens up (to paraphrase the rock critic Robert Christgau, whereas most forms of American popular music have swung with a vengeance, or at least attempted to, punk resolutely *didn't* swing with a vengeance). In Treat Her Right's case, the unlikely combination worked like a charm, proving that the staying power of the blues lies in its ability to disguise itself as anything. "I've got a gun/ I know how to use it," went one of their catchiest chants—and damned if I didn't always find myself chanting along, Gloomy White Guy myself. And damned if Robert Johnson and Skip James weren't saying pretty much the same things in their songs about what they were packing (to say nothing of Ice Cube and NWA).

STEVIE Ray Vaughan wasn't a Gloomy White Guy, though his much-publicized drug problems and his death at the age of thirty-five in a 1990 helicopter crash might tempt us to think of him as one. Vaughan had finally kicked his addiction when that chopper taking him from a gig in Wisconsin to another in Chicago nose-dived. He may also have been on the verge of finding his own voice—and I don't mean metaphorically. He was the first guitarist since Hendrix to win a pop following largely on the strength of his instrumental prowess rather than on his vocals. Along with his older brother, Jimmy (once of the Fabulous Thunderbirds), he helped to focus national attention on the thriving Austin blues bar scene. Before becoming this current revival's first martyr, he was its first superstar, briefly its greatest emissary to hard rock. Even now at blues festivals, you still spot white boys copying his look: shoulder-length hair and pointed sideburns, soul patch, low-topped and wide-brimmed black Texas hat, that deathlike pallor that's the next best thing to blackness for a white junkie playing black man's music or living in a black man's world.

Vaughan was a great guitarist, and as a singer he was—a great guitarist.

This is kinder than saying he was a latterday coon shouter, though I wonder about the contention of his biographers Joe Nick Patoski and Bill Crawford that the fellow members of the Austin blues band he joined as a teenager nicknamed him "Little Nigger" because he was a fuck-up, not because he tried so hard to sound black. Here and there, especially on slower numbers ("The Sky Is Crying," for example), you hear a potentially expressive singer trying to get a sound in edgewise over those profligate guitar licks. Maybe if he had lived long enough to relax, his voice would have found its way out—that's more or less what happened with Eric Clapton.

Or maybe if Vaughan had emulated Lonnie Mack's impassioned vocal style as well as his guitar heroics. Mack is a veteran white performer whose 1963 instrumental hit "Wham!" grabbed hold of the adolescent Vaughan (who went on to produce and add a touch of star power to one of the albums Mack released on Alligator in the early eighties). "He did all that wild-ass, fast-picking, whammy-bar stuff, then he would do a ballad, and it would sound like a cross between gospel and the blues—incredibly soulful and eerie," Vaughan once told Ed Ward. "[He] really taught me to play guitar from the heart, to really tap your insides." Mack offered a similar lesson as a singer, never sounding even on his earliest records like anything but what he was—a white Hoisier with a touch of black Memphis in his soul. Vaughan had similar potential, but we distort his memory if we fail to acknowledge that potential was all it was.

ROBERT Cray, the only young(er) contemporary blues performer aside from Vaughan to gain a foothold with white rock audiences, achieves a better balance than Vaughan between voice and guitar, and between innovation and tradition. I include Cray among the Great Black Hopes, a category that should be self-explanatory. Those who worry that the blues is withering despite the current craze for it take heart in the arrival of gifted younger performers, and it's almost too much to hope for when a few of those younger performers are black. It's taken to mean that the blues is still a living tradition.

A case could also be made for Cray as a Soulster, and not just because he travels and records with horns and occasionally lets loose with a convincing shriek. As classic soul was, Cray's songs are driven by a perception of sex as sin—and by an acceptance of sin as the only thing in this world that affords pleasure, whatever the ultimate cost.

Blues writers designate as "postmodern" anything recorded since the last revival. But Cray qualifies as postmodern in another way. In songs such as "Right Next Door (Because of Me)" from his 1986 breakthrough album *Strong Persuader*, he undercuts the bluesman's traditional machismo while giving a credible approximation of it. It's possible that the lion's share of

Robert Cray
(RAY AVERY'S JAZZ
ARCHIVES)

the credit for this should go to Dennis Walker, Cray's former producer and songwriting partner. It was Walker who wrote "Right Next Door," told from the point of view of a man guiltily listening on the other side of a motel wall as the woman he sweet-talked into bed hours before breaks up with her regular man—a *good* man, better for her than the strong persuader singing the song. In "I'm a Good Man," a much later song co-written by Walker and Cray but with Walker's fingerprints all over it, the singer tells us that he doesn't mean to brag but he's a good man—he'll always be there for his woman. It's left to Cray's guitar to deflate these pious declarations, to reveal how self-congratulatory they are. The unspoken message of the song is that a man who makes such a big deal of his own sensitivity isn't to be trusted.

With Cray and Walker, the blues has come a long way from "It's Tight Like That." I know almost nothing about Walker, except that he's also produced and written songs for a variety of other performers, including Ted Hawkins and Joe Louis Walker. He might be white, he might be black, but I'm willing to wager that he's Southern. So is Cray, but only by birth. The

247

son of a career military officer, he was born in Columbus, Georgia, in 1953, but moved from there with his family before he was a year old. He grew up on military bases all over the map, until his father was permanently stationed near Tacoma, Washington, when Cray was in his teens. Most of the articles on Cray have pointed out that he didn't begin to listen to the blues until he was in his early twenties, by which time he was already a veteran of numerous soul and psychedelic cover bands. On his early albums, Cray often sounded as though he was singing because someone in the band had to. (He's since gained more self-confidence.) In terms of their material, these early albums had a generic feel to them. So did *Shame + a Sin*, a 1993 album which Cray produced himself and which included no songs by Walker. Where Cray goes from here is impossible to say, but his partnership with Walker produced some great music while it lasted—songs of a depth and complexity not often found in contemporary pop or blues.

OTHER Great Black Hopes include the organist Lucky Peterson and the guitarists and singers Larry McCray, Kenny Neal, Lonnie Shields, Chris Thomas, and Joe Louis Walker. By pop standards, none of them is especially young. Nor is Lil' Ed Williams, the guitar-playing leader of Lil' Ed and the Blues Imperials; and nor are the junior members of the Kinsey Report, a Chicago family band led by Lester "Big Daddy" Kinsey. The oldest of these performers is Walker, who once shared a producer with Cray, and whose gospel background is evident in the healthy shake he gives his high notes. Walker was born in 1949. Peterson was born in 1964, which makes him the youngest of those included here. But the emergence of any black performer born after Muddy Waters's Chess debut helps to dispel the widespread notion that the blues is now a form of music in which "black" means ancient and "young" means white. To one degree or another, all of these performers have been influenced by hard rock, not always for the better. McCray, Donald Kinsey, and Thomas (a son of the still-active New Orleans bluesman Tabby Thomas) all sometimes lose track of themselves in Jimi Hendrix. The (relatively) young men to watch in this grouping are Lonnie Shields and Kenny Neal (a son of Raful Neal), both of whom offer up bewitching, funk-influenced variations on the oldest country blues. Before her death in 1993, Valerie Wellington was another promising newcomer—a classically trained singer with a genuine feel for the songs of Ma Rainey and Bessie Smith.

I almost decided to call the Women with Guitars, Chicks with Picks—an admittedly tasteless joke not too wide of the mark in describing the somewhat self-conscious stance occasionally taken by such younger women guitarists as Rory Block, Joanna Conner, and Sue Foley. They face a problem in that blues rhythm is frequently equated with male strut; some members of their mostly male audiences are never going to get over the fact that those are *girls* up there, walking that walk (often in short skirts and spike heels, no less). Sometimes I think these women guitarists have never gotten over it themselves. But Block in particular is an accomplished slide guitarist—one of the best contemporary interpreters of Robert Johnson and other legends of years gone by. Austin mainstay Lou Ann Barton is probably the most consistently satisfying of the younger women singers, though she occasionally overplays her tough-girl side.

Bonnie Raitt and Lucinda Williams warrant special mention here as eclectic pop singers who continue to draw inspiration from the blues. Williams has obviously listened to Memphis Minnie, but never copies her. Raitt's musical mother was Sippie Wallace, just one of the elder blues performers to whom she's called wider attention. In addition to being a tireless campaigner for the blues, Raitt sings and plays them with grace and conviction. It doesn't

Bonnie Raitt
(DOUG FULTON)

249

matter what *kind* of song she happens to be doing—the blues echoes in everything she does. She knows who she is as a performer, and she knows that the blues are a part of her.

The most magnetic figures on the contemporary scene may be those black performers born in the 1930s and early 1940s who missed out on the urban ferment of the 1950s and the folk and electric blues revivals of the 1960s by just a few years. Johnny Copeland, a Texan in his late fifties who could give most other singer/guitarists lessons in stagecraft and dynamics, is beginning to assume the mantle of an elder statesman, and he wears it with dignity. For all his stage antics, so did Albert Collins, whose lean and percussive fretting was frequently likened to an ice pick (thus such album titles as *Ice Pickin'*, *Frostbite*, and *Frozen Alive*), and who was not yet sixty when he died toward the end of 1993. Copeland is never going to be as famous as John Lee Hooker. No matter how old he grows to be, he's never going to have the same mythological mojo working in his favor, or benefit from the same grandfather clause that allowed Hooker to become a star. So, if it takes a blues revival to draw attention to a trouper such as Copeland, let the next revival begin—or let this one never end.

B U T the final words here should be about Ted Hawkins, because he's the contemporary performer who brings us full circle.

No one knows who sang the very first blues. All that anyone knows is that the first blues performer would have been surprised to hear himself or herself called that. To their own way of thinking, the first blues singers were songsters. These were local or itinerant performers who sang any tune that caught their fancy or put money in their cups, occasionally even making up their own songs.

Ted Hawkins, whose affinity to Sam Cooke makes him a Soulster, is also a latterday songster, if ever there was one. Until very recently, he could be found sitting on a milk crate and singing his own songs or Sam Cooke's or John Denver's or Charlie Pride's for spare change on the boardwalk in Venice Beach, California. A tall black man with an intense gaze, his hair and beard just beginning to gray, Hawkins plays his guitar and keeps time by patting his foot on a wooden board among the panhandlers, body builders, and Frisbee tossers. Technically speaking, he doesn't sing the blues. Though born in the Delta, he's a died-in-the-wool soul man in his late fifties who'll also warble a pop or gospel or country tune even without a request for one, especially if he thinks he can sing it better than the original performer—which he usually can. ("He didn't sprinkle enough pepper on it," he says of Charlie Pride's recording of "Crystal Chandelier.") But he performs no blues per se, though the emotion he wrings out of the blue notes on the numbers he does sing should be enough to persuade anyone who's still skeptical that the blues doesn't always fit into those cherished twelve bars. Besides, as Kurt Loder put it in a 1987 issue of *Rolling Stone*:

> His bio, if not his repertoire, is truly the blues—a harrowing chronicle of wino camps, work-gang whippings, and aimless boxcar ramblings, of hunger and homelessness so abject as to make [his] frequent stints in prison camps seem like sylvan interludes. . . .

Romanticized? Slightly. But it leaves out Hawkins's prostitute mother, the father he never met, his troubled relationships with women, his years in detox centers and psychiatric wards. Given everything Hawkins has been through, that boardwalk milk crate must have been heaven, and he might still be on it if not for the promise of greener pastures still.

As I write, in the early summer of 1994, Hawkins is still semiobscure. This could change. About two years ago, an employee of Geffen Records, who was passing through Venice Beach, heard Hawkins on the boardwalk and was immediately smitten. Hawkins was signed to a Geffen contract, and the label's publicity department is doing everything it can to make him a star. When I finally heard him live, it wasn't on the Venice boardwalk. It was on stage at the Bottom Line, in New York.

Amazingly, nobody at Geffen seemed at first to realize that all of this had happened at least twice before—once in the early eighties, when an independent producer flew Hawkins to Nashville to record a session eventually released as *The Boardwalk Tapes*; then again toward the end of that decade when Bruce Bromberg and Dennis Walker recorded him for Rounder. There's potential for bitter irony here. Hawkins's first release for Geffen might sell double what his Rounders sold and still not be enough to satisfy a major label. He might wind up back on that boardwalk. If so, it's a cinch he'll be discovered once again, a few years hence. It's another way in which Hawkins could *be* the blues.

EPILOGUE

· ·

THE BLUES TAKES A HOLIDAY, THE BLUES THUMBS A RIDE

Junior Wells is dynamite with a harmonica in his mouth, another jive James Brown imitator when he sings and starts to step. The opening night headliner of the 1993 Chicago Blues Festival, he kept telling us that he was "the Godfather of the Blues," just in case we had missed the point.

Wells put me in a bad mood, but I couldn't very well blame the weather on him. Memorial Day weekend was much too early for an outdoor festival, especially one in a city whose springtime weather can be as unpredictable as Chicago's. The rain was already falling when I landed at O'Hare, and it didn't let up all weekend. The temperature dropped about fifteen degrees on my drive into the city, and it must have been in the low forties by the time Wells wrapped up his set. Standing there chilled to the bone in Grant Park, just a few hundred yards from the lake, I suddenly knew why the people who live here call the wind "the hawk."

At least the weather kept the crowds down—a calamity from the point of view of the producers, but a blessing from mine. Though even people who know me well think of me as antisocial, my aversion to crowds is actually a symptom of a condition very much like claustrophobia. I not only need *my space*; I need it to be defined in a way that's virtually impossible at an outdoor festival. Maybe I'm in the wrong line of work. But this time, it wasn't the crowd that was bringing me down. It was the music, as enjoyable as most of it was. The nighttime lineup included the Staple Singers, Hank Crawford and Jimmy McGriff, and the Johnny Otis Revue—acts representing gospel, jazz, and R&B rather than the blues per se. Generally, this doesn't bother me. In fact, I'm philosophically in favor of such a broad definition of the blues; and Crawford, in particular, has been a favorite of mine since his days as music director and alto saxophone soloist with Ray Charles. But his presence at a blues festival, along with that of Otis and even Mavis

Staples, was a reminder that anyone who says the blues is as vital as ever is kidding himself. It's true that the blues will never die, but perhaps only in the sense that there will always be something packaged and sold as the blues. We'll go on stretching our definition to incorporate other forms of black music no longer popular with younger black audiences and in which the blues is merely *inherent* (as a radical theologian would say God is in man).

"The uniqueness of a work of art is inseparable from its being embedded in the fabric of tradition," wrote Walter Benjamin in "The Work of Art in the Age of Mechanical Reproduction."

> This tradition itself is thoroughly alive and extremely changeable. An ancient statue of Venus, for example, stood in a different traditional context with the Greeks, who made it an object of veneration, than with the clerics of the Middle Ages, who viewed it as an ominous idol. Both of them, however, were equally confronted with its uniqueness, that is, its aura.

In the case of the blues—"a work of art" in its totality, "imbedded in the fabric of tradition" and (ideally) "never entirely separated from its ritualistic function"—the "aura" is all that remains, and it's only because we insist that it does. Much of what festivals such as this one are intended to preserve is gone forever, or soon will be. In Chicago, the duo of John Cephus and Phil Wiggins (latterday Piedmont bluesmen, in the style of Brownie McGhee and Sonny Terry, but with their own happy vibe) and other acoustic performers were relegated to the daytime hours "crossroads" stage, where even in good weather they would have played for mostly white crowds numbering in the dozens. And the "modern" bluesmen featured on the nighttime bills, like Wells and Johnny Copeland, would have looked as out of place on the South Side as they would on the Miracle Mile. You can always spot a blues musician in a crowd; he's the middle-aged black man whose clothing and hairstyle are a decade or more out of date. Among veteran blues performers, jheri curls are just now catching on.

By Sunday, the final night of the festival, the rain was falling too hard for me to even think of walking to the park. I'd gotten so drenched at the crossroads stage that afternoon that I had to dry my paper money on a bathroom clothesline. As if to tip my mood from annoyance to abject depression, a phone call from home brought the news that the outcat bandleader Sun Ra had died. I had a radio sent up to my hotel room to hear the live broadcast, and as I lay there chain-smoking and watching the sky fall in puddles on Michigan Avenue, I found myself thinking of another miserable holiday weekend a few years before. To my utter astonishment, this unexpected memory cheered me up.

EPIPLOGUE

THE Saturday after Thanksgiving in 1987, my Significant-Something-or-Other and I drove from Philadelphia to suburban Maryland to visit her relatives. Though I'm genuinely fond of my in-laws, I wasn't looking forward to this particular encounter with them. As usual, I was in the middle of an assignment, still in the brooding stages of it, and I guess I resented the interruption. But it wasn't only that. With its emphasis on family values most of us now honor only in the breach, Thanksgiving can be tough going even if you don't have to battle traffic. And at this particular family sitdown, I was going to be badly outnumbered. I was going to be expected to enter someone else's history, as it were—to take sides in or bear silent witness to family arguments couched in the language of reminiscence; arguments that were raging long before I came into the picture and could never be won or lost anyway. Family can be a blueprint for alienation, even when the family's your own and you at least know what the unspoken issues are. With someone else's, you feel as though you've just dropped in from the moon (and want to head back there ASAP).

My girlfriend, who was doing the driving, wasn't in such a good mood, either, and the long and the short of it is that we got hopelessly lost after leaving the turnpike. We drove for hours through faceless suburbs, slowing down to ask directions whenever we spotted a pay phone or a pedestrian. The problem was we didn't quite know how to describe to the few strangers we saw where we were supposed to be, and we weren't able to describe over the phone where we were to the people who were holding brunch for us (and steadily growing more annoyed with us for starting from Philly so late in the first place).

The rain gushed in every time we rolled down the window, and we gradually reached the point where we could no longer bear the sound of the wipers, the cassettes we had brought with us, and each other's voices. So we turned on the radio, to hunt for a public station.

We found a blues show on WPFW-FM, Washington's Pacifica affiliate. The DJ was a middle-aged black man who never gave his name in the hour or so that we listened, and who sounded as soured on the whole idea of home and hearth as we were. He told of how he'd stuffed himself with turkey and filling the night before. Not that he'd been that hungry, you understand? It was Thanksgiving and all, and somebody had invited him over. So he ate to be polite. Understand? He read a public service announcement about a series of documentary films being screened that weekend at Howard University. "Now, I'm not big on things like culture," he admitted after giving the details. "But I plan ta go ta see these movies myself. And I'll tell you what else. I'm gonna bring a lady I just met with me. Impress her, too, I bet."

Then he played a solid half hour of the late O. V. Wright, a somewhat obscure labelmate of Al Green's on Hi Records in the 1970s—Green's contemporary, though he sounded more like the missing link between Green and Bobby "Blue" Bland. The Great Lost Soulster, in other words, a man *hurting* with love and not ashamed to tell the world—slow drumbeats echoing his ache.

As Wright's screams rent the air and the nameless DJ cut in between the tracks to reiterate what Wright had just said ("I would rather be *blind*, crippled, and *crazy*") . . . there was no place I would rather have been than lost on the road in that Toyota, with the rain falling down.

THAT day was a lesson in the blues, a music that has always been about wanting to be someplace else but making the best of where you are. I knew that intuitively even then, and I knew that this is why the blues seems to reach everybody sooner or later. But thinking back on that day as I listened to the radio in Chicago, I realized something else about the blues. In lieu of defining them, you could say that they happened as a result of one group of people being forced to enter another's history. The same with blues revivals, but in reverse and by choice. All of American music is a family argument by this point, with no one content to bear silent witness.

I turned the radio up loud for the Staple Singers, and found myself thinking benign thoughts even about those Blues Brothers for whom the blues is nothing more than a ticket down to funky town. That's the way it's always been with black music, hasn't it? It ain't over till the white man dances. And maybe not even then.

A C K N O W L E D G M E N T S

. . . .

There should probably be more here about minstrels, coon shouters, zydeco, and the relationship of blues to jazz, country, and soul. But each of these could be a separate book. There should also be more about the contemporary blues scene, but a "history" of anything inevitably focuses on the past. Blues supremacists are going to complain that this is a pop critic's history of the blues. So be it. I believe that what we call the blues mutated into a form of pop the moment it was first commercially recorded, and I expect some reviewers to argue.

But enough, for now, about what this history of the blues is or isn't. It's time to roll the credits. So many individuals assisted in the writing of this book—often without realizing it—that I'm bound to overlook a few. I apologize to them in advance.

My first thanks should go to Charles Hobson, of Mojo Working Productions, who initiated *The History of the Blues* as a TV project, and to David Wolff, of WNET-TV, who brought me on board. I thank Charles—and John Williams, of Vanguard Films—for allowing me a free hand in telling my version of the story, even though it often conflicted with theirs (as anyone who bothers to compare this book to the TV series bearing the same name will soon realize). I am also grateful to Claudia Rizzi, Charles's assistant, who provided me with interview transcripts and rounded up the photographs for this book.

James Butler and John Mohead gave up a sunny Saturday afternoon in April to escort me around the Delta, and I value the insights I drew from them. Thanks also to Robert Gordon, Michael Leonard, Ron Wynn, Jim O'Neal and the staff at Stackhouse Records, Kerry Dacon of the Center for Southern Folklore, and Sid Graves and John Ruskey of the Delta Blues Museum for giving me a sense of where I was and what I should be looking for in Memphis and Clarksdale.

Talking with Peter Guralnick is as rewarding as reading him, and the same goes for Sam Charters. They might not realize it, but I owe thanks to both of them for telling me I was on the right track when I was on the right track and setting me straight when I needed to be set straight.

Allen Lowe is going to recognize many of his own ideas here, and I look forward to reading his own book on early popular song. Ira Berger found me books I might otherwise never have located, as did John Szwed, who contributed to this venture in numerous other ways. Donald Elfman of Koch International and the infallible Terri Hinte of Fantasy Records were among several record company publicists who graciously provided me with CDs. Others to whom I am indebted for valuable pieces of information or favors both large and small include Chris Albertson, Carl Apter, Eric Bruskin, John Buckley, Barry Dollins, Stephen LaVere, Milo Miles, Danny Miller, Robert Mugge, Maren Stange, Kevin Whitehead, Valerie Wilmer, and the staff of the Free Library of Philadelphia.

A fellowship from the John Simon Guggenheim Memorial Foundation, intended to facilitate the writing of a biography of John Coltrane, wound up facilitating the writing of this book instead. I promise that Coltrane will be next, and I thank George Andreou, my editor at Alfred A. Knopf, for his patience. I'm grateful to William Whitworth of *The Atlantic Monthly*, Joe Levy of the *Village Voice*, Linda Hasert of the *Philadelphia Inquirer*, and Steve Simels of *Stereo Review* for granting me what amounted to a leave of absence in order to complete this book. Thanks also to Corby Kummer, my fellow castaway on the island of overdue authors these last few months (good luck with the coffee book). I should mention that the chapter on Robert Johnson first appeared in a much different form in *The Atlantic Monthly*, and that the passage on Big Joe Turner first saw print as an *Inquirer* obituary.

No thank you I could muster would be large enough to acknowledge the support I've received from Mark Kelley, my agent, and Patricia Mulcahy, my editor at Hyperion. Thanks also to Yvonne Murphy, Pat's assistant.

Dorothy Davis, my mother, and Terry Gross, identified earlier in these pages as my Significant-Something-or-Other, though that hardly begins to describe what she means to me, have enriched my life with their innumerable goodnesses. As ever, my biggest thanks goes to them—and I promise them, no more chatter about pig's feet and Fred Below's backbeat.

Last but not least, shout outs to Sean of Apple Technical Assistance for his work on my Macintosh Classic II, Drs. Sylvan Hurewitz and Francis J. DuFrayne for their work on my digestive tract, and Elvis Costello for "Every Day I Write the Book"—*my* idea of a blues moan, as that light at the end of the tunnel turned out not to be spring, but early summer.

F.D.
Philadelphia,
June 1994

JOHNNY ACE *Memorial Album* MCA MCAD-31183

JOHNNY ADAMS *I Won't Cry: The Original Ron Recordings* Rounder CD-2083 *Walking on a Tightrope* Rounder CD-2095 *Johnny Adams Sings Doc Pomus: The Real Me* Rounder CD-2109 *Good Morning Heartache* Rounder CD-2125

ARTHUR ALEXANDER *Lonely Just Like Me* Elektra/Nonesuch 61475-2

TEXAS ALEXANDER *Complete Recorded Works in Chronological Order (1927–1950),* Vols. 1–3 Matchbox MBMCD-2001-3

THE ALLMAN BROTHERS BAND *Live at the Fillmore East* Polydor 2-823273-2

DAVE ALVIN *Museum of the Heart* Hightone HCD-8049

ALBERT AMMONS/MEADE LUX LEWIS *The First Day* Blue Note B21Y-98450

PINK ANDERSON *Carolina Blues,* Vol. 1 Original Blues Classics OBCCD-504-2

KOKOMO ARNOLD/CASEY BILL WELDON *Bottleneck Guitar Trendsetters of the 1930s* Yazoo CD-1049

BARBECUE BOB *Chocolate to the Bone* Yazoo CD-2005

ROOSEVELT "BUBBA" BARNES *Heatbroken Man* Rooster Blues R726232

LOU ANN BARTON *Old Enough* Antone's ANT-0021

COUNT BASIE *One O'Clock Jump* MCA-42324

CAREY BELL *Mellow Down Easy* Blind Pig BP-74291

CHUCK BERRY *The Chess Box* Chess CHD3-80001 *The Great 28* Chess 2-CHD-92500

BIG MACEO *The King of Chicago Blues Piano* Arhoolie Folklyric CD-7009

ELVIN BISHOP *Big Fun* Alligator ALCD-4767

BLACK ACE *I'm the Boss Card in Your Hand* Arhoolie CD-374

SCRAPPER BLACKWELL *The Virtuoso Guitar of Scrapper Blackwell* Yazoo CD-1019

BLIND BLAKE *Ragtime Guitar's Foremost Fingerpicker* Yazoo CD-1068

BOBBY "BLUE" BLAND *I Pity the Fool: The Duke Recordings*, Vol. 1 MCA MCAD-2-10665 *Turn on Your Love Light: The Duke Recordings*, Vol. 2 MCA MCAD-10957 *Touch of the Blues/Spotlighting the Man* Mobile Fidelity MFCD-10-00770 *Years of Tears* Malaco MCD-7469

RORY BLOCK *High Heeled Blues* Rounder CD-3061

MIKE BLOOMFIELD *Essential Blues 1964–1969* Columbia/Legacy CK-57631

LOUISE BOGAN (BESSIE JACKSON) and WALTER ROLAND *1923–1935* Story of Blues SB-3535; *1927–1935* Yazoo CD-1017

JUKE BOY BONNER *Gave Me a Dirty Deal* Arhoolie CD-375

JAMES BOOKER *New Orleans Piano Wizard: Live!* Rounder CD-2027

TINY BRADSHAW *The Great Composer* King KCD-653

LONNIE BROOKS *Bayou Lightnin'* Alligator ALCD-4714 *Sweet Home Chicago* Evidence ECD-26001 *Let's Talk It Over* Delmark DD-660

BIG BILL BROONZY *Good Time Tonight* Columbia CK-46219 *Big Bill Blues* Portrait Masters RK-44089 *The Young Big Bill Broonzy* Yazoo CD-1011 *Do That Guitar Rag* Yazoo CD-1035 *Big Bill Broonzy Sings Folk Songs* Smithsonian/Folkways SFCD-40023 *Big Bill Broonzy and Washboard Sam* MCA CHD-9251

CHARLES BROWN *Driftin' Blues: The Best of Charles Brown* EMI E21Y-97989 *One More for the Road* Alligator ALCD-4771 *All My Life* Bullseye Blues CDBB-9501

CLARENCE "GATEMOTH" BROWN *The Original Peacock Recordings* Rounder CD-2039 *Texas Swing* Rounder CD-11527

JAMES BROWN *20 All-Time Greatest Hits!* Polydor 314-511326-2 *Live at the Apollo* Polydor 823479-2 *Star Time* Polydor 4-849108-2

R. L. BURNSIDE *Bad Luck City* Fat Possum FPCD-1001

PAUL BUTTERFIELD *The Paul Butterfield Blues Band* Elektra 7294-2

JOHN CAMPBELL *One Believer* Elektra 61086-2

CANNED HEAT *The Best of Canned Heat* EMI America E21Y-48377

CANNON'S JUG STOMPERS (GUS CANNON) *The Complete Recordings* Yazoo CD-1082/3

LEROY CARR *The Complete Recorded Works in Chronological Order (1928–1935)*, Vols. 1–6 Document DOCD 5134-39

BO CARTER *Twist It Babe 1931–1940* Yazoo CD-1034 *Banana in Your Fruit Basket* Yazoo CD-1064

JOHN CEPHAS and PHIL WIGGINS *Dog Days of August* Flying Fish FF-70394 *Bluesmen* Chesky JD-89

RAY CHARLES *The Birth of Soul—The Complete Atlantic Rhythm & Blues Recordings, 1952–1959* Atlantic 3 82310-2

CLIFTON CHENIER *Zydeco Dynamite: The Clifton Chenier Anthology* Rhino 71194 *Zydeco Blues and Boogie* Speciality SPCD-7039 *60 Minutes with the King of Zydeco* Arhoolie CD-301

OTIS CLAY *I'll Treat You Right* Bullseye Blues BBCD-9520 *The Gospel Truth* Blind Pig BPCD-5005

JAYBIRD COLEMAN and the BIRMINGHAM JUG BAND *Complete Recorded Works in Chronological Order (1927–1930)* Document DOCD-5140

ALBERT COLLINS *The Complete Imperial Recordings* EMI E22V-96740 *Truckin' with Albert Collins* MCA MCAD-10423 *Ice Pickin'* Alligator ALCD-4713 *Frostbite* Alligator ALCD-4719 *Frozen Alive!* Alligator ALCD-4725 *Iceman* Pointblank/Charisma 91583-2 *Collins Mix, The Best of Albert Collins* Pointblank V21Z-39097

ALBERT COLLINS/ROBERT CRAY/JOHNNY COPELAND *Showdown!* Alligator AL-4743

"CRYING SAM COLLINS" *Jailhouse Blues* Yazoo CD-1079

JOANNA CONNOR *Believe It* Blind Pig BP-73289

JOHNNY COPELAND *Texas Twister* Rounder CD-11504 *When the Rain Starts Fallin'* Rounder CD-11515 *Flyin' High* Verve 314-517-512-2 *Catch Up with the Blues* Verve 314-521239

JAMES COTTON *High Compression* Alligator ALCD-4737

ROBERT CRAY *Too Many Cooks* Tomato R2-70381 *Bad Influence* Hightone HCD-8001 *False Accusations* Hightone HCD-8005 *Strong Persuader* Mercury/Hightone 830568-2 *Don't Be Afraid of the Dark* Mercury 834923-2 *Midnight Stroll* Mercury 846652-2 *I Was Warned* Mercury 314-512721-2 *Shame $^+$ a Sin* Mercury 314-518237-2

PEE WEE CRAYTON *Things I Used to Do* Vanguard VMD-6566

IDA COX *Blues for Rampart Street* Original Jazz Classics OJCCD-1758-2

ARTHUR "BIG BOY" CRUDUP *That's All Right Mama* RCA Bluebird 07863-61043-4 *Mean Ole Frisco* Collectables COLCD-5130 *That's All Right Mama* Relic 7036

COW COW DAVENPORT *Charles "Cow Cow" Davenport (1926–1938)* B.o.B. 5

REVEREND GARY DAVIS *From Blues to Gospel* Biograph BCD-123 *Pure Religion and Bad Company* Smithsonian/Folkways CDSF-40035 *Say No to the Devil* Original Blues Classics OBCCD-519-2 *Harlem Street Singer* Original Blues Classics OBCCD-547-2 *Reverend Gary Davis at Newport* Vanguard VMD-73008

REVEREND GARY DAVIS/PINK ANDERSON *Gospel, Blues and Street Songs* Original Blues Classics OBCCD-524-2

JIMMY DAWKINS *All for Business* Delmark DE-634 *Tribute to Orange* Evidence ECD-26031

WILLIE DIXON *The Big Three Trio* Columbia CK-46216 *Willie's Blues* Original Blues Classics OBCCD-501 *The Chess Box* Chess CHD2-16500 *I Am the Blues* Mobile Fidelity MFCD-10-00872

THOMAS A. DORSEY (GEORGIA TOM) *Come On Mama, Do That Dance* Yazoo CD-1041 *Precious Lord* Columbia/Legacy CK-57164

CHAMPION JACK DUPREE *New Orleans Barrelhouse Boogie* Columbia/Legacy CK-52834 *Blues Masters, Vol. 6* Storyville 8006 *Blues from the Gutter* Atlantic 82432-2 *Back Home in New Orleans* Bullseye Blues CDBB-9502

SNOOKS EAGLIN *Country Boy in New Orleans* Arhoolie CD-348 *Out of Nowhere* Black Top CDBT-1046 *Teasing You* Black Top CDBT-1072

SLEEPY JOHN ESTES *I Ain't Gonna Be Worried No More, 1929–1941* Yazoo CD-2004 *The Legend of Sleepy John Estes* Delmark DD-603 *Brownsville Blues* Delmark DD-613

THE FABULOUS THUNDERBIRDS *Walk That Walk, Talk That Talk* Epic Associated ZK-47878

SUE FOLEY *Young Girl Blues* Antone's ANTCD-0019

ARETHA FRANKLIN *The Great Aretha Franklin: The First 12 Sides* Columbia CK-31953 *Queen of Soul* Rhino R2-71063 *I Never Loved a Man the Way I Love You* Atlantic 8139-2

FRANK FROST *Jelly Roll Blues* Paula CD-20 *Midnight Prowler* Earwig CD-4914

BLIND BOY FULLER *East Coast Piedmont Style* Columbia/Legacy CK-46777 *Truckin' My Blues Away* Yazoo CD-1060

JESSE FULLER *Frisco Bound* Arhoolie CD-360 *San Francisco Bay Blues* Original Blues Classics OBCCD-537-2 *Jesse Fuller's Favorites* Original Blues Classics OBCCD-528 *Jazz, Folk Songs, Spirituals & Blues* Original Blues Classics OBCCD-564

LOWELL FULSON *Tramp/Soul* Flair V21Z-86300 *Hung Down Head* Chess CHD-9325 *San Francisco Blues* Black Lion BLCD-760176 *It's a Good Day* Rounder CD-2088 *One More Blues* Evidence ECD-26022-2

AL GREEN *Let's Stay Together* The Right Stuff T21Y-27121 *I'm Still in Love with You* The Right Stuff T21Y-27627 *Al Green Sings the Gospel* Motown 37463-5319-2

TINY GRIMES *Featuring Screamin' Jay Hawkins* Collectables COLCD-5304 *Tiny Grimes and Friends* Collectibles COLCD-5321 *Tiny Grimes and His Rockin' Highlanders, Vol. 2.* Collectibles COLCD-5317

GUITAR SLIM *Sufferin' Mind* Specialty SPCD-7007-2

BUDDY GUY *The Very Best of Buddy Guy* Rhino R2-70280 *Complete Chess Studio Sessions* Chess CHD2-9337 *A Man and the Blues* Vanguard VSD-79272 *Damn Right, I've Got the Blues* Silvertone 1462-2 *Feels Like Rain* Silvertone 01241-41498-2

BUDDY GUY and JUNIOR WELLS *Buddy Guy and Junior Wells Play the Blues* Rhino R2-70299 *Alone and Acoustic* Alligator ALCD-4802

TRAVIS "MOONCHILD" HADDIX *Winners Never Quit* Ichiban ICH-1101

JOHN HAMMOND *Best of John Hammond* Vanguard VCD-11/12 *I Can Tell* Atlantic 82369-2 *John Hammond* Rounder CD-11532 *Live* Rounder CD-3074 *Nobody But You* Flying Fish FF-70502 *Trouble No More* Pointblank/Charisma V21Z-88257

LIONEL HAMPTON *Flyin' Home* Decca Jazz MCAD-42349

SELECTED DISCOGRAPHY

SLIM HARPO *The Best of Slim Harpo* Rhino R2-70169

WYNONIE HARRIS *Good Rockin' Tonight* Charly CD-244

ERSKINE HAWKINS *The Original Tuxedo Junction* RCA Bluebird 9682-2

TED HAWKINS *On the Boardwalk*, Munich MRCD-123 *On the Boardwalk*, Vol. 2 Munich MRCD-126 *Watch Your Step* Rounder CD-2024 *Happy Hour* Rounder CD-2033 *The Next Hundred Years* Geffen/DGC 24627

CLIFFORD HAYES and the DIXIELAND JUG BLOWERS *Clifford Hayes and the Dixieland Jug Blowers* Yazoo CD-1054

JIMI HENDRIX *Blues* MCA MCAD-11060

Z. Z. HILL *Greatest Hits* Malaco MAL-7437-CD

EARL HOOKER *Blue Guitar* Paula PCD-18 *Two Bugs and a Roach* Arhoolie CD-324 *Play Your Guitar Mr. Hooker* Black Top BT-1093

JOHN LEE HOOKER *The Ultimate Collection* Rhino R2-70572 *Boogie Chillun* Fantasy FD-24706 *40th Anniversary Album: Original 1948–1961 Recordings* DCC Compact Classics DZS-042 *House of the Blues* Chess CHD-9258 *John Lee Hooker Plays and Sings the Blues* Chess CHD-9199 *The Real Folk Blues* Chess CHD-9271 *That's My Story* Original Blues Classics OBCCD-538-2 *The Country Blues of John Lee Hooker* Original Blues Classics OBCCD-542-2 *Detroit Special* Atlantic 82365-2 *Don't Turn Me from Your Door* Atco 7-82365-2 *The Best of John Lee Hooker* MCA MCAD-10539 *The Healer* Chameleon 74808-2 *Mr. Lucky* Pointblank/Charisma 91724-2 *Boom Boom* Pointblank V21S-86553

JOHN LEE HOOKER and CANNED HEAT *Hooker 'n' Heat* EMI E2AS-97896

LIGHTNIN' HOPKINS *Mojo Hand: The Lightnin' Hopkins Anthology* Rhino 71226 *Complete Aladdin Recordings* EMI E22V-96843 *The Gold Star Sessions*, Vol. 1, Arhoolie CD-330 *The Gold Start Sessions*, Vol. 2, Arhoolie CD-337 *The Herald Recordings* Collectibles COLCD-5121 *Lightnin' Hopkins* Smithsonian/Folkways SFCD-40019 *The Complete Prestige/Bluesville Recordings* Prestige 7PCD-4406-2 *Lightnin' New York* Candid CCD-79010 *The Texas Bluesman* Arhoolie CD-302

BIG WALTER "SHAKEY" HORTON *Mouth Harp Maestro* Flair V214-86297 *Fine Cuts* Blind Pig BP-70678

SON HOUSE *Son House and the Great Delta Blues Singers (1928–1930)* Document CD-5002 *Delta Blues: The Original Library of Congress Sessions from Field Recordings 1941–1942* Biograph CD-118 *Father of the Delta Blues: The Complete 1965 Recordings* Columbia/Legacy C2K-48867

PEG LEG HOWELL and EDDIE ANTHONY *Complete Recorded Works in Chronological Order*, Vols. 1–2 (1926–1930) Matchbox MBMCD-2004-5

HOWLIN' WOLF *Cadillac Daddy: Memphis Recordings* Rounder CDSS-28 *Rides Again* Flair V214-86295 *The Chess Box* Chess CHCD3-9322 *Howlin' Wolf/Moanin' in the Moonlight* Chess CHD-5908 *The Real Folk Blues* Chess CHD-9273 *More Real Folk Blues* Chess CHD-9279

ALBERTA HUNTER *Amtrak Blues* Columbia CK-36430

ALBERTA HUNTER/LOVIE AUSTIN and HER BLUES SERENADERS *Chicago: The Living Legends* Original Blues Classics OBCCD-510

ALBERTA HUNTER/LUCILLE HEGAMIN/VICTORIA SPIVEY *Songs We Taught Your Mother* Original Blues Classics OBCCD-520

IVORY JOE HUNTER *16 of His Greatest Hits* King KCD-605

MISSISSIPPI JOHN HURT *1928 Sessions* Yazoo CD-1065 *The Best of Mississippi John Hurt* Vanguard VSD-73103 *Today!* Vangard VMD-79220 *The Immortal Mississippi John Hurt* Vanguard VMD-79248

J. B. HUTTO *Sidewinder* Delmark DD-636 *Slidewinder* Evidence ECD-26009

PAPA CHARLIE JACKSON *Complete Recorded Works in Chronological Order*, Vols. 1–3 (1924–1934) Document DOCD-5087-89

ELMORE JAMES *Let's Cut It* Flair V21Z-86257 *The Sky Is Crying: The History of Elmore James* Rhino R7-71190 *The Complete Fire and Enjoy Sessions, Parts 1–4* Collectibles COLCD-5184-87 *King of the Slide Guitar* Capricorn 2-42006

ELMORE JAMES/JOHN BRIM *Whose Muddy Shoes* Chess CHD-9114

SKIP JAMES *Complete 1931 Recordings in Chronological Order* Document DOCD-5005 *Skip James Today!* Vanguard VMD-79219 *Devil Got My Woman* Vanguard VMD-79273

SKIP JAMES/JACK OWENS *1931–1981* Wolf WBS-CD-009

BLIND LEMON JEFFERSON *King of the Country Blues* Yazoo CD-1069 *Blind Lemon Jefferson* Milestone MCD-47022

"BIG" JACK JOHNSON *Daddy, When Is Mama Comin' Home* Earwig CD-4916

BLIND WILLIE JOHNSON *The Complete Recordings of Blind Willie Johnson* Columbia/ Legacy C2K-52835

LONNIE JOHNSON *Complete Recorded Works in Chronological Order (1925–1932)*, Vols. 1–7 Document 5063-69 *Steppin' on the Blues* Columbia CK-46221 *He's a Jelly Roll Baker* RCA Bluebird 66064-2 *Complete 1937 to June 1947 Recordings in Chronological Order (1937–1947)*, Vols. 1–3 Blues Document BDCD 6024-26 *Blues by Lonnie Johnson* Original Blues Classics OBCCD-502-2 *Blues and Ballads* Original Blues Classics OBCCD-531-2 *Losin' Game* Original Blues Classics OBCCD-543-2 *Another Night To Cry* Original Blues Classics OBCCD-550-2 *Blues Masters*, Vol. 4 Storyville 8004 *The Complete Folkways Recordings* Smithsonian/Folkways CDSF-40067

LONNIE JOHNSON and VICTORIA SPIVEY *Idle Hours* Original Blues Classics OBCCD-518

PETE JOHNSON *Central Avenue Boogie* Delmark DD-656

ROBERT JOHNSON *The Complete Recordings* Columbia C2K-46222

TOMMY JOHNSON *Complete Recorded Works in Chronological Order (1928–1929)* Document CD-5001

LOUIS JORDAN *The Best of Louis Jordan* MCA MCAD-4079-2 *Five Guys Named Moe: Original Decca Recordings*, Vol. 2 MCA MCAD-10503

SELECTED DISCOGRAPHY

JACK KELLY and HIS SOUTH MEMPHIS JUG BAND *Complete Recorded Works in Chronological Order (1933–1939)* Blues Document BDCD-6005

JUNIOR KIMBROUGH *All Night Long* Fat Possum FP-1002

ALBERT KING *The Ultimate Collection* Rhino R2-71268 *Born Under a Bad Sign* Mobile Fidelity UDCC-577 *The King of the Blues Guitar* Atlantic 8213 *Best of Albert King* Stax FCD-60-005 *Live Wire/Blues Power* Stax SCD-4128 *Blues at Sunrise* Stax SCD-8546-2 *Albert* Tomato R2-70398 *King Albert* Tomato R2-70395

ALBERT KING and LITTLE MILTON *Chronicle* Stax SCD-4123

ALBERT KING/OTIS RUSH *Door to Door* Chess CHD-9322

B. B. KING *Singin' the Blues/The Blues* Flair V21Y-86296 *Spotlight on Lucille* Flair V21Y-86231 *My Sweet Little Angel* Virgin V21Y-39103 *The King of the Blues* MCA4-10677 *Live at the Regal* MCA MCAD-31106 *Great Moments with B. B. King* MCA MCAD-4124 *Blues Is King* MCA MCAD-31368 *Indianola Mississippi Seeds* MCA MCAD-31343 *Live in Cook County Jail* MCA MCAD-31080 *The Best of B. B. King* MCA MCAD-31040 *Midnight Believer* MCA MCAD-27011 *There Must Be a Better World Somewhere* MCA MCAD-27034 *The King of the Blues: 1989* MCA MCAD-42183 *Live at San Quentin* MCA MCAD-6455 *Live at the Apollo* GRP GRD-9637 *There Is Always One More Time* MCA MCAD-10295

B. B. KING and BOBBY "BLUE" BLAND *Together for the First Time: Live* MCA 2MCAD-4160 *Together Again* MCA MCAD-270129

B. B. KING and DIANE SCHUUR *Heart to Heart* GRP GRD-9767

FREDDIE KING *Just Pickin'* Modern Blues MBXLCD-721 *Freddie King Sings* Modern Blues MBXLCD-722 *Let's Hideaway and Dance Away* King KCD-773 *!7 Original Greatest Hits* Deluxe DCD-7845 *Blues Guitar Hero* Ace CDCH-454 *Freddie King Is a Blues Master* Atlantic 90345-2

LESTER "BIG DADDY" KINSEY *I Am the Blues* Verve 314-519175-2

THE KINSEY REPORT *Edge of the City* Alligator ALCD-4758 *Powerhouse* Pointblank/Charisma 91421

DENISE LASALLE *Hittin' Where It Hurts* Malaco MAL-7447-CD

LAZY LESTER *Harp and Soul* Alligator ALCD-4768

LEADBELLY *King of the 12-String Guitar* Columbia/Legacy CK-46776 *Midnight Special* Rounder CD-1044 *Gwine Dig a Hole to Put the Devil In* Rounder CD-1045 *Let It Shine on Me* Rounder CD-1046 *Sings Folk Songs* Smithsonian/Folkways CDSF-40010 *The Titanic* Rounder CD-1097 *Nobody Knows the Trouble I've Seen* Rounder CD-1098 *Go Down Old Hanna* Rounder CD-1099 *Alabama Bound* RCA 9600-2-R

J. B. LENOIR *His JOB Recordings* Paula PCD-04 *Natural Man* Chess CHD-9323

FURRY LEWIS *In His Prime (1927–28)* Yazoo CD-1050 *Shake 'Em on Down* Fantasy FCD-24703-2

MEADE LUX LEWIS *Blues Piano: The Artistry of Meade Lux Lewis* Original Jazz Classics OJCCD-1759

SMILEY LEWIS *I Hear You Knockin': The Best of Smiley Lewis* EMI E21Y-98824

LIGHTNIN' SLIM *Blue Lightning* Igo CD-2002

LI'L ED and the BLUES IMPERIALS *What You See Is What You Get* Alligator ALCD-4808

MANCE LIPSCOMB *Texas Songster and Sharecropper* Arhoolie CD-305 *You Got to Reap What You Sow* Arhoolie CD-398

LITTLE MILTON *The Sun Masters* Rounder CDSS-35 *We're Gonna Make It/Little Milton Sings Big Blues* Chess CHD-5906 *If Walls Could Talk* Chess CHD-9289 *Grits Ain't Groceries* Stax SCD-8529-2 *Walking the Back Streets* Stax SCD-8514-2 *The Blues Is Alright* Evidence ECD-26026

LITTLE WALTER *The Blues World of Little Walter* Delmark 648 *The Essential Little Walter* Chess CHD2-9342 *The Best of Little Walter* Chess CHD-9192 *The Best of Little Walter*, Vol. 2 Chess CHD-9292 *Hate to See You Go* Chess CHD-9342

ROBERT ''JUNIOR'' LOCKWOOD *Steady Rollin' Man* Delmark DD-630 *Contrasts* Trix 3307 *Plays Robert and Robert* Evidence ECD-26020

CRIPPLE CLARENCE LOFTON *The Complete Recorded Works in Chronological Order (1935–1943)*, Vols. 1–2 Blues Document BDCD 6006-7

LONESOME SUNDOWN *Been Gone Too Long* Hightone HCD-8041

MIGHTY SAM MCCLAIN *Give It Up to Love* Audioquest AQCD-1015

TOMMY MCCLENNON *1939–1942* Wolf WBCD-001

LARRY MCCRAY *Delta Hurricane* Charisma/Pointblank 87784-2

MISSISSIPPI FRED MCDOWELL *Mississippi Delta Blues* Arhoolie CD-304 *Long Way from Home* Original Blues Classics OBCD-535-2

BROWNIE MCGHEE *The Folkways Years 1945–1959* Smithsonian/Folkways CDSF-40034 *Brownie's Blues* Original Blues Classics OBCCD-505-2

BROWNIE MCGHEE and SONNY TERRY *Brownie McGhee and Sonny Terry* Smithsonian/Folkways CDSF-40011 *The Complete Brownie McGhee* Columbia/Legacy C2K 52933 *Blues Masters*, Vol. 5 Storyville STCD-8005 *Sing* Smithsonian/Folkways SFCD-40001 *Midnight Special* Fantasy FCD-24721 *Just a Closer Walk with Thee* Original Blues Classics OBCCD-541 *Sonny Terry and Brownie McGhee* Original Blues Classics OBCD-546

JAY MCSHANN *Blues from Kansas City* Decca Jazz GRD-614

BLIND WILLIE MCTELL *1927–1933 The Early Years* Yazoo CD-1005 *Doin' That Atlanta Strut* Yazoo CD-1037 *The Definitive Blind Willie McTell* Columbia/Legacy C2K-53234 *Complete Library of Congress Recordings in Chronological Order (1940)* Blues Document BDCD-6001 *Atlanta Twelve String* Atlantic 82366-2 *The Last Session* Original Blues Classics OBCD-517-2

WILLIE MABON *Willie Mabon* Chess CHD-9189

LONNIE MACK *Strike Lightning* Alligator ALCD-4739

MAGIC SAM *1957–66* Paula PCD-2 *West Side Soul* Delmark DD-615 *Live* Delmark 2DE-645 *Magic Touch* Black Top BTCD-1085

JOHN MAYALL *Wake Up Call* Silvertone 01241-41518

JOHN MAYALL and ERIC CLAPTON *Bluesbreakers* Deram 800086-2

PERCY MAYFIELD *Poet of the Blues* Specialty SPCD-7001-2 *Volume 2: Memory Pain* Specialty SPCD-7027-2

MEMPHIS JUG BAND *The Memphis Jug Band* Yazoo CD-1067

MEMPHIS MINNIE *Hoodoo Lady* Columbia/Legacy CK-46775 *Ain't No Bad Girl* Portrait Masters RK-44072 *Early Rhythm and Blues* Biograph BCD-124

MEMPHIS SLIM *Memphis Slim* Chess CHD-9250 *The Real Folk Blues* Chess CHD-9270 *Rainin' the Blues* Fantasy FCD-24705-2 *Memphis Slim U.S.A.* Candid CLD-79024 *Tribute to Big Bill Broonzy* Candid CLD-79023

MISSISSIPPI SHEIKS *Stop and Listen* Yazoo CD-2006

LITTLE BROTHER MONTGOMERY *Complete Recorded Works in Chronological Order, 1930–36* Document DOCD-5109 *Chicago: The Living Legends—Southside Blues* Original Blues Classics OBCCD-525 *Chicago: The Living Legends—Piano, Vocal, and Band Blues* Original Blues Classics OBCCD-525 *Tasty Blues* Original Blues Classics OBCCD-554 *Blues Masters*, Vol. 7 Storyville STCD-8007 *At Home* Earwig CD-4918

CHARLIE MUSSELWHITE *Stand Back!* Vanguard VMD-79232 *Memphis Charlie* Arhoolie CD-303 *Memphis, Tennessee* Mobile Fidelity MFCD-10-00775 *Ace of Hearts* Alligator ALCD-4781 *Signature* Alligator ALCD-4801 *In My Time* . . . Alligator ALCD-4818

KENNY NEAL *Big News from Baton Rouge!* Alligator ALCD-4764 *Walkin' on Fire* Alligator ALCD-4774 *Walking on Fire* Alligator ALCD-4795 *Bayou Blood* Alligator ALCD-4809

RAFUL NEAL *Louisiana Legend* Alligator ALCD-4781

ROBERT NIGHTHAWK *Robert Lee McCoy a.k.a. Robert Nighthawk: Complete Recorded Works in Chronological Order (1937–1940)* Wolf WBCD-002 *Live on Maxwell Street* Rounder CD-2022

THE NIGHTHAWKS *Jacks and Kings* Adelphi ADC-4120

JOHNNY OTIS *Spirit of the Black Territory Bands* Arhoolie CD-384 *The New Johnny Otis Show with Shuggie Otis* Alligator ALCD-4726

JUNIOR PARKER *Junior's Blues: The Duke Recordings*, Vol. 1 Duke MCAD-10669

JUNIOR PARKER/JAMES COTTON/PAT HARE *Mystery Train* Rounder CDSS-38

CHARLIE PATTON *Founder of the Delta Blues* Yazoo CD-1020 *King of the Delta Blues* Yazoo 2CD-2001

ANN PEEBLES *Fulltime Love* Bullseye Blues BBCD-9515

PINETOP PERKINS *Pinetop's Boogie Woogie* Antone's ANT-0020

LUCKY PETERSON *Lucky Strikes* Alligator ALCD-4740 *I'm Ready* Verve 314-517-513-2 *Beyond Cool* Verve 314-521-147

ELVIS PRESLEY *The Complete '50s Masters* RCA 5-07863-66050-2 *The Complete Sun Sessions* RCA 6414-2 *Elvis Is Back* RCA 2231-2 *Reconsider Baby: Elvis Sings the Blues* RCA PCD1-5418

SAMMY PRICE *Rib Joint* Savoy Jazz ZDS-4417 *Barrelhouse and Boogie* Black Lion BLCD-760159

PROFESSOR LONGHAIR *New Orleans Piano: Blues Originals*, Vol. 2 Atlantic 7225-2 *Crawfish Fiesta* Alligator ALCD-4718

YANK RACHELL *Complete Recorded Works 1934–1941 in Chronological Order (1934–1941)*, Vols. 1–2 Wolf WBCD-006-7 *Chicago Style* Delmark 649

MA RAINEY *The Paramounts Chronologically, 1924–25*, Vols. 1–2 Black Swan WCH-12001/2 *Ma Rainey's Black Bottom* Yazoo CD-1071 *Ma Rainey* Milestone MCD-47021-2

BONNIE RAITT *Bonnie Raitt* Warner Bros. 1953 *The Bonnie Raitt Collection* Warner Bros. 26242 *Nick of Time* Capitol C21Z-91268

OTIS REDDING *The Very Best of Otis Redding* Rhino R2-71147

JIMMY REED *Jimmy Reed* Paula PCD-8 *The Best of Jimmy Reed* GNP Crescendo 2GNPD-0006 *Compact Command Performances* Motown 37463-9065-2 *Jimmy Reed at Carnegie Hall/The Best of Jimmy Reed* Mobile Fidelity UDCD-566

LESLEY RIDDLE *Step by Step* Rounder CD-0299

JUDY RODERICK *Woman Blues* Vanguard VSD-79197

JIMMIE RODGERS *America's Blue Yodeler, 1930–1931* Rounder CD-1060

JIMMY ROGERS *Chicago Bound* Chess CHD-93000 *Ludella* Antone's ANT-0012

ROY ROGERS *Chops Not Chaps* Blind Pig BP-74892 *Slide of Hand* Liberty C21S-81097

OTIS RUSH *1956–1958 The Cobra Recordings* Paula CD-01 *Cold Day in Hell* Delmark DE-638 *Right Place, Wrong Time* Hightone HCD-8007 *Lost in the Blues* Alligator ALCD-4797 *Tops* Blind Pig BP-73188 *Screamin' and Cryin'* Evidence ECD-26014-2 *Live in Europe* Evidence ECD-26034-2 *Ain't Enough Comin' In* Mercury 314-518769-2

JIMMY RUSHING *The Essential Jimmy Rushing* Vanguard VCD-65/66

SAFFIRE—THE UPPITY BLUES WOMEN *Saffire—The Uppity Blues Women* Alligator ALCD-4779

SON SEALS *Midnight Sun* Alligator ALCD-4708 *Live and Burning* Alligator ALCD-4712

LONNIE SHIELDS *Portrait* Rooster Blues CD-72626

JOHNNY SHINES *Last Night's Dream* Blue Horizon 45285-2 *Traditional Delta Blues* Biograph BCD-121 *Johnny Shines* Hightone HCD-8028

BESSIE SMITH *The Collection* Columbia Jazz Masterpieces CK-44441 *The Complete Recordings, Volume 1: The Empress of the Blues* Columbia/Legacy C2K-47091

Volume 2 Columbia/Legacy C2K-47471 *Volume 3* Columbia/Legacy C2K-47474 *Volume 4* Columbia/Legacy C2K-52838

J. T. "FUNKY PAPA" SMITH   *The Howling Wolf* Yazoo CD-1031

OTIS SPANN   *The Blues Never Die* Original Blues Classics OBCCD-530-2 *Otis Spann Is the Blues* Candid CCD-79001 *Walking the Blues* Candid CCD-79025 *Blues Masters*, Vol. 10 Storyville 8010

OTIS SPANN/LIGHTNIN' HOPKINS   *The Complete Candid Otis Spann and Lightnin' Hopkins Sessions* Mosaic MD3-139

SPECKLED RED   *Blues Masters*, Vol. 11 Storyville 8011

FRANK STOKES   *Creator of Memphis Blues* Yazoo CD-1056

HUBERT SUMLIN   *Hubert Sumlin's Blues Party* Black Top CDBT-1036

SUNNYLAND SLIM   *Slim's Shout* Original Blues Classics OBCCD-558 *House Rent Party* Delmark DD-655 *Blues Masters*, Vol. 8 Storyville 8008

ROOSEVELT SYKES   *The Complete Recorded Works in Chronological Order (1929–1944)*, Vols. 1–7 Document DOCD-5116-22 *The Postwar Years, 1946–54* Wolf CD-WBJ-004 *The Honeydripper* Original Blues Classics OBCCD-557 *The Return of Roosevelt Sykes* Original Blues Classics OBCCD-546-2 *Gold Mine* Delmark DD-616

TAJ MAHAL   *Best of Taj Mahal*, Vol. 1 Columbia CK-36258 *Dancing the Blues* Private Music 01005-82112-2

TAMPA RED   *Bottleneck Guitar* Yazoo CD-1039 *The Guitar Wizard* CK-53235 *1928–1942* Story of Blues CD-3505 *Don't Tampa with the Blues* Original Blues Classics OBCD-516-2 *Don't Jive Me* Original Blues Classics OBCD-549-2

HOUND DOG TAYLOR and the HOUSEROCKERS   *Hound Dog Taylor and the Houserockers* Alligator ALCD-4701

JOHNNIE TAYLOR   *Who's Makin' Love* Stax STCD-4115-2 *The Best of Johnnie Taylor*, Vol. 1 Malaco MAL-7463-CD

KOKO TAYLOR   *Koko Taylor* Chess CHD-31271 *What It Takes: The Chess Years* Chess CHD-9328 *From the Heart of a Woman* Alligator ALCD-4724

SONNY TERRY   *The Folkways Years 1944–1963* Smithsonian/Folkways SFCD-40033 *Sonny's Story* Original Blues Classics OBCCD-503 *Sonny Is King* Original Blues Classics OBCCD-521 *Whoopin'* Alligator ALCD-4734

CHRIS THOMAS   *Simple* Hightone HCD-8043

HENRY THOMAS   *The Complete Recordings 1927–1929* Yazoo CD-1080/81

BIG MAMA THORNTON   *Hound Dog: The Peacock Recordings* Peacock MCAD-10668 *Ball and Chain* Arhoolie CD-305

HENRY TOWNSEND   *St. Louis Country Blues, Complete Recorded Works in Chronological Order (1929–1937)* Document DOCD-5147 *Mule* Nighthawk NHCD-201

TREAT HER RIGHT   *Treat Her Right* RCA 6884-2 *What's Good for You* Rounder CD-9028

"BIG" JOE TURNER *I've Been to Kansas City: Volume 1* Decca Jazz MCAD-42351 *Every Day in the Week* Decca Jazz GRD-621 *Tell Me Pretty Baby* Arhoolie CD-333 *Jumpin' with Joe: The Complete Aladdin Recordings* EMI-99293 *Big, Bad & Blue: The Big Joe Turner Anthology* Rhino 3-R2-71550 *Greatest Hits* Atlantic 81752-2 *Memorial Album: The Rhythm and Blues Years* Atlantic 81663-2 *The Boss of the Blues* Atlantic 8812-2 *Big Joe Rides Again* Atlantic 90668 *Singing the Blues* Mobile Fidelity MFCD-10-00780 *The Best of "Big" Joe Turner* Pablo PACD-2405-404-2 *Texas Style* Evidence ECD-26013-2

"BIG" JOE TURNER and ROOMFUL OF BLUES *Blues Train* Muse MCD-5293

STEVIE RAY VAUGHAN and DOUBLE TROUBLE *Texas Flood* Epic EK-38734 *Couldn't Stand the Weather* Epic EK-39304 *Soul to Soul* Epic EK-40036 *Live Alive* Epic EGK-40511 *In Step* Epic FE-45024 *The Sky Is Crying* Epic EK-47390

THE VAUGHAN BROTHERS *Family Style* Epic Associated 2K-46225

MAURICE JOHN VAUGHN *Generic Blues Album* Alligator ALCD-4763 *In the Shadow of the City* Alligator ALCD-4813

EDDIE "CLEANHEAD" VINSON *Kidney Stew* Black and Blue CD-233021 *Kidney Stew Is Fine* Delmark 631 *Cleanhead and Roomful of Blues* Muse MCD-5282

EDDIE "CLEANHEAD" VINSON and CANNONBALL ADDERLEY *Cleanhead and Cannonball* Landmark LCD-1309-2

JOE LOUIS WALKER *The Gift* Hightone HCD-8012 *Blue Soul* Hightone HCD-8019 *Live at Slim's*, Vol. 1 Hightone HCD-8025 *Live at Slim's*, Vol. 2 Hightone HCD-8036 *Blues Survivor* Verve 314-519063 *JLW* Verve 314-523118

T-BONE WALKER *The Complete T-Bone Walker 1940–1954* Mosaic M6-130 *The Complete Imperial Recordings* EMI E22V-96737 *T-Bone Blues* Atlantic 8020-2 *I Want a Little Girl* Delmark DD-633

SIPPIE WALLACE *Women Be Wise* Alligator ALCD-4810 *Sippie* Atlantic 81592-2

ROBERT WARD *Fear No Evil* Black Top CDBT-1093 *Rhythm of the People* Black Top CDBT-1088

WASHBOARD SAM *Rockin' My Blues Away* RCA Bluebird 07863-61042-2

DINAH WASHINGTON *Mellow Mama* Delmark DD-451 *The Complete Dinah Washington on Mercury, Volume 1 (1946–1949)* Mercury 3-832444-2 *The Bessie Smith Songbook* Emarcy 826663-2

TUTS WASHINGTON *New Orleans Piano Professor* Rounder CD-11501

ETHEL WATERS *On Stage and Screen (1926–1940)* Sony Music Special Products A-2792

MUDDY WATERS *The Complete Plantation Recordings, The Historic 1941–42 Library of Congress Field Recordings* Chess CHD-9344 *The Chess Box* Chess CH3-8002 *The Best of Muddy Waters* Chess CHD-31268 *Rare and Unissued* Chess CHD-9180 *Trouble No More: Singles (1955–1959)* Chess CHD-9291 *Muddy Waters at Newport* Chess HCD-31269 *Folk Singer/Sings Big Bill Broonzy* Chess CHD-5907 *Real Folk Blues* Chess CHD-9274 *More Real Folk Blues* Chess CHD-9278 *Muddy,*

Brass and the Blues Chess CHD-9266 *They Call Me Muddy Waters* Chess CHD-9299 *The London Muddy Waters Sessions* Chess CHD-9298 *Can't Get No Grindin'* Chess CHD-9319 *Live at Mr. Kelly's* Chess CHD-9338 *Blue Skys* Epic Associated/Legacy 2K-46172 *Hard Again* Blue Sky ZK-34449 *I'm Ready* Blue Sky ZK-34928 *Muddy "Mississippi" Waters Live* Blue Sky ZK-35712 *King Bee* Blue Sky ZK-37064

KATIE WEBSTER *The Swamp Boogie Queen* Alligator ALCD-4766

VALERIE WELLINGTON *Million Dollar Secret* Rooster Blues R-72619

JUNIOR WELLS *1957–1963: Messin' with the Kid* Paula PCD-03 *Hoodoo Man Blues* Delmark DD-612 *It's My Life, Baby* Vanguard VMD-73120 *On Tap* Delmark DD-635 *Southside Blues Jam* Delmark DD-628 *Better Off with the Blues* Telarc CD-83354

PEETIE WHEATSTRAW *The Devil's Son-in-Law* (1931–40) B.o.B. 8

BUKKA WHITE *The Complete Bukka White* Columbia CK-52782 *Sky Songs* Arhoolie CD-323

JOSH WHITE Vols. 1–3 (Document 5194–5196)

CHRIS WHITLEY *Living with the Law* Columbia CK-46996

ROBERT WILKINS *The Original Rolling Stone* Yazoo CD-1077

BIG JOE WILLIAMS *Blues on Highway 49* Delmark DD-604 *Shake Your Bootie* Arhoolie CD-315 *Nine String Guitar Blues* Delmark DD-627 *Walking Blues* Fantasy FCD-24724-2 *Blues Masters*, Vol. 2 Storyville STCD-8002 *Classic Delta Blues* Original Blues Classics OBCCD-545-2

JOE WILLIAMS *Every Day, The Best of the Verve Years* Verve 314 519 813-2

LUCINDA WILLIAMS *Happy Woman Blues* Smithsonian/Folkways SFCD-40003 *Ramblin'* Smithsonian/Folkways SFCD-40042

ROBERT PETE WILLIAMS *Free Again* Original Blues Classics OBCCD-553-2 *Blues Masters*, Vol. 1 Storyville STCD-8001

SONNY BOY WILLIAMSON #1 (JOHN LEE WILLIAMSON) *Complete Recorded Works in Chronological Order (1937–1947)*, Vols. 1–5 Document DOCD-5055-59

SONNY BOY WILLIAMSON #1/BIG JOE WILLIAMS *Throw A Boogie Woogie* RCA Bluebird 9599-2

SONNY BOY WILLIAMSON #2 (RICE MILLER) *King Biscuit Time* Arhoolie CD-310 *The Essential Sonny Boy Williamson* Chess CHD-2-9243 *One Way Out* Chess CHD-9116 *Down and Out Blues* Chess CHD-31272 *Bummer Road* Chess CHD-9324 *The Real Folk Blues* Chess CHD-9272 *More Real Folk Blues* Chess CHD-9277 *The Blues of Sonny Boy Williamson* Storyville STCD-4062 *Keep It to Ourselves* Alligator ALCD-4787

SONNY BOY WILLIAMSON/WILLIE LOVE *Clownin' with the World* Alligator ALCD-2700

EDITH WILSON *He May Be Your Man* Delmark 637

JOHNNY WINTER *Guitar Slinger* Alligator ALCD-4735

JIMMY WITHERSPOON *Blowin' in from Kansas City* Flair V21Y-86299 *Spoon So Easy: The Chess Years* Chess CHD-93003 *The Spoon Concerts* Fantasy FCD-24701-2

Evenin' Blues Original Blues Classics OBCCD-511-2 *Baby, Baby, Baby* Original Blues Classics OBCCD-527

O. V. WRIGHT   *The Soul of O. V. Wright* MCA/Duke-Peacock MCAD-10670

JIMMY YANCEY   *The Complete Recorded Works in Chronological Order (1939–1950),* Vols. 1–3 Document DOCD-5041-43

JIMMY and MAMA YANCEY   *Chicago Piano: Volume 1* Atlantic 82368-2

Anthologies

The Alligator Records 20th Anniversary Collection Alligator 2-ALCD-105/6

The Alligator Records 20th Anniversary Tour Alligator Al 107/8

Antone's Tenth Anniversary Anthology Antone's ANTCD-0004

Antone's Anniversary Anthology: Volume 2 Antone's ANTCD-0016

Best of Chess Rock 'n' Roll, Volume 1 Chess CHD-31319 (Includes "Rocket 88")

The Best of Excello Records, Volume 1: Sound of the Swamp Rhino R2-70896

Better Boot That Thing: Great Women Blues Singers of the 1920's Bluebird 66065-2

The Blues: A Smithsonian Collection of Classic Blues Singers Smithsonian Collection of Recordings CDRD-1-1.

Blues in the Mississippi Night Rykodisc RCD-90155.

Blues Masters, Vols. 1–15 Rhino R2-71121-35

Blues Retrospective: 1925–1950 Columbia/Legacy 4-C4K-47911

Boogie Woogie Blues: From Rare Piano Rolls Biograph BCD-115

Canned Heat Blues: Masters of the Delta Blues Bluebird 07863-61047

Capricorn Records Presents the Fire/Fury Records Story Capricorn 2-42009

Chess Blues Chess 4-CHD4-9340

Chicago/The Blues/Today! Vols. 1–3 Vanguard VMD-79216-18

The Cobra Records Story: Chicago Rock and Blues 1956–1958 Capricorn 2-42012-2

The Complete Stax-Volt Singles, 1959–1968 Atlantic 9-82218-2

Deep Blues Atlantic 82450

Drop Down Mama Chess CHD-93002

The Earliest Negro Vocal Quartets (1894–1928) Document DOCD-5061

Fathers and Sons Chess 2-CHD-92522

Grinder Man Blues: Masters of the Blues Piano RCA 2098-2R

The Jewel/Paula Records Story: The Blues, Rhythm & Blues and Soul Recordings Capricorn 2-42014-2

Living Chicago Blues, Vols. 1–4 Alligator ALCD-7701-4

News and the Blues: Telling It Like It Is Columbia/Legacy 46217

SELECTED DISCOGRAPHY

One-String Blues Gazell Documents GDCD-6001

Rare Chicago Blues 1962–1968 Bullseye Blues BBCD-9530

The Roots of Robert Johnson Yazoo CD-1073

Roots of Rock Yazoo 1063

Roots of the Blues New World 80252-2

Sounds of the South—A Musical Journey from the Georgia Sea Islands to the Mississippi Delta Recorded in the Field by Alan Lomax Atlantic 4-82496-2

White Country Blues 1926–1938: A Lighter Shade of Blue Columbia/Legacy 2-C2K-47446

Wild About My Lovin': Beale Street Blues 1928–1930 RCA 2461-2R

BIBLIOGRAPHY

. . . .

The editions cited were those at hand, not necessarily first or most recent editions.

Adero, Malaika, ed. *Up South*. New York: The New Press, 1993.

Albertson, Chris. *Bessie*. New York: Stein & Day, 1985.

Baker, Houston A. *Blues, Ideology and Afro-American Literature: A Vernacular Theory*. Chicago: University of Chicago Press, 1984.

Bane, Michael. *White Boy Singin' the Blues*. New York: Da Capo Press, 1992.

Baralla, Amisi (see LeRoi Jones)

Benjamin, Walter. *Illuminations*. New York: Schocken Books, 1969.

Bergreen, Lawrence. *As Thousands Cheer*. New York: Viking Penguin, 1990.

Berry, Chuck. *The Autobiography*. New York: Fireside Books, 1988.

Bird, Christiane. *The Jazz and Blues Lover's Guide to the U.S.* Reading, MA: Addison-Wesley, 1991.

Blesh, Rudi. *Shining Trumpets*. New York: Da Capo Press, 1976.

———, and Harriet Janis. *They All Played Ragtime*. New York: Oak Publications, 1971.

Booth, Stanley. *Rythm Oil*. New York: Pantheon Books, 1991.

Bradford, Perry. *Born with the Blues*. New York: Oak Publications, 1965.

Broonzy, William, with Yannick Bruynoghe. *Big Bill Blues*. New York: Da Capo Press, 1992.

Brown, Sterling A. *The Collected Poems of Sterling A. Brown*, edited by Michael Harper. Chicago: TriQuarterly Books, 1983.

Cagin, Seth, and Philip Dray. *We Are Not Afraid*. New York: Bantam Books, 1989.

Calt, Stephen, and Gayle Wardlów. *King of the Delta Blues: The Life and Music of Charlie Patton*. Newton, NJ: Rock Chapel Press, 1988.

Cantor, Louis. *Wheelin' on Beale*. New York: Pharos Books, 1992.

Charters, Ann. *Nobody: The Story of Bert Williams*. New York: The Macmillan Company, 1970.

Charters, Sam. *The Blues Masters*. New York: Da Capo Press, 1991.

———. *The Country Blues*. New York: Da Capo Press, 1975.

———. *The Legacy of the Blues*. New York: Da Capo Press, 1977.

———. *The Poetry of the Blues*. New York: Oak Publications, 1963.

———. *The Roots of the Blues*. New York: Perigee Books, 1982.

Chilton, John. *Let the Good Times Roll: The Story of Louis Jordan and His Music*. Ann Arbor, MI: University of Michigan Press, 1994.

Cobb, James C. *The Most Southern Place on Earth*. New York: Oxford University Press, 1992.

Cohn, Lawrence, ed. *Nothing But the Blues*. New York: Abbeville Press, 1993.

Courlander, Harold. *Negro Folk Music U.S.A.* Mineola, NY: Dover Publications, 1992.

Dahl, Linda. *Stormy Weather*. New York: Pantheon Books, 1984.

Dance, Helen Oakley. *Stormy Monday: The T-Bone Walker Story*. New York: Da Capo Press, 1990.

Dance, Stanley. *The World of Earl Hines*. New York: Charles Schribner's Sons, 1977

Dawson, Jim, and Steve Propes. *What Was the First Rock 'n' Roll Record?* Boston: Faber & Faber, 1992.

de Toledano, Ralph, ed. *Frontiers of Jazz*. London: Jazz Book Club, 1966.

Dixon, Robert M. W., and John Goodrich. *Blues and Gospel Records* 1902–1943. 3rd ed. London: Storyville Publications, 1982.

———. *Recording the Blues*. New York: Stein & Day, 1970.

Dixon, Willie, with Don Snowden. *I Am the Blues*. New York: Da Capo Press, 1990.

Ellison, Mary. *Extensions of the Blues*. New York: Riverrun Press, 1989.

Ellison, Ralph. *Invisible Man*. New York: Signet Books, 1964.

———. *Shadow and Act*. New York: Signet Books, 1966.

Escott, Colin, with Martin Hawkins. *Good Rockin' Tonight*. New York: St. Martin's Press, 1992.

Evans, David. *Big Road Blues*. New York: Da Capo Press, 1987.

———. *Nothing But the Blues*.

Faulkner, William. *Wild Palms*. New York: Vintage Books, 1966.

Ferris, William. *Blues from the Delta*. New York: Da Capo Press, 1984.

Field, Kim. *Harmonicas, Harps, and Heavy Breathers*. New York: Fireside Books, 1993.

Friedwald, Will. *Jazz Singing*. New York: Charles Scribner's Sons, 1990.

Garon, Paul. *Blues and the Poetic Spirit*. New York: Da Capo Press, 1979.

———. *The Devil's Son-in-Law: The Story of Peetie Wheatstraw and His Songs*. London: Studio Vista, 1971.

———. and Beth Garon. *Woman with Guitar: Memphis Minnie's Blues*. New York: Da Capo Press, 1992.

Gillet, Charlie. *The Sound of the City*. New York: Pantheon Books, 1983.

Greenberg, Alan. *Love in Vain: A Vision of Robert Johnson*. New York: Da Capo Press, 1993.

Guralnick, Peter. *Feel Like Going Home*. New York: Perennial Library, 1989.

———. *The Listener's Guide to the Blues*. New York: Facts on File, 1982.

———. *Lost Highway*. New York: Vintage Books, 1982.

———. *Searching for Robert Johnson*. New York: E. P. Dutton, 1989.

———. *Sweet Soul Music*. New York: Harper & Row, 1986.

Hadley, Frank John. *The Grove Press Guide to the Blues on CD*. New York: Grove Press, 1993.

Hammond, John, with Irving Townsend. *John Hammond on Record*. New York: Penguin Books, 1981.

Handy, W. C. *Blues: An Anthology*. New York: Da Capo Press, 1990.

————. *Father of the Blues: An Autobiography*. New York: Da Capo Press, 1991.

Haralambos, Michael. *Soul Music*. New York: Da Capo Press, 1985.

Harris, Sheldon. *Blues Who's Who*. New York: Da Capo Press, 1981.

Harrison, Daphne Duval. *Black Pearls*. New Brunswick, NJ: Rutgers University Press, 1990.

Heilbut, Anthony. *The Gospel Sound*. New York: Limelight Editions, 1992.

Herzhaft, Gérard. *Encyclopedia of the Blues*. Fayetteville, AR: University of Arkansas Press, 1992.

Jasen, David A. *Tin Pan Alley*. New York: Donald L. Fine, 1988.

————, and Jay Tichenor. *Rags and Ragtime: A Musical History*. Mineola, NY: Dover Books, 1989.

Johnson, James Weldon, and J. Rosamond Johnson. *The Books of American Negro Spirituals*. New York: Da Capo Press, 1990.

Jones, Jacqueline. *The Dispossessed*. New York: Basic Books, 1992.

Jones, LeRoi. *Blues People*. New York: William Morrow & Co., 1963.

————. *Dutchman + The Slave*. New York: William Morrow & Co., 1964.

Keil, Charles. *Urban Blues*. Chicago: University of Chicago Press, 1991.

Kellner, Bruce, ed. *"Keep A-Inchin' Along": Selected Writings of Carl Van Vechten About Black Arts and Letters*. Westport, CN: Greenwood Press, 1979.

Leadbitter, Mike, and Neil Slavin. *Blues Records 1943–1966*. London: Hanover Books, 1968.

Leigh, Keri. *Stevie Ray: Soul to Soul*. Dallas: Taylor Publishing Company, 1993.

Lemann, Nicholas. *The Promised Land*. New York: Alfred A. Knopf, 1991.

Lichtenstein, Grace, and Laura Dankner. *Musical Gumbo: The Music of New Orleans*. New York: W. W. Norton & Co., 1993.

Lipscomb, Mance. *I Say Me for a Parable: The Oral Autobiography of Mance Lipscomb, Texas Bluesman, as Told to and Compiled by Glen Alyn*. New York: W. W. Norton & Co., 1993.

Lomax, Alan. *The Land Where the Blues Began*. New York: Pantheon Books, 1993.

————. *Mister Jelly Roll*. New York: Pantheon Books, 1993.

Lomax, John A. *Adventures of a Ballad Hunter*. New York: The Macmillan Company, 1947.

————, and Alan Lomax. *Folk Song U.S.A.* New York: Plume Books, 1975.

————, *Negro Folk Songs as Sung by Leadbelly*. New York: The Macmillan Company, 1936.

Lott, Eric. *Love & Theft: Blackface Minstrelsy and the American Working Class*. New York: Oxford University Press, 1993.

Lovell, John, Jr. *Black Song: The Fire and the Flame*. New York: Paragon House, 1987.

McKee, Margaret, and Fred Chisenhall. *Beale Black and Blue*. Baton Rouge, LA: Louisiana State University Press, 1981.

Major, Clarence. *Juba to Jive: A Dictionary of African-American Slang*. New York: Penguin Books, 1994.

Marcus, Greil. *Mystery Train*. New York: E. P. Dutton, 1975.

Marquis, Donald M. *In Search of Buddy Bolden*. New York: Da Capo Press, 1980.

Merrill, Hugh. *The Blues Route*. New York: William Morrow & Co., 1990.

Morgan, Thomas L., and William Barlow. *From Cakewalks to Concert Halls*. Washington, DC: Elliott & Clark, 1992.

Morton, David C., with Charles K. Wolfe. *DeFord Bailey: A Black Star in Early Country Music.* Knoxville, TN: University of Tennessee Press, 1991.

Murray, Albert. *The Hero and the Blues.* Columbia, MS: University of Missouri Press, 1973.

————. *Stomping the Blues.* New York: McGraw-Hill Book Co., 1976.

Oakley, Giles. *The Devil's Music.* London: Ariel Books, 1983.

Obrecht, Jas, ed. *Blues Guitar: The Men Who Made the Music.* San Francisco: GPI Books, 1990.

Oliver, Paul. *Blues Fell This Morning.* Cambridge, Engl.: Cambridge University Press, 1990.

————. *Blues off the Record.* New York: Da Capo Press, 1988.

————. *Conversations with the Blues.* New York: Horizon Press, 1965.

————. *Screening the Blues.* New York: Da Capo Press, 1989.

————. *Songsters and Saints.* Cambridge, Engl.: Cambridge University Press, 1984.

————. *The Story of the Blues.* Philadelphia: Chilton Book Company, 1973.

————, ed. *The Blackwell Guide to Blues Recordings.* Oxford: Blackwell Reference, 1989.

————, Max Harrison, and William Bolcom. *The New Grove Gospel, Blues and Jazz.* New York: W.W. Norton & Co., 1986.

Palmer, Robert. *Deep Blues.* New York: Penguin Books, 1981.

Patoski, Joe Nick, and Bill Crawford. *Stevie Ray Vaughan: Caught in the Crossfire.* Boston: Little, Brown, 1993.

Pruter, Robert, ed. *The Blackwell Guide to Soul Recordings.* Oxford: Blackwell Reference, 1993.

Ramsey, Frederick, Jr., and Charles Edward Smith. *Jazzmen.* New York: Limelight Editions, 1975.

Roediger, David R. *The Wages of Whiteness.* New York: Verso, 1991.

Rooney, James. *Bossmen: Bill Monroe and Muddy Waters.* New York: Da Capo Press, 1991.

Rowe, Mike. *Chicago Blues [Chicago Breakdown].* New York: Da Capo Press, 1981.

Russell, Tony. *Blacks, Whites and Blues.* New York: Stein & Day, 1970.

Sackheim, Eric. *The Blues Line: A Collection of Blues Lyrics.* Hopewell, NJ: Ecco Press, 1993.

Sallis, James. *Guitar Players.* Lincoln, NE: Bison Books, 1994.

————. *The Long-Legged Fly.* New York: Carroll & Graf, 1992.

Santelli, Robert. *The Big Book of Blues.* New York: Penguin Books, 1993.

Sawyer, Charles. *The Arrival of B. B. King: The Authorized Biography.* New York: Da Capo Press, 1982.

Scott, Frank, and the staff of Down Home Music. *The Down Home Guide to the Blues.* Pennington, NJ: A Cappella Books, 1991.

Sharr Murray, Charles. *Blues on CD: The Essential Guide.* London: Kyle Cathie, 1993.

————. *Crosstown Traffic.* New York: St. Martin's Press, 1990.

Shapiro, Nat, and Nat Hentoff. *Hear Me Talkin' to Ya.* New York: Dover Publications, 1966.

Shaw, Arnold. *Honkers and Shouters.* New York: Collier Books, 1978.

Silvester, Peter J. *A Left Hand Like God.* New York: Da Capo Press, 1989.

Southern, Eileen. *The Music of Black Americans.* New York: W. W. Norton & Co., 1983.

BIBLIOGRAPHY

Stewart-Baxter, Derrick. *Ma Rainey and the Classic Blues Singers*. New York: Stein & Day, 1970.

Tracy, Steven C. *Langston Hughes and the Blues*. Urbana, IL: University of Illinois Press, 1988.

Turner, Frederick. *Remembering Song*. New York: Viking Press, 1982.

VanDer Merwe, Peter: *Origins of the Popular Style*. New York: Oxford University Press, 1989.

Watkins, Mel. *On the Real Side*. New York: Simon & Schuster, 1994.

Welding, Pete, and Toby Byron, eds. *Bluesland: Portraits of 12 American Blues Masters*. New York: E. P. Dutton, 1991.

Whitburn, Joel. *The Billboard Book of Top 40 Hits*. 3rd ed. New York: Billboard Publications, 1987.

———. *Joel Whitburn's Pop Memories 1890–1954: The History of American Popular Music*. Menomonee Falls, WS: Record Research, 1986.

———. *Joel Whitburn's Top R&B Singles 1942–1988*. Menomonee Falls, WS: Record Research, 1988.

Whitcomb, Ian. *Irving Berlin and Ragtime America*. New York: Limelight Editions, 1988.

Wilcox, Donald E., with Buddy Guy. *Damn Right I've Got the Blues*. San Francisco: Woodford Press, 1993.

Wilder, Alec. *American Popular Song*. New York: Oxford University Press, 1972.

Williams, Juan. *Eyes on the Prize: America's Civil Rights Years 1964–1965*. New York: Viking Press, 1987.

Williams, Martin, ed. *Jazz Panorama*. New York: Collier Books, 1994.

Wilson, Charles Reagan, and William Ferris, eds. *Encyclopedia of Southern Culture*. Chapel Hill, NC: University of North Carolina Press, 1989.

Wolfe, Charles, and Kip Lornell. *The Life and Legend of Leadbelly*. New York: HarperCollins, 1992.

Woll, Allen. *Black Musical Theatre: From Coontown to Dreamgirls*. New York: Da Capo Press, 1991.

BLUES TIMELINE

• •

	BLUES	JAZZ, POP, THEATER, RELEVANT LITERATURE	HISTORY, INDUSTRY, ARTS, and SCIENCES
1619			The first shipload of African slaves sold to the colonies docks in Virginia
ca. 1830		T. D. Rice introduces blackface and "Jump Jim Crow"	
1831			Nat Turner's slave rebellion
1843	First public minstrel show, in Virginia		
1848		Stephen Foster publishes "Oh, Susannah"	California Gold Rush
1852		Harriet Beecher Stowe's *Uncle Tom's Cabin*	
1862–64			A series of congressional acts facilitates the building of the nation's first transcontinental railroad, the Union Pacific
1863			Emancipation Proclamation
1865			The Thirteenth Amendment abolishes slavery
ca. 1865			In granting basic rights to ex-slaves (including the right to marry and to own land), the "Black Codes"

BLUES	JAZZ, POP, THEATER, RELEVANT LITERATURE	HISTORY, INDUSTRY, ARTS, and SCIENCES
		passed by most Southern state legislatures in the aftermath of the Civil War also ensure segregation of public facilities
1866	Formation of Fisk Jubilee Singers	The Ku Klux Klan founded in Pulaski, Tennessee
1867	First collection of spirituals published: William Allen, Charles Ware, and Lucy McKim Garrison's *Slave Songs of the United States*	
1869		Beef is shipped from Detroit to Boston in a railroad car chilled with ice from the Great Lakes—a primitive form of refrigeration
1870		Section One of the Fifteenth Amendment supposedly guarantees that "the right of citizens of the United States to vote shall not be denied or abridged by any State on account of race, color, or previous condition of servitude"
1876		Custer's last stand at Little Big Horn
1877		Reconstruction ends as Federal troops are withdrawn from the South
		Thomas Edison files patent on a phonograph consisting of a metal cylinder with a fine spiral groove, two diaphragm-and-needle units (one for recording, the other for playback) and a small speaker-horn—a vast improvement over Leon Scott's "phonautograph" of 1855
1881		The Gunfight at the O.K. Corral
1887		Emile Berliner, the inventor of the microphone ten years earlier, files for a patent for the gramophone,

BLUES	JAZZ, POP, THEATER, RELEVANT LITERATURE	HISTORY, INDUSTRY, ARTS, and SCIENCES
		which plays disks rather than Edison's cylinders (Berliner a few years later invents a matrix system whereby an unlimited number of copies can be mass-produced from an original master)
1888		The Kodak box camera is introduced
1889		The Oklahoma Landrush
1890		Mississippi's redrawn constitution includes a clause under which a prospective voter could be required to read and interpret any part of the constitution in order to be eligible to vote. This "literacy clause" becomes the model by which other Southern states disenfranchise blacks
		Columbia enters the record business with recordings of John Philip Sousa
1891	George Washington Johnson's "The Laughing Song" and "The Whistling Coon"	
1892		The boll weevil crosses the Mexican border into Texas and eventually spreads to most cotton-growing regions, including the Mississippi Delta
1893		First public showing of an Edison kinescope
1896		*Plessy* v. *Ferguson*: In upholding an 1890 Louisiana statute mandating separate but "equal" railroad cars for blacks, the U.S. Supreme Court rules that the equal protection clause of the Fourteenth Amendment (ratified in 1866) had guaranteed blacks political, *but not*

	BLUES	JAZZ, POP, THEATER, RELEVANT LITERATURE	HISTORY, INDUSTRY, ARTS, and SCIENCES
			social, equality. Ironically, the railroad lines were among those calling for repeal of the Louisana state law. The court's decision made white compliance with subsequent "Jim Crow" laws mandatory, not discretionary
1898		Bob Cole's *A Trip to Coontown*	Annexation of the Hawaiian Islands
1899	Scott Joplin's "The Maple Leaf Rag"		
1901		Booker T. Washington's *Up from Slavery*	Oil is discovered at Spindletop, near Beaumont, Texas
1902	The Dinwiddle Colored Quartet records for Victor		
1903		Edwin S. Porter's *The Great Train Robbery* made for Thomas Edison W. E. B. DuBois's *The Souls of Black Folk*	The auto industry begins; the Wright Brothers' first flight
1905	The first U.S. movie theater opens in Pittsburgh		
1906	The first of many recorded versions of Bert Williams's "Nobody"		
1910			National Association for the Advancement of Colored People (NAACP) is founded by W. E. B. DuBois and seven whites in response to the lynching of two black men in Springfield, Illinois
1912	Leroy "Lasses" White's "Nigger Blues," Hart Wand and Lloyd Garrett's "Dallas Blues," and W. C. Handy's "Memphis Blues" all are published within a few months of one another. But in a sense, the first published "blues" was Nat D. Ayer and Seymour Brown's "Oh, You Beautiful Doll," a pop hit of 1911 whose opening verse had made knowing use of twelve-bar form	James Reese Europe, the music director for Vernon and Irene Castle, leads his Clef Club Symphony Orchestra at Carnegie Hall	The *Titanic* sinks

	BLUES	JAZZ, POP, THEATER, RELEVANT LITERATURE	HISTORY, INDUSTRY, ARTS, and SCIENCES
1914	Handy's "St. Louis Blues" published		Borrowing an idea from the meat-packing industry, Henry Ford introduces the assembly line to speed production and lowers the selling price of the Model-T (introduced six years earlier)
1915		Scott Joplin's opera *Treemonisha* is staged in New York	D. W. Griffith's *The Birth of a Nation*, based on Thomas Dixon's novel *The Klansman* (also the source for a long-running play), revolutionizes motion pictures and triggers both NAACP boycotts and the revitalization of the Ku Klux Klan (this time a national, rather than an exclusively Southern, organization, as antagonistic toward Jewish and Catholic immigrants as to blacks)
		Bert Williams joins the Ziegfeld follies	
1917	The Original Dixieland Jazz Band becomes the first jazz group to record		The Bolshevik Revolution
			The United States enters World War I
			The *Chicago Defender* announces its "Great Northern Drive," urging blacks to flee the South—an exodus that is already under way
			Birdseye begins to experiment with frozen food, a process not perfected until 1949
1918–19			Influenza epidemic kills 500,000 in United States, over 21 million worldwide
1919			The underside of the migration: bloody race riots in a number of Northern cities, including Chicago

	BLUES	JAZZ, POP, THEATER, RELEVANT LITERATURE	HISTORY, INDUSTRY, ARTS, and SCIENCES
			Commercial air travel begins
1920	"Race" recording begins with Mamie Smith's "Crazy Blues"		Women get the vote
			Westinghouse initiates commercial radio broadcasts
1921		Eubie Blake and Noble Sissle's *Shuffle Along*	
1922			International Harvester manufactures the first row tractor
1923	Bessie Smith's "Down Hearted Blues," Ma Rainey's "Bo-Weavil Blues"	James P. Johnson's *Running Wild* initiates the Charleston craze	
		Fiddlin' John Carson records "The Little Old Cabin in the Lane," arguably the first white rural (or "hillbilly") record, for Okeh	
1924	Papa Charlie Jackson's "Papa's Lawdy, Lawdy Blues"	Gershwin's *Rhapsody in Blue*	
1925		Calvin Dixon becomes the first black preacher to record a sermon; he is quickly followed by Blind Joe Taggart (the first of the "guitar evangelists") and the Reverends J. M. Gates, J. C. Burnett, A. W. Nix, among others. According to Paul Oliver, 750 sermons are recorded over the next 12 years	Electrical recording introduced
		Publication of the anthology *The New Negro*, a touchstone of the Harlem Renaissance, edited by Alain Locke; contributors include Langston Hughes, James Weldon Johnson, and Zora Neal Hurston. Includes essays on jazz and spirituals, though none on blues	Development of the 35-millimeter camera makes it possible to shoot "candid" photographs in natural light, without flashbulbs
1926	Blind Lemon Jefferson's "That Black Snake Moan"	Jelly Roll Morton's "Dead Man Blues" and "Black Bottom Stomp"	

BLUES	JAZZ, POP, THEATER, RELEVANT LITERATURE	HISTORY, INDUSTRY, ARTS, and SCIENCES
	Duke Ellington's first recording of his "East St. Louis Toodle-oo"	
	Carl Van Vechten's *Nigger Heaven; Vanity Fair* publishes Van Vechten's essay on "Negro Blues Singers"	
1927	Jerome Kern and Oscar Hammerstein II's *Show Boat*	The Great Mississippi River Flood
		Al Jolson wears blackface for *The Jazz Singer*, the first "talkie"
		Charles Lindbergh crosses the Atlantic
1928	Leroy Carr's "How Long—How Long Blues," Tampa Red and Georgia Tom's "It's Tight Like That," and Clarence "Pine Top" Smith's "Pine Top's Boogie Woogie"	Louis Armstrong's "West End Blues" and "Weather Bird"	The Southern drought described in Son House's "Dry Spell Blues"
1929	Charley Patton's "Pony Blues" and "High Water Everywhere—Parts I and II"		The stock market crashes, plunging the country into the Great Depression
	Bessie Smith appears on Broadway in *Pansy*		
1930			Nation of Islam founded in Detroit
1931			The left rallies behind "the Scottsboro Boys," nine young black men indicted for raping two white women aboard a freight train passing through Scottsboro, Alabama
1933	Leadbelly (Hudie Ledbetter) recorded by John and Alan Lomax at the Louisiana State Penitentiary at Angola		The first New Deal legislation, including Federal Emergency Relief Association and Public Works Administration. Blacks, traditionally Republican voters, switch parties by the hundreds of thousands before the end of the decade

BLUES	JAZZ, POP, THEATER, RELEVANT LITERATURE	HISTORY, INDUSTRY, ARTS, and SCIENCES
		The Tennessee Valley Authority (TVA) is formed to create a network of dams to control floods, prevent soil erosion, and provide affordable electricity in the rural South
		Prohibition is repealed
		Wurlitzer begins to manufacture coin-operated juke boxes
1934		Formation of Southern Tenant Farmers Union in Arkansas, a historically overlooked alliance between blacks and poor whites that can be seen as a forerunner to the civil rights movement of the 1960s
1935	George Gershwin's "folk opera" *Porgy and Bess* is staged in New York	
1936	Robert Johnson's "Cross Roads Blues"	John and Alan Lomax's *Negro Folk Songs as Performed by Leadbelly*	
	The pianist Teddy Wilson integrates Benny Goodman's trio	
	Count Basie's "Jones-Smith Incorporated" session with Lester Young	
1937	Bessie Smith dies as a result of injuries sustained in an automobile accident on Highway 61, in Mississippi		The Farm Security Administration is founded by the federal government to extend low-interest loans to farm workers to help them start their own family-size farms
1938	First "Spirituals to Swing" concert at New York's Carnegie Hall, featuring Big Bill Broonzy, among others	Benny Goodman's Carnegie Hall concert	

	BLUES	JAZZ, POP, THEATER, RELEVANT LITERATURE	HISTORY, INDUSTRY, ARTS, and SCIENCES
1939		Charlie Christian joins Benny Goodman	
1940		Richard Wright's *Native Son*	A breakdown in contract negotiations between radio broadcasters and the American Society of Composers and Publishers results in a nine-month blackout of ASCAP-licensed songs—eventually leading to the formation of Broadcast Music Incorporated, a rival licensing agency far more hospitable to blues and country music
1941	Alan Lomax records McKinley Morganfield (a.k.a. Muddy Waters) for the Library of Congress on Stovall's Farm		Japanese attack Pearl Harbor; the United States enters World War II First jet aircraft designed
	Sonny Boy Williamson (Rice Miller) debuts on KFFA's "King Biscuit Hour" (Helena, Arkansas)		A threatened march on Washington DC, results in federal legislation forbidding racial discrimination in defense industries
1942		Lionel Hampton's "Flying Home"	*Billboard* initiates its R&B chart The American Federation of Musicians calls for a ban on recording in a dispute over royalties; the "strike" lasts until 1944
1943		Duke Ellington's *Black, Brown and Beige*	
1944	Louis Jordan's "G.I. Jive" reaches top of the pop charts	A "Jazz at the Philharmonic" concert in Los Angeles, featuring Nat Cole, Les Paul, and Illinois Jacquet, among others, yields the first commercially released "live" concert recordings. Jacquet's squealing tenor saxophone solo on "The Blues" helps to plant the seeds for R&B	The mechanical cotton picker is introduced; 20 years later, only 5% of the Delta's cotton crop will be hand-picked
1945		Charlie Parker's "KoKo" and "Now's the Time"	

	BLUES	JAZZ, POP, THEATER, RELEVANT LITERATURE	HISTORY, INDUSTRY, ARTS, and SCIENCES
1946	Arthur "Big Boy" Crudup's "That's All Right"		Network television broadcasts begin
1947	T-Bone Walker's "Call It Stormy Monday"		Jackie Robinson breaks major league baseball's color line
1948	John Lee Hooker's "Boogie Chillen"; Muddy Waters's "I Can't Be Satisfied"		WDIA, in Memphis, becomes the first radio station to switch to all-black programming; B. B. King is later a disc jockey there

The long-playing record (LP) is introduced |
1949	Leadbelly appears in France, becoming the first country bluesman to perform in Europe		
1950		The Weavers' version of Leadbelly's "Goodnight, Irene" sells over 2 million copies	
1951			Libya is granted its independence, followed by twenty other new African nations over the next ten years—a spur to black self-determination in the United States
1952	B. B. King's version of Lowell Fulson's "Three O'Clock Blues" tops *Billboard's* R&B chart for five weeks; later this same year, Little Walter's "Juke" reaches number one	Ralph Ellison's *Invisible Man*	
1954		Ray Charles's "I Got a Woman" and Elvis Presley's "That's All Right" and "Mystery Train"	With its unanimous decision in favor of school desegregation in the case of *Brown* v. *the Board of Education*, the U.S. Supreme Court effectively overturns *Plessy* v. *Ferguson*

The first families move into Levittown, a planned community in suburban Long Island; as a concept, "Levittown" comes to signify white flight from America's inner cities |

	BLUES	JAZZ, POP, THEATER, RELEVANT LITERATURE	HISTORY, INDUSTRY, ARTS, and SCIENCES
1955		Big Bill Broonzy and Yannick Bruynoghe's *Big Bill Blues* published	The Montgomery (Alabama) bus boycott
		Chuck Berry's "Maybellene"	Emmett Till, a black teenager from Chicago, is murdered for talking out of turn to a white woman near Money, Mississippi
1957		Chuck Berry's "School Day" and "Rock 'n' Roll Music," followed by "Sweet Little Sixteen" and "Johnny B. Goode" in 1958	Rev. Dr. Martin Luther King, Jr., is named president of the newly formed Southern Christian Leadership Conference (SCLC)
1958	The end of an era: Muddy Waters's last appearance on *Billboard's* R&B chart with a song called "Close to You"		Stereo is introduced
1959	Sam Charters records Lightnin' Hopkins for Folkways	Sam Charters's *The Country Blues* published	
		John Coltrane's *Giant Steps*, Ornette Coleman's *The Shape of Jazz to Come*, and Miles Davis's *Kind of Blue*	
1960	Muddy Waters and his band get the crowd up on its feets and dancing at the Newport Jazz Festival	The Miracles' "Shop Around," Motown's first top-ten hit (on its Tamla subsidiary)	The Student Nonviolent Coordinating Committee (SNCC) is founded at Shaw University, in Raleigh, North Carolina
1961	Columbia releases selection of Robert Johnson's recordings on LP		First USSR manned space flight Freedom Rides begin
1962	Booker T. and the MG's' "Green Onions," Stax's first hit record		
1963			A peaceful assembly estimated at 250,000 hears Dr. Martin Luther King, Jr., deliver his "I Have a Dream" speech during the March on Washington on August 28. Eighteen days later, four black

BLUES	JAZZ, POP, THEATER, RELEVANT LITERATURE	HISTORY, INDUSTRY, ARTS, and SCIENCES
		schoolgirls are martyred when the Sixteenth Street Baptist Church is bombed in Birmingham, Alabama
1964 The recently rediscovered Delta bluesmen Son House and Skip James are featured at the Newport Folk Festival	*The Autobiography of Malcolm X*	John F. Kennedy is assassinated. Civil rights workers James Chaney, Andrew Goodman, and Michael Schwerner are murdered during Mississippi Freedom Summer
Howlin' Wolf appears on *Shindig*, courtesy of the Rolling Stones	The Beatles conquer America with "I Want to Hold Your Hand"; the Rolling Stones make their first appearance on the U.S. charts with "Tell Me (You're Coming Back)"	Legislative responses to the civil rights movement: the 1964 Civil Rights Act is followed by the Voting Rights Act (1965), the Fair Housing Act (1968), and the Equal Opportunities Act (1972)
1965 The Paul Butterfield Blues Band plugs in at the Newport Folk Festival	James Brown's "Papa's Got a Brand New Bag" and "I Got You (I Feel Good)"	Malcolm X is assassinated in Harlem Watts Riots
1966		Black Panther Party founded in Oakland, California, by Huey Newton and Bobby Seale
1967	Aretha Franklin's "Respect" and "I Never Loved a Man"	
1968		Dr. Martin Luther King, Jr., is assassinated in Memphis
1969 B. B. King and Muddy Waters, both of whom are now playing mostly for white audiences, perform at the Fillmore East	James Brown's "Say It Loud—I'm Black and I'm Proud" Flower-power entrepreneurism finds its fullest expression at Woodstock, New York	
1970 B. B. King's "The Thrill Is Gone"	*Living Blues* begins publication in Chicago	
1971 *Hound Dog Taylor and the HouseRockers* launches Alligator Records		Blaxploitation—Hollywood's ironic acknowledgment of black purchasing power—begins with Gordon Park's *Shaft*

	BLUES	JAZZ, POP, THEATER, RELEVANT LITERATURE	HISTORY, INDUSTRY, ARTS, and SCIENCES
1979		Rap emerges from underground discos with The Sugar Hill Gang's "Rapper's Delight"	
1980	John Landis's movie *The Blues Brothers*, starring Dan Aykroyd and John Belushi		
1982			The compact disk is introduced
1984	Stevie Ray Vaughan's *Texas Flood*		
1986	Robert Cray's *Strong Persuader*		
1989	John Lee Hooker's *The Healer*	Public Enemy's "Fight the Power"	
1990	Columbia releases Robert Johnson's complete recordings on CD		
1991			Breakup of Soviet Union
1992		Ice-T's "Cop Killer"	Los Angeles Riots

INDEX

· ·

Italics indicate pages with photographs.

INDEX